get wired, you're hired

Prentice Hall Canada Inc.
Scarborough, Ontario

get wired, you're hired

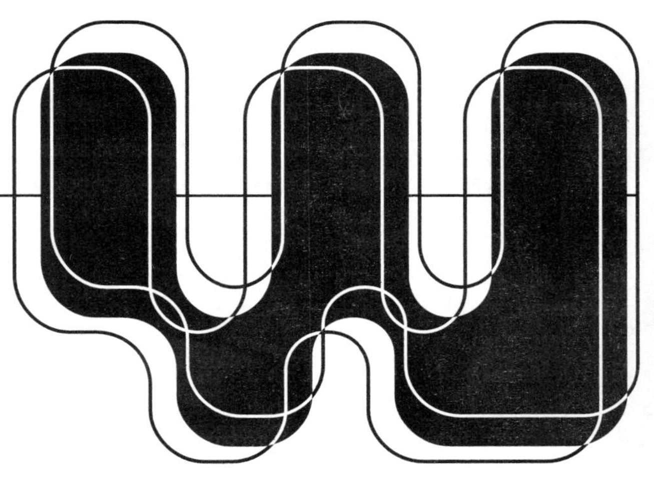

Revised and Updated

Mark Swartz
Canada's Internet Work-Search Authority

Canadian Cataloguing in Publication Data

Swartz, Mark, 1960-
Get wired, you're hired

2nd ed.
ISBN 0-13-974924-1

1. Job hunting – Canada – Computer network resources. I. Title

HF5382.75.C3S93 1998 650.14'0285'4678 C98-932073-1

Prentice Hall Canada Inc.
Scarborough, Ontario
A Division of Simon & Schuster/A Viacom Company

Prentice-Hall, Inc., Upper Saddle River, New Jersey
Prentice-Hall International (UK) Limited, London
Prentice-Hall of Australia, Pty. Limited, Sydney
Prentice-Hall Hispanoamericana, S.A., Mexico City
Prentice-Hall of India Private Limited, New Delhi
Prentice-Hall of Japan, Inc., Tokyo
Simon & Schuster Southeast Asia Private Limited, Singapore
Editora Prentice-Hall do Brasil, Ltda., Rio de Janeiro

ISBN 0-13-974924-1

Director, Trade Group: Robert Harris
Acquisitions Editor: Dean Hannaford
Editor: Madeline Koch
Assistant Editor: Joan Whitman
Production Coordinator: Shannon Potts
Art Direction: Mary Opper
Cover Design: Overdrive
Interior Design: Julia Hall
Page Layout: Dave McKay

1 2 3 4 5 W 02 01 00 99 98

Printed and bound in Canada

Visit the Prentice Hall Canada Web site! Send us your comments, browse our catalogues, and more. **www.phcanada.com**

In loving memory of my exceptional father,
Syd Swartz, 1930-1998. May you be at rest, while
thoughts of you are cherished forever.

ACKNOWLEDGMENTS

Can't a book on technology pretty well write itself? Not a chance (at least...not yet!). It takes a team of dedicated people to pull this project together. That's why I'd like to express my gratitude to the following individuals.

Marianne Swartz—my wife and soulmate. Your support and love make all of this possible.

Stacia and Jonah Swartz—my children who buoy my spirits and keep me grounded.

Helen Cameron—otherwise known as my Mom, who is always there for me.

Alex Spilberg: my father-in-law, who treats me like a son (though he already has four daughters).

The good folks at Drake Beam Morin—especially David Park and Dennis St-Amour, for their unwavering support. And to those who help me in their own special ways, such as Rob Hood, Kay Scott, Gary Fryatt, Jim Roode, Paullette Baker, John Williams, Day Merrill, Naome Howe, Eileen Anderson and Cheryl Wine—to name but a few.

Jim Carroll: He took time out of his incredibly busy life to lend me a hand at a critical stage.

Janis Foord-Kirk: Career advisor, author, columnist—and source of inspiration.

Kevin Hood: Small-business authority and great personality predictor.

Kerry Mahoney: Supervisor of the Career Resource Centre at the University of Waterloo.

Margaret Riley: A pioneer who has led the way for the rest of us online career advisors.

Gary Will: Creator of the Archeus career information Web site.

The people at my publishing company: Thanks to everyone behind the scenes at Prentice Hall for bringing this all together. And to those I worked with personally, Dean Hannaford, Robert Harris and Karen Alliston, a special note of appreciation.

Madeline Koch: Editor extraordinaire.

Shelly Steele and Debbie Cantrell: Friends when you need them most.

TABLE OF CONTENTS

INTRODUCTION

WELCOME TO THE *WIRED* ERA!

Every period of transition forces us to think up new approaches. That's where we, as Canadians, find ourselves when looking for employment. Gone is the age of the "job for life." Say hello instead to concepts like contingency work, Just-In-Time hiring and fixed-term contracts. In other words, our very notions of work and security are changing.

On top of this, the tools we use to find and secure employment are evolving rapidly. A mere decade ago, you were ahead of the crowd if you could fax a copy of your résumé to a potential employer. Compare that to what we're seeing now: requests for e-mailed résumés; the rise of Internet-based job application forms; and an increasing shift to online recruiting tactics.

How This Book Can Help You

Quite simply, I've written the second edition of *Get Wired, You're Hired* to help you look for work as we approach the year 2000. Here's my basic premise: job hunting is extremely competitive. At a minimum, you have to meet the demands of employers who are hiring. If they're now asking you to visit their Web site before applying for work, or if they want you to submit a scannable résumé via e-mail, then that's what you should be doing.

Unfortunately, employers aren't handing out technology instruction guides to job applicants. That's where this book comes in. It provides you with plain-language, step-by-step directions to make the most of the Internet for your work search. For instance, if you've never e-mailed your résumé in response to an advertised job before, turn to Chapter 7 for a complete tutorial. If you're wondering how to research companies and tap into the hidden work market online, Chapters 8 and 9 show you the way.

What If I've Never Used the Internet? Some folks believe that a book like this is only good for people who already use the Net, or for those with computers at home. The reality is that pretty well anyone can take advantage of the techniques that I'll be talking about. Part 1 uncomplicates matters by explaining basic Internet terminology and showing you how to use things like e-mail, the World Wide Web and Discussion Groups. It also tells you how to get access to the online world if you don't have your own equipment.

Thinking that maybe it's too late for you to get started? Don't worry, you're not alone. I give seminars regularly to people who have refused to try the Net for years. When I ask them why they've resisted so strongly, they tell me things like "I never had to use a computer in my previous job," or "I was afraid that it's developing so quickly, and changing so frequently, that I'd never be able to catch up." I'm happy to say that within several hours of instruction, these self-declared cyber-phobes can point and click their way onto the Internet. Then the more they practise, the easier it becomes.

What If I'm Already an Advanced Surfer? I've made sure that even experienced Netizens will benefit from this book. Why spend hours plowing through search engines and newsgroups randomly? I've provided you with a roadmap to the sites and resources that can hasten your job hunt. In addition, each chapter includes proven strategies for finding and securing employment, plus tips on maximizing your efficiency the electronic way.

What If I've Read Version 1? This second edition of *Get Wired, You're Hired* builds on the foundation established in the previous version. You'll find the same basic career management principals. You'll also see fully updated Web addresses plus a host of new Net resources. Additionally, there are now sections on Automated Voice Response and Video-Conferencing.

More Than Just a Job Hunting Guide

As a professional career consultant, I know that it's hard enough to find employment, never mind work that truly suits you. That's why you can use this book in a variety of ways to meet your own requirements. See which one of the following categories you identify with best.

I Must Find a Job—Right Away! If the pressure's really on and you simply *must* find employment—*any* employment—as quickly as you can, you could try the fast track. Jump first to Chapter 3. Review your skills and achievements as the foundation of your résumé. Chapter 6 is where you create a powerful résumé and cover letter, while Chapter 7 teaches you how to convert and send your material via e-mail or Web Form.

In Chapter 10, you go online to seek out advertised jobs. There are thousands of them out there, for sure. You'll see them on company home pages, in electronic job banks, posted in Newsgroups and through recruitment firm Web sites. There's also the option of uploading your résumé to post it on many of these sites.

I'm telling you honestly, though, that the likelihood of finding work very quickly by taking this approach is not good. Keep in mind that advertised jobs make up only 10 to 20% (on average) of the total employment market. And that the Internet captures only a portion of these. Plus almost three-quarters of the jobs you see on the Net are for so-called "techies" (people in the computer and engineering fields). What I'm saying is that going online to find immediate work may not be the instant solution you're looking for. I suggest instead that you use the Net as part of an overall work search strategy.

I Need to Find Work, but Not Necessarily *Tomorrow* Maybe you've found yourself "between jobs." Or perhaps you're employed but it's not working out for one reason or another. Then again, you might be a recent graduate who's trying to get a foot in the door. The point is that right now you're looking for work, not your dream job. If this is you, you could take the following route:

- Chapter 3: Start by Knowing Yourself Well
- Chapter 5: Make a Plan and Upgrade Your Skills
- Chapter 6: Create Superb Marketing Materials
- Chapter 7: Know How to Send Your Material Electronically

- Chapter 8: Research Before You Search
- Chapter 9: Network into the Hidden Job Market
- Chapter 10: Look for Jobs and Post Your Résumé Online
- Chapter 12: Hone Your Other Work Search Skills

This structured approach will enhance your odds of finding and securing employment. I'm not promising that it will be easy or quick. You will, however, learn how to search proactively rather than passively. You'll also be better equipped to market yourself to employers based on who you are and what you have to offer, taking into account the needs of the companies who are hiring.

I Have (or Will Have) an Opportunity to Enhance My Career Some people have the good fortune to approach work as more than just something you have to do in order to pay the bills. But please don't take me the wrong way here. I understand only too well the responsibilities that we face. Often keeping a roof over our heads and meeting our financial obligations prove to be more than enough challenge. I do want to acknowledge, though, that your career can also be a source of personal satisfaction: a place where you use your natural skills and abilities, let your true personality and values shine, and derive rewards from the work you've deliberately chosen to pursue.

If you're striving to be in this category, you'll find many useful resources throughout this book. I suggest that you begin by following the path outlined above in "I Need to Find Work," while adding in the remaining chapters:

- Chapter 4: Take Some Time to Explore Your Options
- Chapter 11: Find Special Resources for Specific Groups
- Chapter 13: Get Wired, Not Mired

By adopting this broader-based approach you'll open yourself up to the process of self-discovery. Yes, it requires time and effort. But you also give yourself the chance to explore new options. This could range from leaving one industry for another to making a full-scale career switch or becoming self-employed—all the way to planning your retirement.

What Does It Take to *Get Wired?*

While this book focuses on the Internet, it also recognizes that other technologies have made an impact on job hunting. Word processing software, fax machines, CD-ROMs, voicemail, video-conferencing—they've all burst onto the scene in recent years. At first they were expensive, hard to get hold of and awkward to use. Not so anymore. Today they're user-friendly and widely available. Best of all, they've evolved to the point where they can truly help you reach your career goals.

Anyone Can Do It! By now I hope that at least one thing is clear: it's not just computer geniuses and techno-wizards who are taking their work search online. Literally anyone can get plugged in to increase his or her chances of finding work—no matter what that work is! Whether you're a graduating student or mid-life career changer, senior executive or administrative assistant, blue-collar worker or budding entrepreneur, there's something worthwhile for you in cyberspace.

If You Don't Do It, Someone Else Will The bottom line is that searching for work the *wired* way gives you a distinct competitive edge. But if you stop to think about it, soon everyone will be doing it. That's the way our marketplace works. The harsh truth is that if you don't make at least some effort to keep up, you could find yourself in an even tougher situation in the future.

My Personal Commitment to You

I don't like to over-promise. So before you go off hoping that this book will single-handedly turn your life around let's come back to earth. It's time to go over what you can realistically expect from using this guide.

What's Inside? Throughout each chapter, there is advice on looking for work and taking charge of your career. At every stage there are Internet and other techno-resources cited to make your search more effective. There are also elements that bring ideas and hints into focus for you, in particular:

- **Cyber Tips**: Clear, concise instructions on how to locate information and use the electronic tools that are critical to every stage of your career planning process.
- **Real Life**: Short pieces of advice on how to get to where you really want to be by following tried-and-true practices.

- **Wired Wrap-ups**: Summaries at the end of each chapter tie the information together and reinforce what it means in terms of finding and securing work.

What's Not Inside I believe in being upfront. This book doesn't pretend to answer every single career-related question ever posed by humankind. It will definitely point you to resources that can be of assistance, but don't count on it to do the following:

- provide simplistic or instantaneous solutions to difficult situations (you're going to have to do the legwork yourself)
- guarantee you a fantastic new job (it's up to you to decide for yourself what you really want, and how to best use the tools that I describe to help get you there)
- turn you into a technological genius (I do provide basic instructions on using technology to advance your career, but you'll have to practise and experiment *a lot* if you're thinking of becoming a pro).

Proudly Canadian You might be wondering how this book differs from other job hunting guides you've come across. For one, it superimposes user-friendly technology over proven methods for planning your career and searching for work. As well, it's exclusively for Canadian work searchers by a Canadian career professional. That means you'll learn about resources that can assist you from Vancouver to St. John's, while not ignoring the rest of the world.

Take It from Someone Who's Been There

Just so you know, I've found myself on the receiving end of a downsizing more than once. (Translation: I've experienced the gut-wrenching trauma of losing my job when I worked in the corporate world.) I know how unsettling and harrowing being out of work can be. Searching for employment is a hard, grim fact in today's marketplace. Well over one million unemployed Canadians will attest to that.

Why Not Give the New Techniques a Shot? The bright side is that the newest tools can make your search more efficient. At the very least, you'll be able to:

- show employers that you have the technical skills they're looking for today

- search for work or promote yourself worldwide
- take advantage of resources 24 hours a day, 7 days a week
- network into the hidden job market—right from your computer console.

Using the methods I describe will give you a leg up, especially on those who count only on the old techniques to find work. This could be the competitive edge that you've been looking for, and you may very well find work more quickly than otherwise. My real hope is that you use this book to help you uncover—and secure—the type of employment that you genuinely want!

Mark S

p.s. We all know that technology is changing rapidly, and this book is designed with that in mind. Once you're hooked up to the Net, surf over to **www.wiredhired.com** for regular updates to the resources you'll find inside.

PART 1

WIRED BASICS

CHAPTER 1

Internet Essentials

I. THE BASICS

There's nothing more frustrating than watching the bus leave while you're left behind to choke on its dust. If that's been your experience with the Internet, then this chapter is your first step to becoming active in the expanding universe of online resources (well, second actually, if you count picking up this book). And many of those online resources are invaluable employment tools.

I've written this opening chapter specifically for new users. I'll even throw in some words of encouragement to get things going: If you've never used the Internet before, or if you have but still feel overwhelmed, it's not too late for you! At the time of publication, perhaps 25 percent of Canadians had access to the Net. That means you're about to escape from the dreaded 75 percent who are missing out on the dawn of a brand new age. Good news, considering how important the Net is becoming in business, personal communications and—most important for you—in finding work and managing your career.

To help you move forward, this chapter gives you useful background and tips about the Net, including:

- what the Internet is, and what it is not,
- how it got started,
- the key components to consider, and
- basic instructions on using e-mail, discussion groups and the Web.

One thing you won't find here, or anywhere else in this book, is techno-babble geared to folks with PhDs in advanced computerology (is there such a word?). My rationale goes something like this: You do not have to be a technical expert to use the Net effectively. In fact, anyone who can use a basic word-processing package, such as Word or WordPerfect, or a spreadsheet program, such as Excel or Lotus 123, can learn the essentials in less than a day. The truth is that it's far easier to go online today than it was even a year or two ago.

CYBER TIP If you already have access to the Net but need to find instruction guides for any aspect of surfing, check out Yahoo's list of Beginners' Guides at **www.yahoo.com/computers_and_internet/internet/information_and_documentation/beginner_s_guides/**. Or stop at your bookstore and pick up a copy of the *Canadian Internet New User's Handbook* (**www.handbook.com/hnd_user.htm**) by Jim Carroll and Rick Broadhead.

What the Internet Is

The word *Internet* literally means a network of networks. In itself, the Internet comprises thousands of smaller regional networks scattered around the globe. On any given day it connects roughly 40 million users in more than 100 countries. Not bad for a bunch of wires and invisible connections.

When I conduct Internet seminars I am constantly astounded by the assortment of opinions people hold when it comes to the Net. For some, it's just an easy way to send e-mail back and forth to friends and colleagues, across town or around the world. Others have seen the extraordinary power of information that appears at their fingertips once they've logged on. And, of course, there are those who insist on describing the Net as an "information swamp" or a "waste of time and energy." However, at least one or two folks per session say something like "This is incredible! I'm gonna use it from this moment on to help me find work."

Such variety tells me one thing: just about everyone has now heard of the Net, but relatively few have taken the time to tap into the real potential of this expanding, ever-changing resource.

So what is this thing they call the Net, anyway? Let me try to explain in some simple, straightforward terms. It certainly is a way to communicate with people all over the world, as long as they too are hooked up. It's also a huge assemblage of data, facts, articles and information—some of it useful, much of it useless and some of it potentially harmful (like bomb-building instructions or hate literature).

Three Basic Parts Essentially, the Net can be viewed as having three distinct components. First, there are the *physical components* of this international electronic system. Computers, modems, software (including browsers such as Netscape and Internet Explorer), telephone lines, cable, satellites and other equipment constitute the heart of this seemingly ungainly beast.

Next you have the *transmission components*. Here you'll come across terms ranging from the everyday, such as telephone lines, cable and satellites, to arcane jargon such as routers, ISDN, ADSL and packet switching. These allow for the almost instantaneous transfer of data to just about anywhere on earth.

Fortunately, that's already more than you really need to know about the inside workings of this stuff. True, this technical background can be fascinating (maybe not to me and you, but surely to an information systems professional, who will likely skip this chapter anyway). What will help you most in your work search is the third part: the *information component*. This includes industry databases, company Web sites, labour market information, press releases about specific organizations, trends, job postings, current events and all those other critical details you need to make sound career decisions.

How It All Started

So far it may sound as if the Net was a gift hand-delivered to us mortals by good Samaritans who floated down from cyber-heaven. The truth is somewhat more frightening. Back in 1969, the U.S. Department of Defense was given a mandate to fortify its computer system against nuclear attack. This was the beginning of Arpanet, the network developed by the Advanced Research Projects Agency (you gotta love those military acronyms).

Here's what it comes down to, really. The U.S. army built a system whereby if the entire continent was consumed by a horrific nuclear

Table 1.1 What the Net Used to Consist Of

Before the World Wide Web came to be in the early 1990s, cyberspace was dominated by text only. Here are some of the components of the early Internet.*

COMPONENT	DESCRIPTION
Archie	A program used to search files at FTP sites
Gopher	A menu of text-only databases
Veronica	A search engine for data in "Gopherspace"
FTP	File Transfer Protocol based on text messages
Finger	A primitive way of finding who is online

*Purists can still find these but *you* needn't worry about them.

holocaust, causing life as we know it to become nothing more than ashes swirling in the wind, there would be at least two computers left to exchange data between themselves. A comforting scenario, wouldn't you agree?

Arpanet gradually matured into a series of independent computer networks. These were used mostly by scientists, academics and, of course, the military. The fact is that up until 1993, you pretty well needed a degree in computer science to be part of the Net. That's because it required knowledge of specialized coding language (UNIX, to be exact) just to send an e-mail message.

In 1993, all that changed with the invention of linked pages and a user-friendly interface called the World Wide Web. This suddenly enabled regular people like you and me to point and click our way through the growing volumes of information online and send messages to one another without having to know programming language. Today things have leaped ahead by giant bounds. The Internet has become the latest form of mass media. It is easy to access, full of information and filled with text as well as audio and video clips.

What the Internet Is Not

While there is a great deal of good to be said about the information highway, there are still some things to be careful of. It is still at a relatively early—some even say "embryonic"—stage of development. So, be forewarned that:

- The Net is not well organized. One thing you might find interesting is that nobody actually owns the Internet. There are companies and organizations that help manage different parts of the networks that tie everything together, but there is no single governing body that controls what happens online. The networks within different countries are funded and managed locally, in accordance with local regulations. Also, because millions of people around the world are accessing and broadcasting information from their homes, schools and workplaces, finding specific information can quickly become a chore.
- The Net is not completely free. There was a time when you could surf the Net endlessly without having to pay for anything other than your computer, modem and telephone connection. Nowadays we're seeing the rise of electronic commerce (e-commerce, for short), which involves using your credit card—or one of the new electronic payment devices now being tested—to buy products and services online. Personally, I'm not so sure this is a bad thing. After all, when you pay for information, it's often more detailed, recent and quickly retrievable than what is available at no charge. Still, in many cases, most of what you see online is included in your monthly fee for Internet access.
- The Net is not glitchless. If you've ever surfed before (on the Net, that is), you're probably well aware that things do not always go smoothly. You might, for instance, get the dreaded "404 error," telling you that the Web site you had been dreaming of reaching is no longer there. Or you could be dialling up at 8:00 in the evening only to find that it takes forever to download even a single page of information (due to the volume of users online at the same time). In other words, don't look for perfection here. But do expect things to improve continually as faster connections and automatic site searching are introduced.
- The Net is not static. Remember the expression "moss doesn't grow on a rolling stone"? The Net makes that rolling stone look like a moss-free, jet-propelled fireball. In other words, change happens so quickly on the Net that it's impossible to stay completely updated. The great Web site you viewed last month may now have a differ-

ent address, or perhaps it's disappeared altogether. You may have just gotten used to your browser when a brand new version comes along. Perhaps you've mastered the basic techniques, only to discover that yet another "killer app" (useful application) has sprung to prominence overnight.

- The Net is not private. The ugly truth about online privacy is that when you surf the Net, you are not completely anonymous. You might leave a trail behind you as you hop from site to site that can be traced by professional data gatherers. Each time you send an e-mail or post a message to a newsgroup or discussion forum, your e-mail address can be "harvested" for marketing purposes. Fortunately, it is not very easy to follow these trails directly back to you (your name and address, for example, are not necessarily available just from your e-mail address). It does suggest, however, that you should consider using a program such as Pretty Good Privacy (**www.nai.com/products/security/security.asp**) for a measure of protection.

II. THE MAIN PARTS OF THE NET

CYBER TIP One way to keep up with all the changes on the Net is to get updates regularly. There are several options here. You could regularly review certain sites, such as *The Toronto Star*'s Convergence (**www.theconvergence.com**). On the other hand, why not have free updates sent to you automatically by e-mail, such as the Berst Alert at **www.zdnet.com/anchordesk**. Or else just bookmark your own favourite sites and visit them from time to time.

For career seekers and job hunters, the Net has become a genuine bonanza of information. It's also an electronic meeting place for people with similar goals and interests from across Canada and around the world. There is a common misconception, however, that the Net is a single, cohesive entity. It most certainly is not. It consists of several disparate parts, each linked in its own way through the Internet's network. Each of these

Table 1.2 Key Components of the Internet

NAME OF COMPONENT	BRIEF DESCRIPTION
E-mail	Electronic mail with text and file attachments
World Wide Web	Information with graphics, text, sound and video
Usenet Newsgroups, forums and mailing lists	Discussion groups based on e-mail messages
Internet Relay Chat, Internet Phone, Bulletin Boards	Used to communicate with others instantly on the Net
FTP, Gopher, Telnet, Archie	Older Internet applications that are not often used

elements can be viewed as a tool in its own right, with increasingly seamless connections.

To help unravel the Net's networks, I've provided brief descriptions of the important components in Table 1.2. This includes e-mail, the World Wide Web, Usenet newsgroups and Internet Relay Chat. Each element is introduced here, along with practical tips and instructions for getting started, except for Internet Relay Chat, which is described in Chapter 9. There's more on newsgroups in that chapter, too.

E-mail: The Winged Messenger

The most popular aspect of the Internet, by far, is e-mail. You may already have it at home, and odds are that you've used it if you've worked in an office. But what is it and what can it really do? In its simplest form, e-mail is an electronic message sent from one computer to another. You can send or receive personal and business-related messages with attachments of pictures, word-processed files or other documents. You can even send World Wide Web documents back and forth on some of the more recently released mail programs.

How E-mail Works Just as a letter stops at different postal stations along its delivery route, e-mail is passed from one computer to another as it travels through the network. Each computer receives the e-mail address and routes it to another computer until it eventually reaches its destination. It's then stored in your electronic mailbox, where it waits until you access it with your private password. With the Internet, the whole electronic mailing process usually takes only a few minutes, allowing you to communicate quickly and easily with virtually anyone in the world who has an e-mail address, day or night—and it's all included in your monthly Internet access fee.

Getting Set Up What do you need to be able to use e-mail? If you're working from home, you'll need a personal computer, modem and an Internet account (see Chapter 2). You must also have an e-mail program. You automatically get one from your Internet Service Provider (ISP) when you subscribe.

Then comes the ever-popular e-mail address. Your ISP gladly issues you at least one at no extra charge, and it will sound something like yourname@netservice.com. Not bad, until you consider that this ties you to a specific ISP. Consider the repercussions. If you put an e-mail address on your résumé, which I strongly suggest in most cases, you'd better be sure that your provider will still be around three months from now. If it happens to go out of business or merge with another provider, you could lose your mailing address—just as employers are trying to contact you for interviews!

Is there an alternative? Yes—free, third-party e-mail accounts that you can use no matter what service provider you choose. Examples are Hotmail from Microsoft at **www.hotmail.com** and Excite from the Excite search engine at **www.excite.com**. There are many benefits to taking this approach. You free yourself up from having to stay with one provider just to keep a consistent e-mail address. You can access your e-mail from any computer in the world that is hooked up to the Net, just by visiting the Hotmail Web site for example. The disadvantages are that you're relying on the free service to a) remain free and b) remain in existence over a long period of time. There are also the flashing banner advertising and intrusive information gathering that go along with these services, but these could be worth it for the convenience and portability.

Something else you'll need to know is your username and a password. These allow you to keep the contents of your mailbox private, although not impenetrable. Of course, you'll also need to know the e-mail address of the person you want to send your message to.

Understanding Your E-mail Address Your e-mail address has the following structure: yourname@domain. The *yourname* portion is your user name (e.g., mswartz or mark, in my case), and the *domain* is the address of the mail server (either that of your ISP or the one supplied by the third-party e-mail service). You can always tell the difference between an e-mail address and a Web site address. The e-mail address invariably has the @ (pronounced as "at") symbol somewhere in the middle; Web sites never do.

Getting Your Mail—A Non-Techie Explanation To retrieve new messages, you need to go online first (that is, boot-up your computer and log on to your Internet connection). Once this has been done, you run your mail program. (Note: some browsers do this for you automatically.) Then you click on the "Get Mail" or "New Mail" icon.

The e-mail program does the rest for you. It logs in to your POP (Point of Presence) server, sends the username and password (which you've stored in your mail program so you don't have to type them in each time), and downloads (transfers) any new mail on to your hard disk. Depending on your mail service, you will see a status message during this process saying how much mail is on your server and perhaps the sender and subject line for each message. You then click on the message you want to read and...voilà!

CYBER TIP You usually don't have to use the e-mail package that comes as part of your browser. If you want more control and variety of features, consider downloading a different e-mail program, such as Eudora (**www.eudora.com**).

Sending New Mail Composing an e-mail message is very much like creating a regular letter or memo. The difference is that you can send your message across the city—or across the globe—in the blink of an eye (try that with Canada Post!). Most e-mail programs now enable you to type in your message offline, when you are not plugged into the Net. Personally I prefer this approach because it gives me time to draft and edit before I send the message out—forever!

Try to make sure that you fill out the address information correctly. You'll be asked who you're sending the message to (that is, the recipient's e-mail address), what the subject is and if there are any attachments. Note that your subject line is very important. It tells the recipient what this message is about, and is often the first thing displayed in his or her mailbox. Keep your subject line concise and accurate. Even so, there's nothing wrong with an attention-getting subject line. But do make it short, relevant and inoffensive.

The procedure of connecting to your server and uploading your mail (transferring your mail to the server) is automated by your mail program. Once you've made the Internet connection, you only have to tell your mail program to transmit your new mail by clicking on the "Send" icon. Normally there is no delay. The message is uploaded to the SMTP (Simple Mail Transfer Protocol) server, which sends it right away. It may take a few moments or more to reach its destination, depending on the size of the message, attachments (if any), the routing involved and how busy the routes are.

A Word of Caution Sending an e-mail message is very easy. So easy that it could get you into trouble if you're not careful. One of my clients once sent off a nasty e-mail to her former employer a few days after her job was terminated. About two hours later she realized that this was, in her own words, "not a good move." It could have jeopardized her future dealings with the company (as in getting a positive letter of reference).

Fortunately, the former employer recognized that this message was sent by someone who was extremely upset at a time of emotional vulnerability and wisely let the matter go without further incident. The point, however, is clear: Can you always rely on the goodwill and understanding of your e-mail recipient, or should you take a few moments before hitting that irreversible "Send" button? My advice is to give yourself some time to check your spelling and grammar, and ask yourself "does this really say what I want it to say?"

The Look of Your Message The content of your message is not the only thing that makes an impression on your reader. E-mail expert Kaitlin Sherwood has some interesting advice in this area. As she says, "words on a computer screen look different than on paper, and usually people find it harder to read things on a screen than on paper." Some people actually go so far as to print out their e-mail just to read it!

Remember that the resolution of the computer screen may not be as crisp as it is on paper, especially if the recipient is using a small computer screen. Sometimes the screen flickers, or the font may be too small, or it may just be plain ugly. After all, unlike the printed page, you have no control over the size or even choice of font the recipient uses to read your message. Any of these factors can detract from the impact of your message.

Your recipient's mail program may also impose some constraints upon the formatting of your message. For instance, some do not automatically wrap the text, so the lines might not run together in a paragraph. That means that if your margin setting is 80 characters per line, it could appear ragged to a reader whose margins are fixed at 72. One way to get around this is to set your own default to 70 characters. That way you increase your odds of having your message come out cleanly at the other end. On top of this, your e-mail message may be read in a window with scrollbars, particularly if it's long. While scrollbars let you move up and down the page to view more text, they can make it harder to see long paragraphs in a small window. What all this really means is that an effective e-mail page layout may be different from that of a paper document.

Hints on Improving the Appearance of Your Message

To help make your message more readable, consider the following hints:

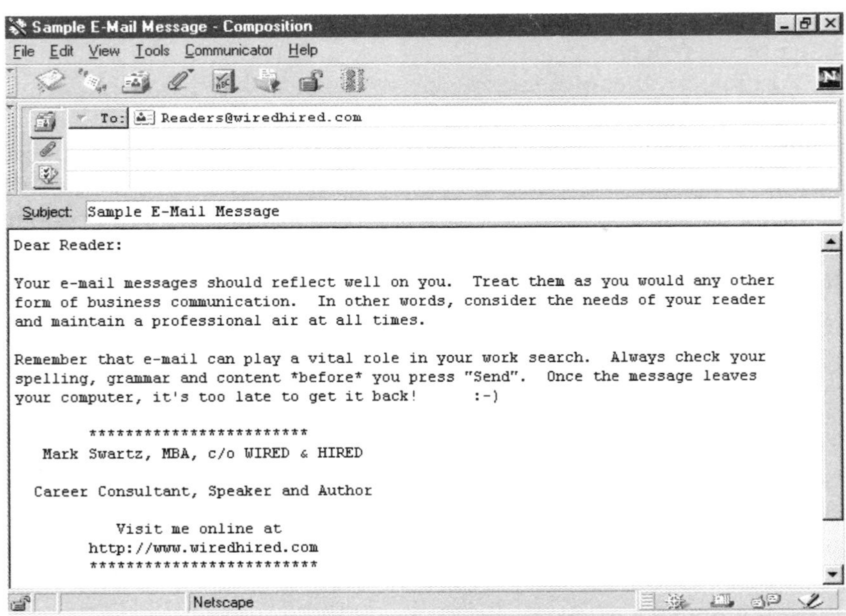

- Break up paragraphs to only a few sentences apiece.
- Set the line length to 70 characters.
- Use concise, clear terms instead of big words and overly long sentences.
- Use headings where appropriate to break up your paragraphs.
- Keep the whole message as brief as possible.

CYBER TIP For more information on using e-mail, try the Kaitlin Sherwood site at **www.webfoot.com/advice/email.top.html** or the Guide to Effective E-mail from the University of Prince Edward Island at **www.upei.ca/~access/emaillinks.html.**

Sending Attachments with E-Mail Most mailers now support *attachments*, which means you can send along a document or Web page (even a binary file, such as a computer program) with your mail. If your correspondent has a mail reader that can handle attachments (as most people do), this works very well. The file can be opened at the convenience of the recipient, in the format that you sent it.

In some ways e-mail is better than a fax. When you send your e-mail message, it gets stored in the recipient's mailbox until he or she is ready to open it. With a fax, the message is there for everyone to see. Plus a fax won't go through if the recipient's line is busy. This is almost impossible with e-mail. You can also send your e-mail to anyone who has access without incurring long-distance charges, even if you're sending it halfway around the world. Try that with a fax!

The Formatting Quandary Best of all for work searchers, you can send more than just regular text via e-mail. With an Internet protocol called Multipurpose Internet Mail Extension (MIME), you can also include formatted documents, photos, sound files, Web pages and video files as attachments. That means you can send your fully formatted Word or WordPerfect résumé to potential employers—if they are equipped to read it.

Does this mean that you could e-mail your finely tuned, highly targeted résumé and cover letter to a potential employer, only to have that person unable to open or read your file? You betcha. You need first to understand that you can choose how you send your message out: *as is* or *universally readable.* Here's a quick look at what that means.

- *As is* means your document retains all its original formatting. You can only do this when you attach your document as a file to the body of the e-mail (by clicking "attach" or "attachment" on your mail program, then navigating your folders to select the right file). It can only be read by the recipient if he or she has the same or higher version of the software you used to create the file. For example, if you send a file as Word97, and your recipient has Word95, that person will not be able to read your attachment (without going to the Microsoft site to download the appropriate update patch, which you can't count on).
- *Universally readable* means that if you want your message to be accessible by your recipients, no matter what type of computer or e-mail reader they have, you'll have to go the plain-text route. This converts your file to ASCII (American Standard Code for Information Interchange) format. The downside here is that all your fancy formatting such as bold lettering, underlining, bullet points, centring and so on gets removed. (More on this in Chapter 7, Know How to Send Your Material Electronically.)

Discussion Forums via Usenet Newsgroups

Humans do not live by the exchange of e-mail messages to specific individuals alone. This is where the Usenet part of the Internet comes into play. Don't be put off by the name. Usenet is simply an area on the Net where people exchange public and private messages about particular subjects. These e-mail interchanges are popularly called *discussion groups.* There are more than 200,000 of these groups (and counting). Topics cover almost every subject imaginable, ranging from poetry to politics and, oh yeah, job hunting or starting a business. Career-related newsgroups often have job postings and self-employment opportunities, as well as interactive advice areas. (More on this in Chapter 9, Network into the Hidden Job Market.)

Of Discussions and Netiquette Think of Usenet as a virtual coffeehouse (unlike Starbucks, where you can also purchase a double mocha cappuccino java). If you're the shy type, you can hang back and read what others are posting without responding. This is called, appro-

CYBER TIP The Net is becoming increasingly seamless. Until recently the only place you could find discussion groups was in the Usenet area. Today you can go directly to the World Wide Web and find thousands of discussion groups on the "My Deja News" service (**www.dejanews.com**).

priately enough, *lurking*. Or you can post a reply to existing messages. You can even create a brand new topic (called a *discussion thread*). The great thing about newsgroups is that anyone can participate in them, although not all ISPs offer access to every single newsgroup.

How do they actually work? If you intend to go through Usenet, as opposed to the World Wide Web (see Cyber Tip), you usually need a newsreader program. Your Internet Service Provider should automatically provide you with one. If not, Netscape Navigator and Microsoft Internet Explorer come with a built-in newsreader program. Next, determine which newsgroups interest you. Bear in mind that there are so many of them that you will only want to choose a few that really interest you (a number of career-related ones are listed in Chapter 11, Find Special Resources for Special Groups).

You can easily subscribe to (that is, join) a newsgroup by following the instructions that come with your newsreader. Taking part in discussions is a whole other matter, although it's technically as easy as e-mail. It requires a certain flair, so you might want to spend a moment reading a bit about Netiquette, which is covered in Chapter 9. Ignore this section at your peril—many a "newbie" (new Internet user) has been "flamed" (besieged by angry e-mailers) for posting without knowing the informal rules of online networking.

REAL LIFE You may find that people send you e-mail written in an informal style. They may get lazy with their sentence structure and punctuation, or they might not take the time to spell-check. *Don't be lulled into a false sense of security by this.* The e-mail that you send is the same as any of your other formal business correspondence (e.g., memos and letters). Take time to check spelling, grammar and content before you press the "Send" button—your professional image rides on it!

Untangling the World Wide Web

Once you've got the hang of e-mail, it's time to go surfing. The *World Wide Web* (also known as WWW or the Web) has been described as a wide-area hypermedia information retrieval initiative that provides universal access to interfaced information. Is this exciting, or what?

Alright, so that definition is in the techno-babble I promised to avoid (but hey, it felt so good to say it!). Even so, the Web itself is nothing less than spectacular. It has provided computer users worldwide with access to a variety of resources in a simplified fashion. The Web has changed the way people view and post information—it has created the first true global data network that anyone can use.

Just Browsing To view the Web, you need a piece of software called a browser (after you've signed up with an ISP, described in Chapter 2). A browser is the graphical interface between you and all the data stored on the World Wide Web. The most popular are Netscape Navigator and Microsoft Internet Explorer. There is almost always one included with the software provided to you by your ISP. It can usually do everything you need it to do: view all sites on the Web, access newsgroups, participate in chat sessions and support technical developments such as frames and Java (which are new ways to view the Web).

How the Web Works Web pages are really just files stored on computers (called servers) located all over the world. The Internet is basically a *client–server* system. Your computer is the client, and the Web site publisher's computer is the server. Here's an example: one of the great Canadian career sites is Canada WorkInfoNet. When you browse their Web site (**www.workinfonet.ca**) and request a page from their server in Ottawa, the server that hosts the WorkInfoNet site sends the page over the Internet to your computer. Since this Web site has links to hundreds of other career-related resources, you can click your mouse and immediately connect to pages in Banff or Charlottetown, or anywhere else in the world.

Let's Get Hyper The glue that holds the Web together is called *hypertext*, which is used to create *hyperlinks*. These allow files on the Web to be connected in a way that lets you easily jump among them. Hypertext is basically the same as regular text. It can be stored, read, searched or edited. There is, however, a critical distinction: hypertext contains encoded connections that can automatically transfer (or link) you to other related online documents. This is commonly known as browsing or *surfing* the Web.

Hypermedia is hypertext with a difference. Hypermedia documents contain links not only to other pieces of text, but also to other forms of information—sounds, pictures and movies. Images themselves can be selected to link to sounds or documents. Hypermedia simply combines hypertext and multimedia. Let's say you're using a CD-ROM and you click on a link that automatically takes you on to the World Wide Web; there you click on another link to view a video clip of a typical job interview. That's using hypermedia.

Upgrading Your Browser If you're not satisfied with the browser supplied by your ISP, you can easily get hold of a better program—for free! The latest version of Netscape is always available directly from the Web at **www.netscape.com**. The nearest competitor to Netscape is Microsoft's Internet Explorer, which is available at the Microsoft Web site (**www.microsoft.com**). An early version of this browser is included free with Windows 95, and it can be upgraded at no charge on Microsoft's Web site, too. While there are many more browsers available, you're better off sticking to the well-known ones when starting out. That way you're assured that they can handle the newer protocols and HTML codes.

Three Main Ways to Search for Information As I mentioned before, the Web is a bonanza for career transitioners. It can help you at every stage—from choosing a profession to preparing yourself for your marketing blitz, right up to locating leads for work. The hardest part, to be frank, is sorting through all the junk that's floating around in cyberspace. Finding exactly what you need, precisely when you need it, will be your greatest challenge.

As it turns out, there are three basic ways to search for information. The simplest way (without overstating the obvious) is to know exactly where to look for it. On the World Wide Web, this means having the correct address of the Web page you're seeking. For instance, you could be scanning a newspaper's employment section and come across an ad for MegaCompany that urges you to "visit our Web site." The ad includes an Internet address, such as www.megacompany.com. A Web address is unique—only one page on the Web per address. In this way, it is akin to a telephone number.

REAL LIFE Every single Web page has its own address, known as a Universal Resource Locator, or *URL* for short. It typically starts with *http://*, which stands for hypertext transfer protocol, but with most browsers you no longer have to enter this as part of the address. In the example of MegaCompany, you would simply go to the address box in your browser and enter www.megacompany.com. For this reason, all the Web sites you'll see in this book have the http:// part omitted.

Searching by Subject or Category Another way to look for information is to use what's known as a *search directory* or *search engine.* A search directory arranges links to relevant Web sites under subject headings or categories. A search engine is basically just a big index, which allows you to seek information using keywords (e.g., the name of a particular company). There are dozens of search tools out there, with names like Yahoo!, Excite, WebCrawler, AltaVista, Maple Square, HotBot, Canada Yellow Pages and so on.

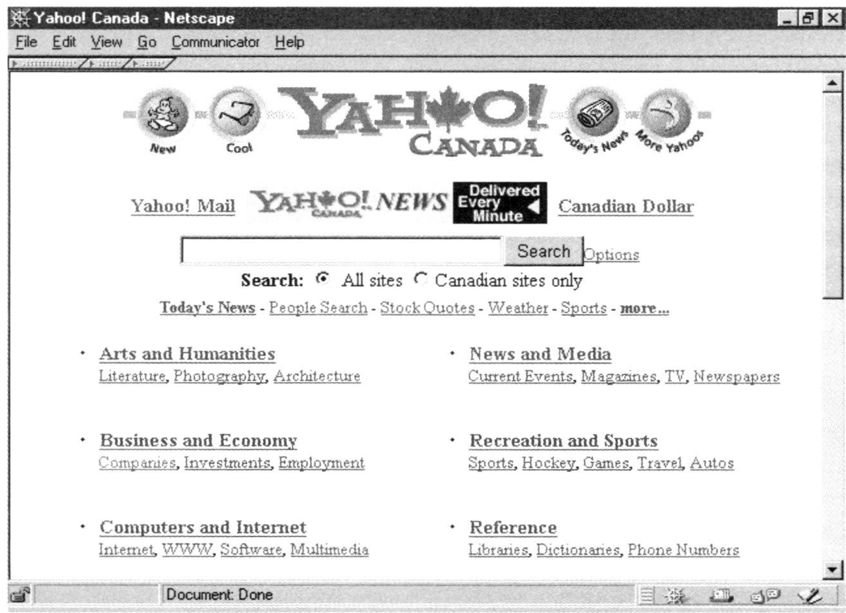

Search directories are great when you're first starting out, especially if you're not quite sure what you're looking for. Let's say you're thinking about finding work in the automotive industry. If you try the Yahoo Canada search directory (**www.yahoo.ca**), you might find around 14 main headings (like I did in the figure on the previous page). You could start by clicking on Business and Economy, then clicking again on Companies, then again on Automotive. From there you can select from about 20 micro-categories, such as Dealers, Manufacturers, Organizations or Consulting.

Each of these micro-categories gives you a list of links to related Web sites, which you can then surf individually. This process of starting broad then focusing in is a classic rule of research, called *drilling down.* Note, however, that the directory does *not* go to every Web site on the Net. Someone has selected maybe 10 to 20 percent of the millions of available sites. Hopefully this means that your search is more targeted and relevant.

Searching by Keyword or Topic There will be times when you know precisely what you want to find, but haven't the slightest clue where to start. Sticking with the automotive example, maybe you've decided that you'd like to work for General Motors. But how do you find its Web site? A fairly straightforward way is to go back to the Yahoo Canada main page, and use the "Search" portion instead of the directory. In this instance, you'd type in the keywords *"general motors"* (quotes and lower-case letters included), then click on the "Search" button. What comes up is a list of Web sites that contain both *general* and *motors.* You've just done an advanced search, meaning that you've combined words and forced the search engine to find only those pages that contain both items.

One thing to remember when searching via keywords is that when the engine sifts through the actual Web it finds just about every page on which your search term appears. So don't be surprised if, for example, you use AltaVista Canada and come up with 486,513 matches (no kidding) when you type in the word *jobs.* Once you start sorting through the responses, you'll see that many of these so-called matches are way out in left field, but somewhere on the page the word *jobs* happens to appear. That's why I recommend using the keyword approach only for finding specific companies, people, places and things.

III. WIRED WRAP-UP

So how are we doing so far? I'm willing to bet that if you've never used the Net before, the whole thing still seems like some mystical, impenetrable Goliath, even if you've read this far. "Let some other brave and sophisticated soul tackle this beast," you're probably saying to yourself.

Try not to give up too easily. Remember that this chapter is specifically for new users of the Net. We looked at what the Internet is and isn't, how it got started and the key components with regard to career matters (e-mail, the World Wide Web and discussion groups). Each of these Internet components has its own features, quirks and benefits. The important thing to keep in mind is that *you don't have to be a high tech guru to use this stuff.*

Of course, I can scream that until my face turns purple and it still won't mean much unless you go online yourself. How to do so and where to find access are the focus of Chapter 2. Meanwhile, make an effort to give yourself some development time. That is, allocate an hour or two each day to practice your surfing skills. I guarantee that you'll move from *beginner* to *user* within a couple of sessions.

CHAPTER 2

Getting Hooked (Up)

Sometimes my lack of techno-depth embarrasses even me. Take the first time I bought a computer (you know, back when you had to hand crank 'em). I raced home and set everything up as quickly as I could. I was dying to try out the Internet. So I switched my computer on and searched my file menus frantically. Aha! There was the Net icon. I clicked on it anxiously and waited for my adventure to unfold before my eyes. Then I waited some more...then waited longer still.

After about five fruitless hours I threw up my hands in disgust, kicked my computer (not too hard, though, so as not to void the warranty) and called the manufacturer to complain loudly about its faulty equipment. Guess what the first question was that the company's service person asked me. You got it: "Is your modem plugged in?" I responded deftly, displaying that technical brilliance for which I have become highly renowned. "Um, what's a modem?"

OK, so it turns out that you need more than just a basic computer to get onto the Net. You must also have a modem (modulator/demodulator unit), which, thank goodness, is built into almost every computer sold today. The other component needed is an Internet Service Provider (a company you pay to link you directly to the Net), and there are lots of them around too. Fortunately, even if you don't own a computer or have ready access to one through a friend or relative, getting connected to the Net is getting much easier. Here's what you really need to know to make it happen.

I. CONNECTING FROM HOME

Let's start with the following scenario: you already have a computer at your disposal, or plan to soon. Like I said, in terms of equipment, all you actually need is a computer (minimum 386 processing speed, but preferably Pentium, or a Macintosh with at least an 030 processor, but preferably a Power Mac) and a modem (with a download rate of 28.8 kbps, or kilobytes per second, preferably 56.6 kbps or higher). You can buy a perfectly suitable computer these days for under $1,500, including just about everything you need to get surfing. You may even be able to lease one of these babies for $40 to $60 a month. The faster your equipment is, the quicker you get to see your information. Of course, it's always nice to have the most up-to-date equipment, but you definitely don't need a $4,500 super hotrod or a dedicated 1,000 kbps cable modem for career-related surfing.

Of course, it's not only the hardware that you'll need. The other thing you must have is a connection to the Internet. This can be arranged by signing up with an Internet Service Provider (ISP). You need one of these because they're the folks who have a direct trunkline link to the Net. In essence, when you sign up with an ISP, you're renting an Internet connection from them, much like the way you rent your telephone number. Your monthly fee for a phone-line modem hook-up may range from as little as $9.99 for five hours of use up to $25.99 for unlimited access (all prices quoted in Canadian dollars, which are automatically devalued by practically 50 percent beyond our lovely borders).

Finding an Internet Service Provider

Luckily, your choice of ISPs has increased dramatically. You can select a local provider or one with a national or international presence. There are full-service providers, as well as those that offer limited services. You've also got commercial online services, such as America Online or Prodigy. They provide access to their own networks and promote their own content in addition to giving you a gateway to the Net. Any ISP will get you up and running to get you started.

Finding one (or more) of these services is fairly easy. You can start with your local Yellow Pages directory. Look up Internet, then check for listings of Services or Service Providers. Make a few calls to see which service is best for you (some criteria to consider are listed on page 32).

REAL LIFE No matter what ISP you choose, once you have Net access you should be able to surf worldwide without incurring any long-distance charges whatsoever. Just make sure that your provider has a *local access phone number,* so that you don't get dinged each time you dial in. Once you're on the Net you've got everything at your disposal; it's not like one ISP gives you more Web sites to choose from than another (although some public-access connections might filter out sites known to post pornography or hate literature). The Net is the Net.

Try It...You'll Like It

Another way to find an ISP is to go to the closest store that sells computer software. This could be a computer retailer, a software outlet or one of the business supplies stores that seem to be springing up everywhere. Survey the Internet section of the software display. You're bound to see two or three boxed versions of Internet sign-up packages, usually from national ISPs such as Sympatico. With these, you'll typically receive software to get up and running, an instruction manual and a free trial. If, at the end of your trial, you decide to cancel, make sure that you call the ISP promptly to notify them. They'll have your credit card number on file and will happily bill you until the end of time unless otherwise instructed.

Are there other methods to load up your computer for free (at least initially)? How about getting a trial software package directly from an ISP? Some of the major Canadian and U.S. services often send out free diskettes to households to encourage you to try them and sign on—have you checked your mailbox lately? Shrink-wrapped computer magazines often contain free trial diskettes as well. If none of the above has materialized for you, simply call up your local ISP and ask them to send you their software for a free trial. Most will do this gladly—just make sure you understood the credit card warning above!

Of course, there's always the online solution. If you already have a way of getting on the Net, surf over to "the list," at **www.thelist.internet.com**. It contains links to more than 5,000 ISPs, searchable by country, province, city or area code.

Selecting the Best ISP

Your choice of ISP should be driven by your intended use, not by flashy displays or fancy trial offers. Here are some questions to ask yourself regarding your usage patterns:

- Will I spend most of my time online sending e-mails, taking part in discussion groups or surfing the Web?
- About how many hours per week do I plan to spend on each of the above activities for work-search purposes? How about for entertainment?
- What time(s) of the day do I intend to be online? (Most casual users go online during the evening, so you want to make sure that you can get connected when it's convenient for you.)
- Will other members of my household be using the Net too? If so, for how many hours per week, and for what purposes?
- Will I need a connection as I travel around the country, or will most of my time be spent at one location (e.g., home)?

When you do call an ISP to inquire about their services, there are some pointed questions that you could put to them:

- Do you offer a "no busy signal" policy so that I can surf whenever I want?
- Do you provide round-the-clock, live technical support?
- Do you ship out your start-up software free, with a complete manual?
- How many separate e-mail addresses are included in my monthly fee?
- Do you give me free storage space if I want to host my own Web site? How many megabytes?

Why Cheaper May Not Be Better No matter which ISP you choose, make sure that it gives you what you require. Look for reliability, user-friendliness, customer support and simplicity. Also, make sure your ISP has a track record and is not likely to go belly up some time in the near future.

The most important thing to grasp is this: the gap between the most expensive phone-line service and the cheapest one is very small. There are, however, some critical differences. At the higher end, you can be reasonably confident that your ISP will be around a few months from now—just when employers are receiving your résumé and want to start contacting you via e-mail. Also, you can be confident that you'll be able to connect any time of the day or night. You will also have access to excellent customer support, no matter how basic or complicated your questions may be. The verdict? Those few dollars extra you spend per month could very well mean the difference between Net satisfaction and total frustration.

How Important Is Speed? There's an argument that, when it comes to the Net, "faster is always better." Here are some words that may bring you comfort. Without sounding like a Luddite, I don't agree that you always need to be at the cutting edge of modem technology. You can adequately use the Net for career purposes with a basic 28.8 kbps phone connection. Sure, a 56.6 kbps hook-up is nice to have. But when you start to consider that a modem rated at 56.6 kbps usually operates at 46 to 48 kbps at the most, the differential becomes less noticeable.

So why is there such a fuss about the new, so-called high-speed Net services? Because they really are fast! Phone companies, for example, are falling over themselves to introduce Internet access at speeds beginning at 2 to 100 times quicker than conventional modems. You may have heard the terms ISDN (Integrated Services Digital Network) or ADSL (Asynchronous Digital Subscriber Line)—these are the phone companies' answers to the question, "How do you squeeze more juice out of a plain old telephone line?"

Unfortunately, these services are considerably more expensive than your basic offerings. With ISDN, you get speeds from 64 to 128 kbps. In addition, you can use your phone while surfing the Net—no extra phone lines needed. Your actual monthly fee may be the same as with a conventional hook-up. But you must have an ISDN phone line, and there is a dollar-a-minute usage charge during the day. Ouch! Plus there may also be an initiation fee of about $100, an installation charge of $200, and you must purchase a special modem for $250 to $500. Double ouch!

Think that this may not be the route to go just yet? Then look at the ADSL path. For $60 to $70 per month, plus an installation charge ranging from $150 to $300, you could zoom away at up to 2 mbps (millibytes per second). The hitch? Service is available in very limited areas, although the rollout continues unabated.

CYBER TIP Check out the ultra fast Net alternatives for yourself. Sympatico's ADSL, called the High-Speed Connection, is at **adsl.sympatico.ca.**

You knew, of course, that once the Net took off everyone would want in on the act. Consequently, there are several emerging ways to hook up at high speed other than ISDN and ADSL connections. Here are the most common:

- Cable: Bypasses the phone system completely. Cable companies set customers up with a dedicated Internet line that runs at 150 to 500 kbps, with dramatic increases in speed expected in the future. Prices are running at $35–$60 a month, with the set-up fee usually ranging from $50 to $200, depending on where you live.
- Satellite: Direct transfer of data from satellite transmission to a specialized modem. Extremely fast, and frees up your phone line. However, the equipment alone could cost upward of $1,000, and the monthly connection could run from $50 to well over $100. But you do get to have that cool parabolic antenna thingie sticking out from your roof.

REAL LIFE A good rule of thumb with Internet service is to keep things simple. Unless you plan to use the Net for working from home, it might be best to stick with a regular telephone modem or cable access.

II. CONNECTING AWAY FROM HOME

Not everyone has the luxury of owning a home computer (although it is quickly becoming more and more of a necessity). Even fewer folks have an up-to-date laptop computer to give them Net access when they're away from home. If you have neither of these, does it mean that you're frozen out of the cyber-revolution? That you can't e-mail your résumé to employers or search for information on work opportunities?

Not at all. Fortunately, you're not out of the ball game just yet. Increasingly, you can opt for "remote" access (neither home- nor office-based) to computers and the Internet. Sometimes this is free, sometimes

> **REAL LIFE** If you happen to be working already and have an online connection, can you use company equipment to surf for new employment? Tempting though that may be, my advice is to take the high road (or is that hire road?) on this one. Employees in Canada have been fired for using the Net on company time for personal purposes. Plus your employer technically owns any e-mail you send or receive. In other words, stay away from this approach and play it safe. If you just can't help yourself, ask for a copy of your company's Internet Usage Policy—that ought to bring you back to reality!

you pay for it. Either way, not having a home computer is no longer an excuse to drop out of the game.

Libraries Get Wired

Have you dropped into your local library recently? You might be amazed by what you discover. Sure, there are books galore on using the Net. You may even find a well-used copy of *Get Wired, You're Hired* there. Of more relevance, your library may now have a computer terminal or two set up for surfing the Internet.

According to the librarians I've spoken to across the country, this form of Net access takes many forms. In some places, you can book a 30-minute or 1-hour session online for free. Other libraries charge a nominal fee for surfing, like $1 an hour, to help recoup costs. In large metropolitan centres such as Toronto or Vancouver, you might just find yourself paying up to $15 an hour (or 25¢ a minute) for the privilege of surfing. In some libraries surfing is free, but it might cost you a dime or quarter to print out a hard copy of each Web page you're interested in.

Note too that not all libraries have this service available, and some of the ones that do use a filter to block out certain sites. Not that being prevented from downloading a 45-minute video version of "Lusty Vixen Stewardesses" is going to hinder your work search (unless you're considering a career as a sex therapist in the airline industry). Of course, the sites you're probably looking for in your work search are not likely to be filtered out. It's just that you should know what you're getting into. Don't forget to call your local college or university library, too, to see if they allow public access to their Net-enabled computers.

CYBER TIP Good news: *Remote e-mail* is now a reality! Even if you don't have a home computer and Internet Service Provider, your very own e-mail address is but a few clicks away. Just about every major search engine or directory now offers free e-mail service accessible from any Net-enabled computer in the world (e.g., at a library, Employment Resource Centre or friend's place). In other words, you don't have to already have an account with an ISP somewhere to be able to set up a free account with one of these services. Two examples are Hotmail (**www.hotmail.com**) and Excite (**www.excite.com**). By signing up, you can send and receive e-mail to employers no matter what your situation is. Just remember to check your inbox on a regular basis!

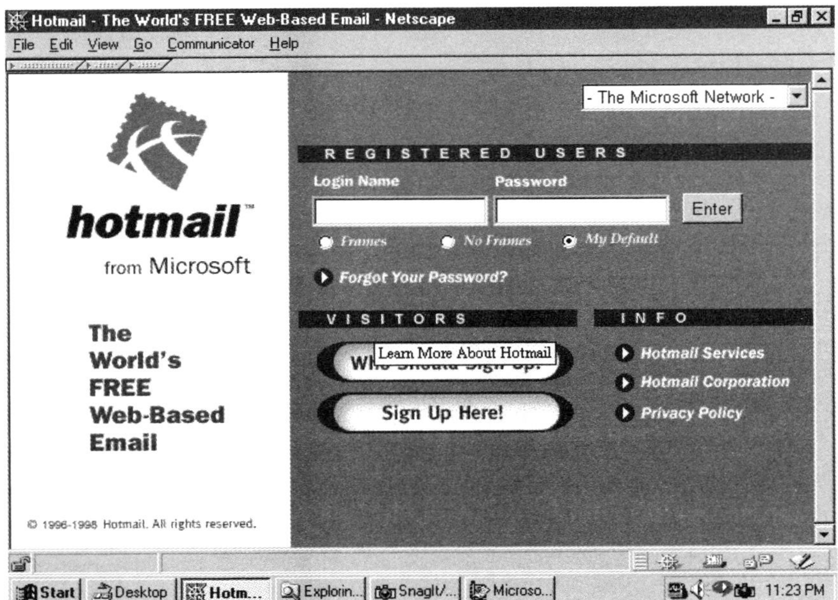

HRDC to the Rescue

If you're like me, you probably give more thought to Revenue Canada than you do to Human Resources Development Canada (HRDC). Until you're unemployed, that is. In which case your employment insurance centre becomes a transition lifeline (been there, done that!). But did you know that the folks at HRDC are also involved in a huge effort to make the Net accessible to just about anyone?

It's not just the unemployed who benefit from HRDC's largesse. For instance, just about anyone can stop into one of the growing number of Employment Resource Centres to use their computers, faxes, phones and library for work-search purposes. To find out about facilities and programs that may be available to you, and whether you qualify or not, call your local HRDC office, listed in the government pages of your phone book. If you already have access to the Net, zip over to their main site at **www.hrdc-drhc.gc.ca/common/home.shtml**.

One thing you'll quickly realize is that many of these outreach programs are still in the early stages. Hence, some cities or regions are not yet fully served. In fact, the services you will find range widely, depending on where you live. For an online look at what's available in your own area, **www.hrdc-drhc.gc.ca/maps/national/canada.shtml** is your best bet. In the meantime, these are some of the possible facilities that you will find when you call or visit your HRDC office, according to Susan Stone at the Metro Toronto office of the Possibilities Project (**www.possibilitiesproject.com**):

- HRDC-funded Assessment Centres. A large number of community organizations receive funding to help people who receive employment insurance (EI) or are eligible for Reachback to determine a suitable course of action in today's labour market. (Reachback clients are those who have received employment insurance in the past three years or those who have received EI in the past five years if the original EI claim was for maternity or paternity reasons.) Referrals for these kinds of programs are generally made after people attend an information session or booster club sponsored by their local Human Resources Canada Centre (HRCC). Many of these organizations offer other employment-related services such as resource centres and workshops.
- Employment Resource Centres (ERCs). ERCs are really self-help, one-stop outlets for relatively employment-ready individuals who want a complete resource base during usual business hours. Here you'll find computers for preparing and sending out résumés, free Internet access, magazines, newspapers, photocopying, faxing, etc.—in other words, all you really need to stay wired without investing in a home office. Of note is the fact that you needn't be unemployed or on social assistance to use these

facilities. Just come as you are, and take advantage too of the free courses and workshops. Self-employment coaching and planning may also be offered.

- Community employment resources. These tend to be targeted at designated groups with special needs. This covers a wide territory, such as people who are homeless or socially disadvantaged, or those who are partially house-bound or have physical disabilities or some form of mental illness. Some of these centres are specifically geared toward women, youth, Aboriginal peoples or recent immigrants. The spectrum of resources is broad, and may include individual counselling, workshops on careers and life skills, wage-subsidy programs, English as a second language courses, labour market trends, computer training, employer information, volunteer opportunities and help with résumé writing. A local job-posting board is often available as well.
- Job-finding clubs. People receiving EI or who have received EI in the past are often referred to job-finding clubs by HRDC. These programs vary in length, although a three-week program is common. You can now look up some of these clubs on the Net. For example, in Quebec there is the Club de recherche d'emploi at **www.cre.qc.ca/english/index.cgi**, and in British Columbia's Fraser Valley region there is **www.bc.hrdc-drhc.gc.ca/fraservalley**. You can also use the AltaVista Canada search engine (**www.altavista.ca**) and type in the words "job finding club" (quotes included). Features of a job-finding club may include:
  - access to the "hidden job market,"
  - after-club support with networking and goal setting,
  - drop-in days for networking,
  - Internet and e-mail access, and
  - computers equipped for word processing, spreadsheets and graphics.
- Social assistance offices. A number of social services have opened their own ERCs in their offices to help recipients of social assistance who are seeking work. All these offices have access to telephones, fax machines, photocopiers and a wide variety of resource materials. However, they might limit an individual to a reasonable amount of use, and long-distance telephone and fax transmissions may not be allowed. You can usually find career assessment and planning booklets and software, job-search strategies reference

guides, business directories and business plan development tools for people seeking self-employment. They may also have CD-ROMs with helpful information for career selection, understanding the workplace or financial planning. Social assistance offices are also good places to find other more general community information.

Business Service Centres Are Turning Up Everywhere

Let's say that you go to your local library to use the Net but the computer is booked up for the day. So you call up the local HRDC office but they haven't installed computers for public use yet. Where do you turn? To the private sector, that's where. Pop into a Chapters bookstore, for instance, and there may be Net-enabled computers available to rent by the minute or hour. Same with other Canada-wide chains such as Willson Stationers, Staples, The Office Place and Mailboxes etc.

Then there are always the smaller business service outlets that are popping up in cities and towns across the country. A good place to look is your Yellow Pages directory, under Office Supplies. Call up some local establishments and ask them if they rent Internet time to the public. Same with all those new computer schools and training institutes. In their non-peak hours, they are often looking for ways to generate additional income. You could even look for an Internet café—a place where you can surf while having a cup of coffee.

III. WIRED WRAP-UP

As the Net evolves, so too does its accessibility to an ever-broadening spectrum of users. Personally, I think this is great. The more people online for career-related reasons, the better the content and services become (and vice versa). Of course, as demand for Net use surges, it must be matched by new and easier ways of getting connected.

What I've seen since the first edition of this book is nothing short of phenomenal: an infrastructure catering to the needs of those without their own computers has begun to develop across the country. Primarily, this is a result of the efforts by Human Resources Development Canada—either directly through its Employment Resource Centres, or indirectly through grants to community outreach programs. Canadian libraries are also rising to this challenge. Not just places to borrow books anymore, they

REAL LIFE If you just can't seem to find a third-party outlet for Net access, there's always the tried-and-true method of "schnorring." This means calling on friends, relatives, colleagues and acquaintances to lend you an old computer, sell you one for next to nothing or let you into their home once in a while to surf or send and pick up your e-mail. If they resist, point out (gently) that it might very well be them asking you for this favour next time around.

now often offer Internet access and computer workshops at reasonable rates (if not for free). And, of course, companies that offer business services have recognized that there is a market for remote Internet access. Drop by the store that sells stationery and office supplies. More likely than not it has at least one Net-enabled computer available for you to use, on a pay-as-you-go basis.

So what does this widespread Internet access mean? Simply put, there is almost no excuse for not being online as part of your search for work. Now when you see the employment ads inviting you to "send in your résumé via e-mail" or to "visit our Web site for more information," you can't just shrug your shoulders in resignation—if you do, you are giving your competition an edge. The gauntlet has been thrown down. It's up to you to decide what way to run with it. The remainder of this book is geared toward helping you, step by step, to become a front-runner in the ever more cyber-dominated race for employment!

PART 2

GET WIRED AND READY

CHAPTER 3 Start by Knowing Yourself Well

I. JUST WHO THE HECK ARE YOU?

As any competent career consultant will tell you, success and satisfaction in work (and in life) depend on the strength of the choices that you make—or don't make. And solid career choices are based on an honest appraisal of who you really are. This includes looking at what you are genuinely good at doing, the things you truly want from life and how you can best match all this up with the current and future needs of employers (or customers, in the case of self-employment).

Unfortunately, many people don't get the chance to undertake such a thorough self-examination. They write up résumés, fall into a career and market themselves without delving into such critical areas as their skills, accomplishments, values, personality type and long-term goals. Then they continue to seek out employment based on what they think they're expected to do, or on their immediate needs, instead of taking a strategic approach to career building.

How This Chapter Can Help You

Do you count yourself as one of the people I described above? If so, you're definitely not alone. Our hurry-up world and the demands it places on us are not exactly contemplation-friendly. In other words, we all have obligations and pressures to find work—any work—to pay our bills, keep spouses and families happy, or simply to get our start in the work arena.

That's where this chapter comes in to play. For those of you who are currently employed, think of it as a moment of calm in an otherwise helter-skelter life. It will give you an opportunity to look inward to help you determine what's best for you in the future. If you are currently seeking work, this is an ideal opportunity to step back and create a strategic career plan. In either case, you'll have a better chance at making meaningful decisions about the direction you take in work and in life. Here are a few more of the immediate benefits:

- You'll know how to position your strengths for the employment market.
- You'll put together a targeted résumé that gets results.
- You'll be able to give exceptional responses to typical interview questions.
- You'll be able to choose a career and organization that truly suit your style.
- Your self-confidence and overall self-esteem will increase.

CYBER TIP Looking to find the meaning of life—*your* life, that is? I highly recommend a software program called LifePlan from Mind Tools Ltd. You can find it on the Web at **www.mindtools.com/lifeplan.html**. It helps you look at your career and life in the short, mid and long term. LifePlan is shareware, which means you can try it for free.

From Fired to Inspired

I vividly remember the first time I was forced to confront my own career demons. It happened when I was "let go" from a job for the first time. Back in the fall of 1988 it was, when I was a marketing manager at an established firm. The pay was very good, I had a wonderful office and the commute was a breeze. Aside from losing my job, there was only one problem—I strongly disliked what I was doing! I was completely unmotivated by the type of work I had chosen.

The shock of being suddenly unemployed was enormous. Fortunately, I had immediate access to some excellent career advice. As part of my severance package from the company that laid me off, I was given the benefit of career transition counselling (also known as outplacement assistance). For me it was a lifesaver. I'm forever thankful to the folks at Drake Beam Morin (**www.dbmcanada.com**), the career management firm into whose lap I dropped precipitously.

Looking Inward The transition consultant who worked with me was a real pro. In one of our first sessions together, he startled me with a deceptively simple question: "Who are you?" Without hesitating, I stammered out the predictable response. It went something along the lines of "I recently worked at (the company who fired me) as a marketing specialist." Pretty revealing stuff, eh?

My consultant looked me straight in the eye, then repeated the question slowly. This time he added, "Let's try it a bit differently. Tell me more about who you are as a person, without focusing so much on what you do." Well, now the floodgates opened. I began to pour out my soul, describing everything from my background and current situation to my frustrations and aspirations. Over the next few sessions, my recollections were assisted by a series of questions that the people at Drake Beam Morin had drawn up. For instance, I had to make a list of my strengths and weaknesses. Then list ten achievements of which I was most proud. Of course, there were questions to answer, too. What did I consider my most important values to be? What factors in my work and life made me happiest? What ones stressed me out the most? How did I think other people saw me? And the killer question: Where did I see myself in five years, ten years, twenty-five years?

REAL LIFE One of the important lessons I learned in my self-evaluation is that honesty lies at the core of everything. Personal honesty, that is. That means being open to yourself in ways that, most likely, you don't normally have a chance to do. Not that it is easy to be so candid. After all, we spend so much time constructing an acceptable image of ourselves that it becomes harder and harder to get back in touch with our basic selves.

You Owe It to Yourself All right, so maybe you don't feel the need to describe yourself intimately to every person you encounter. But wouldn't it be neat if, just once, you could get back in touch with the "real" you—just for you? Now that I'm a practicing career consultant myself, I'm amazed (and thrilled) when my clients start to tear down their barriers and reveal to themselves the dreams they've suppressed or forgotten about after years of "making a living." The rest of this chapter is devoted to this very process of breaking down those barriers.

II. STARTING WITH YOURSELF

One area where the Net has advanced since the first edition of this book is in the availability of online career self-help. Gone are the days when you had to rush out and buy a book or call your career counsellor. Now so much information is available online. It ranges from Web sites with quizzes and exercises to newsgroups and forums where you can discuss your results.

What we're about to cover is based on a conventional, widely used approach to career management. The big difference is that I'll point you to online resources for each specific area. Are you ready to look inward? Here goes.

Table 3.1 Areas to Focus on During Self-Assessment

THINGS TO CONSIDER	WHAT TO LOOK FOR SPECIFICALLY
Personal Strengths	Highlights of your abilities and skills, knowledge and personal traits
Accomplishments	Things you've achieved, and what that shows about you
Interests and Values	What you like, love and hate in your work and personal life
Personality Type	Your moods, ideas and ways of seeing and interacting with the world

What Are Your Skills and Abilities?

Your abilities generally include the things that you are naturally good at, such as the ability to run very fast or judge the spatial perspectives of objects. While you might work at these abilities to improve them, they are likely to be part of your original hard-wiring. Skills flow from those abilities, and you can hone them and use them to get along at work and in life. (If this all sounds a bit confusing, don't worry. The exercises I point you to next will clear it all up.)

Jump right in and get started. Type the following URL into the address line of your browser: **www.ns.hrdc-drhc.gc.ca/english/career/pathways/look.htm**. You'll find yourself at the very heart of the Nova Scotia Human Resources Development Canada site. The particular page I've pointed you to is all about assessing your skills. You list the ones you think you already have, and identify those you think you might need in the future. Then you can go about identifying the training or education you'll need to fill the gap (see Chapter 5). Other good skills sites are:

- Knowing Ourselves, Youth Employment Services B.C. (**207.194.203.151/index.asp**, register and go to "Skills" section). A brief questionnaire to get people, especially students, thinking about their strengths.
- Skills Defined, Bowling Green State University (**www.cba.bgsu.edu/class/webclass/nagye/career/competen.html**). A huge list of skills to help you identify your own.

How Do You Learn?

Knowledge is critical in our society. We obtain it in many ways. Interestingly, it's been estimated that we only derive about 20 percent of what we know from formal education. This includes everything we soak in during high school, college and university courses or vocational training. The rest we learn by informal means. This could be everything from on-the-job experience to volunteering, to everyday living and reading books, or even to watching TV. (To think I actually went back to get a second master's degree when I could have been home watching Star Trek reruns!)

Knowing Is Different from Doing It turns out that the old adage is true: it's not just what you know, it's how you use it (or something like that, anyway). Just knowing about a topic won't do you much good. You have to be able to apply that knowledge in a meaningful way. Find out what your preferred learning style is at Career Paths Interactive (**207.194.203.151**, then — if you've already registered and logged in — "Instructions," and "Step 3"). This site can really help you when you're putting your résumé together. It will help you show how you've applied your knowledge by what you've accomplished. You can also use this information to help point you in the direction of a career that's right for you.

What's Your Personality Type?

Personality is such an unquantifiable thing. That one term embraces our thoughts, feelings, moods and behaviour, often in ways we don't even understand. In fact, we're generally taught that personality (who you are) is less important than accomplishments (what you've done). If you're having trouble understanding what I mean, try this. Think back to your last job interview. Did the interviewer light up when you described yourself as a happy, caring and loving person? Or was the interviewer snoozing until you mentioned that you're a workaholic who could single-handedly boost the company's sales by 200 percent?

To Thine Own Self Be True My clients often start out with ingrained images of themselves that are impressive and acceptable to the outside world. This often shrouds their true sense of themselves. One client I worked with initially characterized himself as a "hard working, get-things-done manager with a staff of 12 employees." Sounds pretty good, eh? Unfortunately, he was absolutely miserable. After many conversations and much soul-searching, this same person came to describe himself as "somewhat shy and highly emotional, with a strong desire to nurture and do good." That's the level of insight that can help you make the right life decisions.

Doing the "Type Thing" Online Psychologists and career practitioners have been trying for years to bring some scientific credibility to the realm of personality. One way they have managed this is through research that sorts out specific personality types. There's a huge body of literature on this field. (See for yourself, at **www.smartbiz.com/sbs/arts/abu4.htm**.) Still, the theories are just that: potential explanations for the way we behave.

Doing a so-called personality "test" can be an eye-opening experience. Keep in mind, however, that these aren't really tests at all. They're more like inventories or exercises that can help you to identify and measure who you are, and what kind of work environment you might thrive in. Just remember—personality tests are only one component of an overall career and lifestyle assessment. They should be used with caution, and should be interpreted with the help of a trained career professional. Now that I've said all my warnings, here are some of the places to check out for free:

- Kiersey Temperament Sorter (**www.keirsey.com/cgi-bin/keirsey/newkts.cgi**). You input your scores on the screen to get a brief printout of your personality. Based on the Myers-Briggs Type Indicator.
- Self-Image (**www.virtent.com/familyent/testcntr/selfimage.html**). An entertaining test that may point out some of your blind spots when it comes to how you perceive yourself.
- Your Supervisory Style (**www.worksearch.gc.ca**, then "English," "Site Map," "Knowing Yourself," "Styles of Supervision"). The results may surprise you.
- Personal Styles (**www.freshy.com/personality/persprofile.html**). How do you react to certain situations? Do you have a preferred style? Find out by taking this informative (although not entirely scientific) test.

CYBER TIP Let's say you want to talk to other people about personality typing. Where do you turn? To a listserv (mailing list), of course. Try the Psych-Type Mailing List. To subscribe, send e-mail to **psych-type-request@sacam.oren.ortn.edu** with the word *subscribe* in the body (not in the "Subject" field) of the message. There's also a digest version available. Plus there is the newsgroup **alt.psychology.personality** for more information.

The Intelligence Factor

Measuring intelligence is not, in my opinion, the best way—or even a very suitable way—to predict your employability. Questions of cultural bias and relevance are raised all the time in conjunction with intelligence tests. Nonetheless, a number of counsellors still include one in the battery of tests they use. Hence I've thrown in a few for your viewing pleasure.

Your Intelligence Quotient (IQ) There are many ways to measure your intelligence. In fact, there are so many ways that you begin to wonder which one is right. Here are a few Web sites to visit to explore your own IQ.

- Self-Discovery Workshop (**www.iqtest.com/welcometest.html**). A 13-minute problem-solving quiz. Fun to do.
- Braintainment Five-Minute IQ Test (**www.brain.com/iq/5mintest/**). You must fill in the right word in a sentence.
- The Mensa Workout (**www.mensa.org**). Not an IQ test, but a brain teaser from the genius folks.

Emotional Intelligence (EQ) One of the more recent additions to the personality assessment arsenal is the emotional intelligence test. This is supposed to give you a good idea of how you're equipped to deal with change, manage stress and generally conduct your life. You can find a few versions around:

- The Utne Reader (**www.utne.com/cgi-bin/eq**). While you're at the Web site of this American magazine, check out the interactive discussion forums and compare your thoughts with folks from around the world.
- Enterprise Rent-A-Car (you heard me right) (**www.erac.com/recruit/EQ.htm**). An EQ test designed for post-secondary students.

Tell Us What You've Accomplished

The things that you've done in your past (those that you can mention in polite company, anyway) can be very relevant to your future. Often your achievements tell a great deal about you. They may indicate your hidden abilities, skills, knowledge and personality traits. Sometimes they reveal things about you that even you wouldn't normally see.

Showing What You're Capable of Doing An accomplishment is anything you've done that demonstrates your strengths. You can draw on all of your past experiences, including your achievements from school, work, your personal life or outside activities (e.g., hobbies or social groups). What you're looking for in each accomplishment is:

- what you did,
- how you did it,

- why you did it,
- what the results were, and
- what you learned from it.

The results of this analysis will be used directly in your résumé and cover letter (see Chapter 6). They'll also assist you in selecting an appropriate career and work environment. If you'd like a guide on listing your achievements, check out the Career Development Manual at **www.adm.uwaterloo.ca/infocecs/CRC/manual/skills.html**.

Assorted Assessments

Although personal analysis is very important, I don't like to carry this thing too far. After all, you really just want a chance to clarify who you are, what you're good at, what to improve on and what your long-term goals are. Keep this in mind while you check out some of these additional quizzes and inventories.

- Testing Your Career Competencies, Job Trak (**www.jobtrak.com/jobmanual/assess.html**)
- Employment Search Readiness Inventory, CareerWeb (**www.careerweb.com/inventory**)
- How Creative Are You? from Virtual Entertainment (**www.virtent.com/familyent/testcntr/creativity.html**)
- What Are Your Values As A Consumer? SRI Consulting (**future.sri.com/vals/survey.html**)
- Self Esteem: Do You Believe In Yourself?, Body–Mind Queendom (**www.queendom.com/selfest.html**)

III. SEEKING PROFESSIONAL HELP

There's no doubt that rediscovering who you are can be exhilarating and liberating. It can also be exhausting and time-consuming. Be warned, though—if you try to do all of this analysis on your own, it may be tough to see all the different perspectives. That's why I strongly advise you to seek advice from a professional career advisor, in addition to doing any online exercises and resources that you find.

Table 3.2 How Career Counselling Can Help You

STAGE OF SEARCH	WHAT A CAREER ADVISOR CAN DO FOR YOU
Self-Evaluation	• Suggest appropriate exercises and career inventories to use • Work with you to interpret and apply results of inventories (like those described in this chapter) • Discuss personal issues that may affect your search
Career Exploration	• Direct you to specific careers for you to explore further • Suggest creative ways to learn about potential careers • Help you integrate your skills, values, personality and goals when choosing potential career options • Give unbiased reactions when you're deciding what to do
Creating Marketing Materials	• Review your résumé and cover letter before you send them out • Propose strategies to target your marketing efforts
Finding Work	• Give advice on networking and following-up • Prepare you for interviews • Refer you to other relevant resources, as needed • Provide support and motivation during difficult periods

Getting Good Counselling

Some people don't really know what a career practitioner does. Don't feel bad if you fall into this category. I shudder myself when I think back to my early recollections of career counselling. Fortunately, things have changed. A professionally trained career advisor can actually be useful in many ways. He or she can assist you in specific stages of your search for work or can help you to plan and manage the entire process, including lifestyle aspects too. You're the one who gets to decide. Table 3.2 outlines some of the ways that you could use a career advisor's services.

Different Ways to Get Career Advice It used to be that if you wanted to get career advice, you had two basic choices. One was to travel to a career consultant's office to meet in person. The other was to buy a book on career management, then sit at home doing the exercises in a feedback vacuum.

Today you can find career consulting in a wide variety of formats. There is the traditional approach, which lets you work—one-on-one or in groups—with a real, live person. If face-to-face is not your thing, there are online methods too. These range from simple question-and-answer Web-based services to live chats with trained counsellors via the Internet. You can select the one that's right for you or mix and match to get customized advice. Although each approach differs in its level of detail and the scope of its services, there are some common features. You may be asked to do some written career interest tests. Then you'll probably review the results together with your counsellor and generate some ideas about your future.

Career Counselling the Non-Electronic Way

Let's put aside for a moment the Net-based career resources that have proliferated in the last while. You can find traditional (that is, face-to-face) career counselling services in many different settings. A lot of these are provided by government and not-for-profit agencies, while others can be found in the post-secondary school system, with more still offered by practitioners in the private sector. Below is a sampling of what's available.

Government and Not-For-Profit Agencies Thank goodness for free and low-cost career counselling services. They put vital resources within reach of pretty well everyone. Plus you usually get to meet other people in similar situations, with whom you can share ideas and experiences. Your best bet is to start with Human Resources Development Canada. Their main site is at **www.hrdc-drhc.gc.ca/common/home.shtml**, and localized resources can be located at **www.hrdc-drhc.gc.ca/maps/national/canada.shtml**. Refer back to Chapter 2 for a look at not-for-profit agencies, Employment Resource Centres, job-finding clubs and other community-based career programs.

REAL LIFE Be a smart consumer. Try not to settle for just any career advisor. If possible, arrange to meet with a few to see what their styles are and what programs they offer. In the final analysis, you have to trust and have confidence in the person who you work with, and be able to afford the appropriate services.

College and University Career Centres I bet you thought that you had to be a student to have access to college and university career centres. Wrongo! Almost every single post-secondary institution has a career centre. These centres often provide a full range of occupational advice and employment assistance to alumni and the public, in addition to their students. Although you may be asked to pay a fee for these services, they can be well worth it.

You can quickly find out what's available at your local college or university career centre by surfing the Web. For a partial listing of these Canadian centres online, go to **www.cacee.com/edandemp/eecu.html**. This helpful page can link you directly to the career centre at the institution of your choice. It's maintained by the Canadian Association of Career Educators and Employers (CACEE), which can be found at **www.cacee.com**.

Private Career Counsellors The private sector is full of consultants who can help you with your career decisions. Some are individuals who work on their own; others are employed by small to mid-sized career management firms. Because prices and services vary widely, it's best to shop around. Of course, you could always pick up your local Yellow Pages and look under Career Counselling to get started. Then you can call several services to find out what they offer and how much they charge. This can be just as fast, or faster, than the Web route. But hey, that's not the Wired way, now is it!

CYBER TIP To find a comprehensive online listing of career counselling services in your area, go to Infospace Canada. You'll find it at **206.129.166.151/categ/cancategory.html.** Scroll down to the bottom of the page, where it says "Specify a Topic" and enter the word *career.* This will take you to the Career and Vocational Counselling section. Select a province and city, then click on "Find." Browse alphabetically to see listings with full addresses and phone numbers.

Career Counselling the Wired Way

Have you tried any of the new services offered by the emerging breed of online career counsellor? You won't find them in your phone book. Instead, they respond automatically via the Web, answer your questions via e-mail or even interact live through chat sessions. This recent wave of cyber-counselling has some definite advantages (such as round-the-clock accessibility) and disadvantages (no face-to-face contact). I'll describe a few of these online methods in this section. The simplest, most generalized approaches are discussed first, moving on to more personalized services.

Basic Questions and Answers At the most basic, de-personalized level, you can get general answers to career-related questions electronically. Sound a bit impersonal? It can be, but it can also save you some time and effort. Many basic employment concerns are shared by lots of people. It therefore makes sense to provide standardized responses that can be accessed quickly and easily. A prime example of this is "Query the Chat Career Coach," at **rick.dgbt.doc.ca/career.html**. You just type in your question in plain language, and out comes a pre-packaged piece of advice.

General Advice There are all sorts of online articles and electronic magazines (e-zines) with career advice. They tend to address specific aspects of the work search. Some examples of article collections are listed below:

- CareerConnect at the Globe and Mail, under "Articles of Interest" (**careers.theglobeandmail.com/careerconnect**). Each month find new articles by prominent Canadian career professionals.
- Drake Beam Morin Canada Inc. (**www.dbmcanada.com**). A career management firm's take on the work market and on embracing change.
- Archeus, from Gary Will (**www.golden.net/~archeus/covlet.htm**). One Canadian's collection of articles on all facets of the work search.

As for e-zines, here are a few to consider:

- Next Steps (**www.cadvision.com/next/current.html**). Targeted to youth, this site focuses on Alberta but is Canadian all the way.
- Career Options (**www.cacee.com**, then click on "Career Options"). Meant for post-secondary students, with a national reach.
- The Node (**ngr.schoolnet.ca/sites/companies/newsletter/home.htm**). Another student-oriented e-zine, with input from various experts.
- Canada Prospects (**www.hrdc-drhc.gc.ca/hrib/ocd/prospects/index.html**). A treasure trove of articles and advice pieces for Canadians.

Replies from Professionals Here's another way to use the Net for advice: Send in your question to a trained career professional for a free response. A wonderful example of this (if I do say so myself) is courtesy of yours truly. Surf over to "Swartz's Resources" via **www.wiredhired.com**. I can't promise to answer your questions individually, nor can I guarantee that this portion of the site will still be active by the time you're reading this. However, you can review my previous responses, surf the Archives for the Site of the Week and take part in discussion forums with other work searchers across the country. Other Canadian question-and-answer sites to consider:

- The Node, from the National Graduate Registry (**ngr.schoolnet.ca/sites/companies/newsletter/guest.htm**).
- Ask A Career Counsellor, from B.C. WorkInfoNet (**workinfonet.bc.ca/wsearch/wsearch.html**).

For a U.S. perspective, check out **www.careertalk.com**, the site of Damir Joseph Stimac. He claims to be the Internet's first syndicated career columnist. JobSmart's "Ask Electra," by Mary Ellen Mort, at

jobsmart.org/electra/question/index.htm has a California twist on things. There's also Dave Soss, a career consultant who answers questions at **www.dnai.com/~career/sosscc.htm**. Then you have the father of all career consultants, Richard Bolles, author of *What Color Is Your Parachute?* He has his own Q&A forums. To take part, you must register (for free) with his sponsor, the *Washington Post* (**www.washingtonpost.com/wp-srv/talk/front.htm**). Once there, click on "Career Talk," and follow the enrolment instructions step by step.

High Tech, High Touch Career Counselling Up to now, I've talked about online products or services that, although useful, lack the human touch. To get more individualized services, you can stay with multimedia (if you want to), but add a personal dimension.

One such virtual experience is the Career and Personal Planning (CAPP) site (**www.cln.org/provdocs/careers/capps.html**). This distance education course, which is geared toward high school students, gives participants "the opportunity to gain a better understanding of their professional futures and increase their confidence" by preparing them for going out into the workforce and planning for the future. During the CAPP course, participants communicate with their counsellor and peers via telephone, e-mail and the World Wide Web. The cost of the course is around $350, and it even includes a work experience component. It's offered by the Open Learning Agency, a Canadian online learning institution. Their Web site is **www.ola.bc.ca**.

Adults haven't been ignored here, especially those who live in Alberta. If you do, there's a service called "Hotline Online" at **www.aecd.gov.ab.ca/hotline**. It's hosted by the Alberta Department of Advanced Education and Career Development. You can access one-on-one career counselling, over the phone, for free. There are also resources on the Web that you can dip into when needed.

Personalized Service There are, of course, faster (and costlier) alternatives. One such option is a live, one-on-one chat with an online career counsellor. This service is beginning to become available in Canada. It is already well established on several of the major commercial online providers (e.g., America Online and Prodigy).

A good example is the Career Center on America Online. Here you get confidential access to one of their counsellors. The session is booked in advance. At the appointed time, you meet online in a private chat room, and you converse by typing in your comments. Convenience does have its price. To take part in one of these sessions, you must first have a paid subscription to America Online (starting at around $9.95 U.S. monthly for five hours of surfing). On top of that, counselling fees range from $50 to $100 U.S. per hour and must be booked with a credit card. So while it's convenient, this may not be your preferred way to go—especially if you're a slow typist!

IV. WIRED WRAP-UP

Planning your career has never been more important. And knowing who you really are is the foundation of a solid career plan. The Net has made it relatively easy to start a self-evaluation on your own. Many of my clients love the freedom it provides. Any time, day or night, they can take a few moments and do the work that will form the basis of their entire career planning process.

But Is This Enough?

Not by a long shot! Happily, we still have humans to talk to. Remember that career decisions and personal discovery don't happen in a vacuum. They can affect virtually every facet of your life, so it's vital to get input from others. My advice is to involve people when you're feeling some uncertainty or just want to bounce ideas around. Talk to your family members. E-mail your friends to get feedback. And talk to (or chat with!) a career advisor when it comes to the difficult parts. This, in combination with the new electronic tools, will help you to understand your true self—so you can make decisions that are right for you.

CHAPTER 4 Take Some Time to Explore Your Options

I. TO BE OR TO DO (OR "DO-BE-DO-BE-DO")

Whether you're happily employed and starting to think about your future or actively seeking work, or considering a career change, someone is bound to hit you with a devastatingly simple question: "So...what do you want to be when you grow up?" This chapter is all about investigating your options. It can assist you with making a solid career decision, for the short term as well as the long term.

So what happens to you when you're faced with this deceptive query? I'll tell you what my experience is, both from my own personal perspective and from that of my clients. It doesn't matter if you're 25 or 65. When some well-meaning friend, relative or colleague does the "so what do you want to be" thing (no matter how they phrase it), it usually causes people to freeze in their tracks.

Just think about it for a minute. This question is charged with dynamite. First of all, it's like, whoa, you mean I've got to choose just one thing that I want to be and then do it for the rest of my mortal existence? Is that a big decision, or what? The next hardest part about answering quickly is the use of the word *be*. In my own case, it led to years of frustration, trying to "be" something I wasn't. I kept trying to fit in to established roles. For instance, I chose to "be" an MBA, and sought work in large corporations in order to "be" secure and respected (neither one of which came to pass).

Asking the Right Question Amazingly, it was a simple inquiry from my transition consultant at the career management firm of Drake Beam Morin that turned the tide for me. He asked me, "What do you like to do?" instead of what I wanted to be. Wow! What a shift in thinking! You mean I don't have to force fit myself into some pre-existing designation, like marketing manager, or lawyer, or plumber, or financial analyst?

How liberating it was to answer my consultant wholeheartedly. "What I really like to *do*," I said excitedly, "is to write, to lead workshops and seminars that help people to reconnect with their true selves, and to work one-on-one with people in transition." I felt as though I no longer had to be someone I wasn't. I could actually choose to do the things I was good at, which I enjoyed, and which ignited a passion in me. That's when my career (and life) really started to turn around.

How This Chapter Can Help In Chapter 3, we looked at self-evaluation in terms of who you really are. Chapter 4 builds on this by examining what you enjoy doing and how that ties in to your employment options. You have a chance to do some more self-assessment. This time, though, it will focus on the kinds of occupations and work environments you're most suited for. You'll also learn how to find out about nearly every occupation in Canada, so you can make an appropriate career choice. Plus we'll look at how to upgrade your skills and education—if need be—the virtual way. Finally, we'll tie it all together by looking at sites where you can assemble a personalized career plan.

II. WHAT KIND OF WORK IS RIGHT FOR YOU?

What kinds of things do you truly enjoy doing? You probably haven't heard this question lately, especially at work. Can you imagine your boss coming up to you one morning and saying, "Hey, you don't seem very happy here. Would you kindly tell us the role that you would genuinely like to play in our company? I will gladly adjust your assignment to fit with your expressed strengths and the activities you enjoy doing most."

Nice fantasy, eh? Particularly when many of us are either clinging to our jobs or facing the prospect of finding new employment. Nonetheless, enjoyment and a sense of fulfillment are important career considerations, particularly over time.

So, what do you enjoy most about work? Is it the work itself, the people or just the comfort of having someplace to go everyday? Do you find the work you've been doing satisfying? Or is it merely a regular paycheque? And what kind of work do you prefer: something unpredictable and creative, or stable and well defined? Do you like to work alone or in large groups? What about self-employment—have you ever considered it?

Defining Your Interests and Values

You'll be asking yourself these questions when you take a look at your interests and values. Your answers paint a picture of you in terms of the work environment that will best suit you. Here are some sites to visit to clarify the things you enjoy doing and the values that are most important to you.

- Interest and Values Assessment, University of Waterloo's Career Manual (**www.adm.uwaterloo.ca:80/infocecs/CRC/manual/values.html**). A neat and simple way to list your work and lifestyle preferences. There's no scoring here, unfortunately, but it makes a great reference list.
- 10-Step Career Planning Guide, Career Paths Interactive (**207.194.203.151**, then "Instructions," "Step 1"). Select those values that apply to you, then get a reading of your styles (you have to enrol first, if you haven't done so already).
- WorkSearch (Human Resources Development Canada) (**www.worksearch.gc.ca**, click on "English," then "Frames," then look for "Site Map," "Taking Care of Basics," "Knowing Yourself," and "Identifying Values"). A very good way to summarize your values as they pertain to employment.

The Self-Employment Option Ever had the inkling that the corporate world just isn't for you? Or that being an employee in the private, public or not-for-profit sector is too constraining? If so, welcome to the world of self-employment. This growing sector now accounts for close to 20 percent of the entire Canadian workforce. That amounts to more than 2.6 million adults who have given up working for a company or organization (either voluntarily or involuntarily) and have chosen to do work where it needs to be done (either voluntarily or involuntarily).

Is this option right for you? It takes more than just a bright idea and good intentions. Determination, creativity and the ability to endure uncertainty are a few of the qualities required to succeed on your own. I go into much greater detail about this in Chapter 11. For now, I've provided a few Web-based questionnaires so that you can get a feel for your entrepreneurial leanings.

- How Entrepreneurial Are You? TD Bank and Larry Easto (**www.tdbank.ca/tdbank/succeed/quiz.html**). Twenty questions with automatic scoring to show you where you stand.
- Could You Succeed In Small Business? Occupational and Career Development, Federal Government (**www.hrdc-drhc.gc.ca/hrib/ocd/minding/mind-eng/succ.html**). Part of the "Minding Your Own Business" course. A great resource.

Where Do You Belong?

Up to now, we've mostly looked inward without really considering what's out there. In other words, although you may know a great deal about yourself by now, what about the marketplace and the needs of potential employers and customers? Matching who you are with what's available is part science, part art.

REAL LIFE Don't be overly concerned with the score you get on a career-matching test. It is actually an attempt to measure how closely your skills, interests and values align with people who are successful in particular fields. Getting a higher score has no correlation with being smarter or better than anyone else—it merely indicates the types of work that you might do well at.

The science comes in with employment assessment tests and inventories. We'll look at a few in a moment. The art is all about exploring the realities and complexities of the careers that your tests point you toward. That we'll do later in this chapter. The idea here, as with all self-evaluation, is to be as honest with yourself as possible. Try to give your most immediate response without over-thinking or second guessing. Here are some of the more popular tests, online and for free:

- Self-Directed Search, by John Holland (**www.career-pro.com/profile.htm** or **www.missouri.edu/~cppcwww/holland.html**).The SDS is a "self-administered vocational interest inventory used in career exploration and selection based on John Holland's theory of personality types and work environments." As a result you'll find possible careers to consider. It starts with your vocational interests, looks at your preferred work environment and then examines your personal values.
- What Career Is for You? (**www.ventura.com/jsearch/unique/29063/jshome2e.html**). This exercise helps you identify what career may suit your personality. You are asked 21 simple questions that require you to make a choice between one activity or another.
- The Birkman Method® Career Style Summary (**www.review.com/birkman/birkman.cfm**). This questionnaire guides you to possible careers of the most interest to you. Your answers to 24 questions are analyzed to determine your most likely interests and work style. This information can help you choose fields, jobs and organizations suited to your strengths and occupational preferences.

CYBER TIP You can find a homegrown Canadian quiz from Dr. James Sofia, PhD, in Hawkesbury, Ontario (**www.hawk.igs.net/careers**). You get a reasonably priced interest inventory that you can order online. Dr. Sofia claims that "you will have taken a constructive step toward learning about yourself, your vocational interests and how they compare to a representative group of people working in a variety of career areas." The cost is $49 and includes a personalized, 12-page report that you receive by mail.

III. INVESTIGATING CAREERS

Do you really know what you want to do with your life? Probably not entirely. Even if you think you do, it's likely to change as you enter different stages of life. I recommend that you examine your options sooner than later. This way, you reduce the likelihood of feeling trapped or out of place. Plus if you know what your transferable skills are and what the current employment trends are, you can market yourself to employers effectively. As well, knowing your transferable skills and understanding employment trends enable you to choose the appropriate career and market yourself to employers in a very targeted way.

I realize, however, that it's not so easy to decide on the right kind of work for you, even after doing all the tests and inventories. How do you take it a step further and break through the mystery? By learning all you can about what really goes in different career settings. But the first task is to choose a career field or two that appear to be a good fit for you, based on the self-evaluation and networking you've done so far. This is just as true if you're a recent graduate unsure of the future as if you're already established in your career but want to be aware of your alternatives (just in case, know what I mean?).

REAL LIFE If you're already in the workforce, you may want to consider exploring your career options while keeping your current job. This is highly recommended when you can't afford to make sudden changes. While you stay in your current career, you can upgrade your education or moonlight in your chosen field (part-time for pay or by volunteering). This way, you can continue to earn an income, build your experience base and create a bridge toward future change.

How Do You Examine a Career?

Exploration allows you to do some important information gathering. It builds on all the self-evaluation that you've done. Now is the time to ask

CYBER TIP Looking for a place to describe your ideal work situation? Try the Carnegie Mellon School of Industrial Administration's Web site at **www.gsia.cmu.edu/afs/andrew/gsia/coc/student/assess.html#jobdescription**. Don't be intimidated by the site's name. It's a neat place to list the attributes of the work you really want. When you're done, print out the results and put the hard copy somewhere close by—you'll want to refer to it when you reach the decision-making part of your career journey.

such vital questions as "What do you actually do in this type of job?" "How much can I make?" "Do I need more education to get into this field?" "Should I start my own business instead?"

You can identify potential careers and work environments that interest you in several ways: with the help of a career advisor, through the results of your completed interest inventories or from your own experience. What you don't want to do is to waste your energy searching down every possible alley. By the same token, it would be a shame to miss out on something that might be a potential fit.

Finding Out Details of Specific Occupations

Once you've selected a few occupations to investigate, it's time to learn all you can about them. Only then can you decide on the right choice. And only then can you begin to target your marketing for specific companies in particular industries (whether it's a job or self-employment you want). We take a detailed look at that in the next few sections.

What You'll Want to Know About For now, you'll want to discover if the potential careers or jobs you've identified are truly right for you. There are lots of unknowns that need to be addressed. Here is a list of some of the main questions to investigate when you're considering a particular career:

- What does the work involve on a daily basis?
- Are there any special educational requirements?
- How do starting and mid-point salary ranges compare to other careers?
- Will this work allow me to have the kind of lifestyle that I want (in terms of hours of work, location, stress levels, salary and benefits, security)?
- Is the work itself in line with who I am (e.g., structured versus non-structured, creative versus predictable, independent versus team-oriented)?
- What are the best and worst parts of this type of work?
- Will I work mostly from the company's location? Will I be on the road? Can I work from a home office, if I want?
- How do people generally break into this field?

Gathering Information

There are some tried and tested ways to find out about different careers. You can always go to the library and read about them in books on careers, occupation guides or industry trade publications. You can also learn about them on career-related videos, available through school and community employment centres or at your local library. Or you can meet with people who work directly in the field that you're investigating. This is done by means of information interviews (more about this in the section on networking in Chapter 9). You can also try to arrange job shadowing and volunteer apprenticeships, where appropriate (e.g., college, university and trade school career offices).

CYBER TIP Let's say that you want to talk to someone about potential careers, but there's no one around. How about doing the discussion-group thing online? For example, there are great forums for Canadians at a wonderful site called Your Mining Company. Go to **jobsearchcanada.tqn.com**, then click on "Bulletin Boards." From there, choose the e-mail–based discussion group that best suits your needs. You can also take part in a real-time discussion by selecting "Chat," then registering, then picking "Careers and Education," followed by "Careers."

Finding Out the Wired Way When you're online, you can start directly at the premier site for occupational descriptions in Canada: Job Futures (**www.hrdc-drhc.gc.ca/JobFutures/english/index.htm**). This informative Web site is hosted by Human Resources Development Canada (HRDC). It includes full outlines of 211 occupational groups, which cover pretty well all the jobs available in Canada (with the exception of self-employment). Information on each occupational group includes:

- job duties and responsibilities,
- types of employers who hire workers,
- the level and type of education, training and experience required,
- main labour market characteristics,
- current prospects of finding work, and
- job prospects for the next five years.

Other career exploration sites can be found at the following:

- Exploring Occupations, University of Manitoba Career Centre (**www.umanitoba.ca/counselling/careers.html**). Dozens of occupational profiles, with links to take you further.
- What Can I Do with a Degree in...? Washington State University (**wwgate.wustl.edu/careers/major**). The place to go if you're wondering where your BA in psychology, certificate in marketing or other degree will take you. It's based in the U.S., but highly relevant to anyone.
- OccInfo, Alberta Occupational Information (**www.aecd.gov.ab.ca/occinfo**). More than 500 occupations profiled. Need I say more?

REAL LIFE Still feeling stuck in terms of choosing your career direction? Time for a visit to your friendly career consultant. He or she may have more sophisticated tests available, such as the Myers-Briggs Personality Type inventory, or the Campbell Interest and Skills Inventory, among others.

IV. WHERE IS THE WORK?

There's yet another step to finding your fit into the marketplace. It involves determining if your chosen path has positive growth prospects, or if it's a declining industry with a limited future. I often see my clients experience this clash. They get all worked up about a new career path, then—after doing the research—discover that the employment prospects in that industry are lousy.

Of course, the opposite situation can be equally frustrating. This often happens when people ask me where the hot jobs are. People seem to think that if you can tap into a growing market, you will be assured of career success. The computer field is a great example. I mean, does it really matter that work prospects and salaries are soaring there, if you happen to be someone who has a low tolerance for detail, a desire to work with people rather than machines and an aversion to anything technical?

In any case, you'll be able to find some of the predictions you need when you search the occupational profiles we talked about earlier in this chapter. You might find comments like, "Prospects for this industry are predicted to be stable for the next five years." Note that these are estimates only, based on information that may already be a few years old. So it behooves you to do a bit of additional research. Fortunately, I have some suggestions on where to go.

The Canadian Economy in General

Want some broad strokes on how the economy is doing? Or perhaps you're looking for facts on specific sectors. Either way, Statistics Canada has it all. At their main site (**www.statcan.ca**), you'll find a menu to get you going. Two spots I suggest you refer to are:

- the latest economic indicators (**www.statcan.ca/english/econoind**), and
- a profile of the economy (**www.statcan.ca/english/Pgdb/economy.htm**).

Note that the stuff you'll come across here may not directly answer the "where is the work" question. However, it can certainly give you some perspectives on where we're heading nationally, provincially and by city.

Trends by Industry and Location

So arcane economic statistics aren't your idea of a career-exploration picnic. Maybe you're looking for simplified, direct data. First, you have to figure out what kind of information you want. There's labour market information, which describes specific occupations in terms of who's working where and what the prospects are over the next few years. This information is compiled by government sources and put into an easy-to-read format. Or maybe you prefer expert predictions. This is where you'll find prognostications by economists and futurists. It's interesting to see what the pundits say, and how their views sometimes conflict dramatically. So where can you find this neat stuff?

Labour Market Information Kudos to the federal government for organizing and standardizing job information on the Net. You can now go to one central source to locate the career prospects info that you need. The site to begin with is **lmi-imt.hrdc-drhc.gc.ca/lmi.html**, HRDC's Labour Market Information homepage. You can select your province and gain entry to a world of helpful data.

Let's say that you choose "Quebec" as an example. First, you get to select the specific region you're interested in. I picked the Eastern Townships, just to see what's available. I found that information is grouped into three main headings:

- Occupational Profiles: "Detailed information on occupations, including duties, employment requirements, terms and conditions of work, potential employers, census information, wage trends, training availability and professional associations."
- Industrial Profiles: "General status report provided for each industry, number of businesses, evolution of employment, main occupations wage ranges, and industry issues relating to human resources."
- Potential Employers: "Employers who may possibly employ persons in a selected occupational group."

You won't believe how powerful this resource is until you try it. Let's say you're now at the Occupational Profiles section for the Eastern Townships. You are presented with two choices: you can either find a specific occupation via the site's internal search engine or click on an extensive list of "significant occupations." If you choose the latter, you are presented with around 100 occupations to choose from. I clicked on "Program Leaders and Instructors in Recreation and Sport," which falls under National Occupation Code 5254 (see Cyber Tip).

CYBER TIP You can look up just about any career or job classification by its National Occupation Code (NOC). Surf over to the NOC (**hamilton.london.hrdc-drhc.gc.ca/english/lmi/noclist.html**), which classifies and describes more than 25,000 occupations in the Canadian labour market. These are categorized into three levels: 26 major groups, 139 minor groups and 522 unit groups. It's a nice companion to the Job Futures site described earlier.

There I found such delights as Example Titles (e.g., aerobics instructor, fitness instructor, swimming instructor, golf professional), Related Occupations (e.g., recreation and sports program and service directors), Duties and Requirements, Employment Requirements (e.g., completion of a college program in recreation or physical education or extensive experience in a specific recreational or sports program activity is usually required), Employment Statistics by Age and Gender for the Census Region, Average Employment Income and Employment Trends/Outlook. Pretty good for a free, regularly updated site, *n'est-ce pas*? And there's one for every province! Other such sites to consider are:

- Using Labour Market Information, Virtual LMI Toolkit (**www.paxar.bc.ca/LMI-VT**)
- Canadian Labour Force Development Board (**www.clfdb.ca**).

Expert Predictions It seems that almost everyone has an opinion when it comes to looking at where work is headed. Some folks end up being right, while others are way off the mark. Since there's no such thing as a crystal ball that really tells the future, your best bet is to consult several sources (online as well as through live networking and article searching via CD-ROM at public libraries). Here are a few Web sites to get you started:

- The New Economy™ (**www.neweconomy.com**). This site is maintained by well-respected Canadian economist Nuala Beck. She is one of Canada's gurus when it comes to predicting where the hot employment markets are and what to expect in the future. A site well worth visiting, when it's been updated.
- Strategis (**strategis.ic.gc.ca/sc_indps/engdoc/homepage.html** for national information, and **strategis.ic.gc.ca/sc_ecnmy/mera/engdoc/04.html** for additional information). Industry Canada's marvellous site has a sector-by-sector analysis of future growth prospects. It is updated regularly and is simple to follow.
- CareerPaths Online (**www.careerpathsonline.com/scaping**). Overviews of key industries and potential growth patterns for each. An interesting read.

V. OTHER USEFUL INFORMATION

What About Relocating?

Wouldn't it be nice to work on a quiet tropical island, surrounded by deep blue oceans and the gentle breeze of an eternal summer? Dream on, my fellow Canadian. Unless El Niño creates a tropical haven in Saskatchewan, it ain't likely to happen.

However, if you are considering a move, there are lots of resources available. One terrific Web site is City.Net. It's at **www.city.net** and has just about everything you'd want to know about virtually every major city in the world (and many not-so-major places, too). You can find links to local employment opportunities, chambers of commerce, industry associations and general information here. There are also discussion forums to ask specific questions and exchange ideas with folks from around the globe.

There's even a way to compare the potential salary you'd need to earn if you moved to a new location. Once you've selected a city or town, go to The Salary Calculator (**www.homefair.com**, then "Salary Calculator"). It takes what you currently earn and estimates what you'd need to make in the new destination, based on the cost of living and real estate price differences. Pretty neat, eh?

VI. WIRED WRAP-UP

You could spend weeks or even months researching industries, occupations, jobs and self-employment opportunities. Indeed, you may have to. However, I'm well aware that most people don't have the luxury of stopping their lives for that long. That's where the Net can really help. If you use it properly, you can find up-to-date occupational and industry data to speed along your search.

What I'm not saying, though, is that this is the ultimate solution. Yes, the Net creates wonderful opportunities to investigate the work that you would really like to do. But before we go galloping off, let's rein ourselves in for a second. The enormous amount of information that's available has its darker sides too. First, not everything you read online is accurate or timely. Second, the deluge of data can be overwhelming, to the point of paralysis. Third, well...I can't actually think of a third thing right now. But keep in mind that all this is in addition to the fact that existing occupations and industries are constantly dying off, while new ones sprout up almost daily. Even with all the available technology, a huge question remains: How do you know which decisions are best for you in terms of career and lifestyle?

Happily, we still have humans to talk to. Remember that career decisions don't happen in a vacuum. They can affect every facet of your life, so it's vital to get input from others. My advice is to involve people when you're feeling a bit uncertain or just want to bounce ideas around.

Remember—talking to your family members and e-mailing your friends are excellent ways to get feedback. And meet with a career advisor when it comes to the difficult bits. This, in combination with the new electronic tools, will help you to make the decisions that are right for you.

CHAPTER 5

Make a Plan and Upgrade Your Skills

Now that you've completed Chapters 3 and 4, give yourself a pat on the back. You've done a lot of the work needed to assess yourself and define your employment path. By now you're probably thinking along the lines of "So how do I get hired already?"

Patience, *mon ami*. It's at this very stage that I inject a strong note of caution to my clients. That is, you do yourself a huge disservice by skipping two more critical steps. One is to incorporate your lifestyle and personal goals into your career plans. The other is to consider upgrading your skills or education to maximize your marketability.

This chapter is all about these two important processes. Without them, you run the risk of a) ignoring a major component of your life, namely the time spent when you're not working, and b) ignoring the needs and requirements of potential employers. Either one of these could divert you from your quest for a satisfying career and lifestyle, so I encourage people to deal with them head on.

I. CAREER/LIFE PLANNING: PUTTING IT ALL TOGETHER

There's something you should know about me. I'm a big fan of career/life planning. In other words, I strongly believe that your career choice dramatically affects your way of life. The ultimate impacts are seen in your physical and emotional well-being. When you are unhappy in your career, it is bound to show up in your life, and vice versa. Fortunately, the opposite is true as well—being happy in your career has a positive effect on your life, too.

Taking the time to put the pieces together can be very rewarding. For example, one of my clients came to me with a common complaint. Her work was very satisfying. However, it usually took up 60 hours or more of her week, leaving little time to do the socializing and volunteer work that she loved to do. She felt unfulfilled and empty on certain levels. The key here was to find a happy medium. This involved cutting back a little in her work and earning slightly less money, which allowed more time to do the things that left her feeling happier and more satisfied.

Career/Life Planning Web Sites

I wish it were always this easy to rectify a situation of imbalance. Obviously this isn't always the case. However, you do have to start somewhere. And there is no better place to begin than on the Net. It is full of self-directed career material, as we've already seen. It also has some excellent resources that combine career choices with your personal goals and vision.

A good case in point: the WorkSearch site from Human Resources Development Canada (HRDC). You won't believe what you'll find when you surf over here (**www.worksearch.gc.ca**). Start by clicking on "Map Your Route." This takes you to a brief questionnaire, which actually personalizes the rest of your site visit. Follow the links in the map designed especially for you. You can choose from among the following areas (and more):

- preparing a household budget (critical for those planning a work search);
- finding and using community support agencies;
- identifying your skills, interests, aptitudes, values, learning styles, supervisory approaches and the like;
- assistance in decision making and narrowing down your choices; and
- education and training resources across Canada.

What you get here is a mixture of articles, tips, self-scoring exercises and links all geared toward helping you with your career and life. Thanks again, HRDC!

More Career/Life Planning Web Sites

There are a number of other sites you can access to create a comprehensive plan for work and play, including:

- The Online Career Manual, University of Waterloo Career Centre (**www.adm.uwaterloo.ca/infocecs/CRC/manual-home.html**). This one is classic. More than a terrific self-evaluation tool for everyone, and it's not just for students. You can examine yourself in detail, then link to career exploration and work-search sites. Highly recommended.
- Careerpath Adventures, Careerpath Counselling Services (**www.islandnet.com/careerpathadventures**). You'll want to thank Margaux Finlayson, the founder of this site, once you've checked it out. You build a Personal Career Profile, starting with who you are and then looking at where you want to be. Very simple and easy to use.
- The 10-Step Career Planning Guide, Youth Employment Services (**207.194.203.151/index.asp**). Explore your personality, aptitudes, values, options and more at this intuitively designed site. Once you enrol (for free, of course), the world of work is your oyster. You can even create short-term action plans to get going.
- The Career Planning/Competency Model, Bowling Green State University (**www.bgsu.edu/offices/careers/process/process.html**). Geared toward post-secondary students, this U.S.-based site starts with a self-assessment and includes advice on academic options and work searching. It's a top-notch site, and has been around for several years.

CYBER TIP There is a nifty life-mapping program online at **www.lifemapping.com**. It allows you to provide an overview of your history, guided by computer commands. It then looks at your coping and adjustment strategies, leading to future action plans. Look for the demo (demonstration) version on the homepage. A CD-ROM version can also be ordered online.

Lists of Career-Related Links The self-help sites I've just listed are great for those of you who prefer a pre-packaged approach. If you're already comfortable surfing the Net, you may also want lists of Net resources that you can explore on your own. Perhaps the best Canadian site of career-related links of all is the Canada Work Information Network (CanWorkInfoNet). These folks, again sponsored by HRDC, have compiled the mother of all list of Canadian links. Head over to **www.workinfonet.ca** and see what I mean.

There are hundreds and hundreds of sites listed here. All of them are classified in a few major categories, including Jobs and Recruiting, Career Planning, Training and Qualifications, Labour Market Information and Financial Help. Better yet, you can view them (and their accompanying brief descriptions) by province. When you get done with these links—which could take some time—remember to look at other great Canadian career-related link sites.

- Canadian Jobs Catalogue (**www.kenevacorp.mb.ca**). This incredible site has more than 2,000 Canadian career-related links. It focuses on the work search, as opposed to self-evaluation or career exploration. The cost for a year's membership is $10, and it's worth every cent!
- Job Search Canada via The Mining Company (**jobsearchcanada.tqn.com**). Look for the Net Links section, which is organized in an accessible way. There's also lots of great career planning and work-search stuff to check out while you're there.
- Maple Square Search Directory (**www.maplesquare.com/business.asp**). Under the Business and Money category, choose "Employment." Up comes a list of about 50 useful sites, which you can surf at your leisure.

Self-Help Software

The Web-based career/life-planning tools are terrific—if you happen to be hooked up to the Net. What if you want something portable and customizable? It's at times like these that career software comes in handy. At the lower end, there are several CD-ROMs that take you through the career planning process. Most of these sell for about $40 to $80 at your local software or business supply store, or by special order online. Note that in this range you're essentially purchasing a résumé creation package. Since they're on CD-ROM, they have plenty of room to hold self-evaluation exercises, overviews of various occupations and things like video clips of job interviews. To learn more about specific titles, here are some of the corresponding Web sites.

- Achieving Your Career, Upsoftware (**www.upsoftware.com**, then "Home Use by Individuals," then "Achieving Your Career")
- Résumé Maker Deluxe (**www.individualsoftware.com**, click on Résumé Maker Deluxe)
- WinWay Résumé (**www.winway.com**)

CYBER TIP Would you like a free copy of careerware just by asking for it? The folks over at Chivas Regal (yes, the liquor company) are offering you their Career Toolbox CD for the cost of shipping ($9.95 U.S.). This is no joke. For details, surf over to **www.careertoolbox.com**, then look for the free CD offer. While you're at their site, scope out their excellent career resources, including articles, tips and forums. Sure, it's all American, but after a few glasses of Chivas, will it really matter?

Upscale Software for Greater Depth At the higher end, you can spend from $100 up (make that way up). Here you get programs that are completely dedicated to career planning. I'll give you an example. The Employment Coach at **vvv.com/ai/counsel/ec/ec.html** is made in Canada. The producers describe it as "a user friendly expert system which provides information about the basic steps that should be followed to find appropriate work. The steps are presented in four major areas. Each step provides a list of issues that should be addressed and offers employment tips on how to deal with them." At $199 plus shipping, this option may not be for everyone. But if you are looking in this range, here are the Web sites of some higher priced career software:

- YouthWorks CareerQuest (**www.youthworks.ca/yw-cdrom.htm**)
- Jump Start Your Job Skills, **www.upsoftware.com**, then "Home Use By Individuals," then "Jump Start Your Job Skills" (U.S.)

Industrial Strength Software If you're really into the software scene, but want a good, thorough one that is Canadian, try one of the "institutional" products. These tend to be very expensive (anywhere from $400 to well over $1,000). That's why they're mostly purchased by college and university career centres, high schools and employment resource centres, which may let you use them on-site (for free or for a reasonable fee). For instance, Choices is a program for high school students and young adults, while Choices CT is for adults. Both are superb products. Offered by ISM Corporation, an IBM company, English and French trial versions can be downloaded for free at **www.canibm.com/ism/career ware** (click on "Products," then "Canada," then choose the desired product). Or call their toll-free number, 1-800-267-1544, for a site close to you. Also look up Discover in the pull-down menu (or Découverte in the French version) from ITP Nelson at **www.nelson.com**. You can learn more and download a free demo.

II. UPGRADING YOUR SKILLS AND KNOWLEDGE

We've already come a long way in this book. I hope that you're gaining insight into the type of work and lifestyle that you really desire. Along the way, you may have discovered that you need to acquire new skills or more education. Some fields require you to have a specific degree. Many assume that you already possess skills and knowledge specific to that area.

You'll learn more about these requirements as you explore your selected career paths. But what about upgrading skills? Let's face it: employers' needs are changing rapidly, and the demand for skills upgrading and education grows constantly. But does this mean that you have to become a full-time student?

Not necessarily (thank goodness!). It depends on your circumstances, as well as the expressed prerequisites of employers and the competitiveness of your field. For many people, it's a simple matter of taking an accredited course or two. Others might only need to attend a seminar or workshop. Some folks, however, have to get a recognized degree or diploma from a college, or else a degree (undergraduate or postgraduate) from a university. The question is: How do you source these conveniently and quickly?

Edu-Net

It probably won't surprise you that education and cyberspace are natural partners. At a minimum, you can search for courses, workshops and degree programs online. This can be genuinely convenient. Think of the time you'd spend if you had to travel to a library, career centre or guidance office, locate all sorts of school calendars and catalogues, then thumb through them for hours on end.

Did you know, though, that you can also take entire courses and degrees online? The distance education route is growing every year. Well over half a million Canadians are taking some kind of course electronically, according to StatsCan. This ranges from Web-based university lectures to e-mailed college tutoring sessions, all the way to educational CD-ROMs that anyone can purchase and use.

Searching for Courses

Let's start with looking for courses to take the conventional way, that is, by attending a class or workshop. The Net has come a long way in the last few years when it comes to finding learning resources. You no longer have to use a general search engine, such as Yahoo or Excite, to look for specific courses or degrees. This method continues to be unnecessarily complex and time-consuming. I mean, why use the shotgun approach when someone else has already collected the information for you?

Colleges and Universities It is becoming a cinch to find these listings online. Let's assume for the moment that you're planning to attend a credit course at an institution near you. Visiting the Web sites of colleges and universities within travelling distance is as simple as entering **www.theinfoguide.com/gradcap.htm** into the address box of your browser, then pressing the Enter key. About halfway down the page that appears you can select from over 180 university and college homepages across Canada. Other such guides are:

- The Central Index of Canadian WWW Servers (**www.csr.ists.ca/w3can/scope/scope_university.html**). Universities and their various faculties across Canada, although it could use some updating.
- Association of Canadian Community Colleges (**www.accc.ca/english/members**). Links to the 175 colleges and technical institutes in Canada.
- The College Net (**www.collegenet.com**). Comprehensive links to post-secondary educational institutions in the U.S.

If you're searching for degree information, start with a school's homepage. Once there, look for headings such as Day Programs, Applied Degrees, Divisions/Programs, Academic Calendar and the like. These will take you to the degree-granting portion of the school's calendar. From there, look for Degrees, Diplomas and Certificates Awarded, etc. This should lead you to individual programs (such as Business Administration) and the details you need to know. Most schools also allow you to order a hard (paper) copy of their calendar by filling in an Internet form, should that be your preference.

For accredited and general interest courses, it's the continuing education calendar that you'll need. Here's where you can choose from a single course on, for example, public speaking, or a credit course in accounting, or even a full degree or diploma offered in the evenings over a period of a year or two (or three or four).

Vocational Schools and High School Equivalencies For many people, education was not a high priority when they were younger, or maybe circumstances prevented them from getting formal learning in the past. Relax. It's never too late to go back for upgrading. If it's a trade that you intend to practice, you might need to check out vocational training. For instance, budding bartenders could look at the Master School of Bartending in Halifax, at **www.bartending.com**. Meanwhile, potential pet groomers can take a correspondence course from JKL Pet Grooming School, in Queen Charlotte City, B.C. (**www.jklgrooming.com**), which offers "Diploma Trade Programs of Professional Dog and Cat Grooming." All you need to do is surf over to the Yahoo Canada search directory at **www.yahoo.ca**, choose the Education category (be sure to select the "Canada Only" option!).

As for a high school diploma, these are available at a wide variety of institutions across the country. One way to see what's near you is to use the AltaVista Canada search engine, at **www.altavista.ca**. In the search box, type in "high school diploma" (quotes included to force all three words to appear together). Then see if there is a school or correspondence course near you.

Workshops and Seminars

Even though workshops and seminars abound in Canada, finding relevant ones—when you need them—is not easy. As I write this, only one province has assembled this type of information on one site (please let me know if you find others!). It happens to be Ontario at **www.trainingiti.com**. They've developed a comprehensive listing of non-

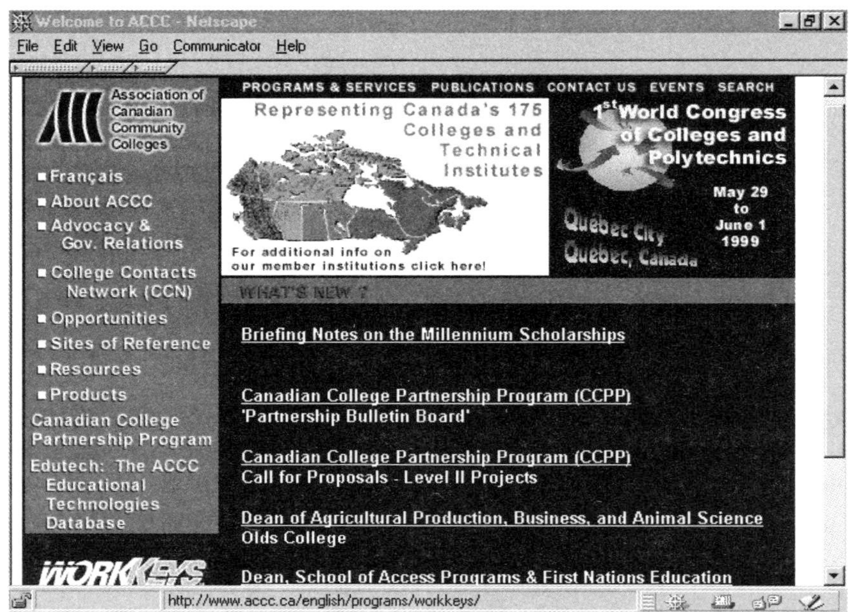

credit courses including professional development, general interest and career-related topics.

Upgrading Yourself the Wired Way

Even if you do need a full degree or diploma, you may not have to strap on your knapsack and trudge off to a classroom. More and more college, university, vocational and high school programs are being offered electronically. This expanding mode, known as *distance education,* is taking on numerous shapes and delivery formats.

How Distance Education Works Learning from afar generally translates into a home-study program. You typically use a variety of resources as educational tools. This can include well-established things such as textbooks, workbooks and audio tapes.

These days you're just as likely to get your course delivered over the World Wide Web. This gives you hyperlinked text, full audio and graphics. Even video is becoming standard course fare, as Internet speeds increase.

CYBER TIP A growing number of professions and trades insist that you have an approved designation. How do you find out who wants what? Try going to the Web site of the association or professional association for that particular trade. From there you can look for the Designation or Courses section. A good list of associations is available at Strategis (**strategis.ic.gc.ca/engdoc/main.html**). Click on "Canadian Business Map," then "Start," then look in the left-hand corner for "Industry and Professional Associations." Alternatively, type in **strategis.ic.gc.ca/scdt/bizmap/nav.html**.

With electronic learning, you get your instruction from a teacher you'll probably never meet in person. Your assignments are evaluated by a grading assistant you'll never see. This can be disconcerting for some, and liberating for others. It all depends on your learning style and how you like your social interaction.

To reduce the possibility of experiencing cabin fever, a number of online schools offer a link to a live human or two or three. There could be a phone, e-mail or chat connection with a tutor, and opportunities to talk to other students. Several programs are offered with computer-mediated communications support, such as teleconferencing or Internet chat.

One thing that's made this whole concept more attractive is the ease of signing up. The faxed application has been with us for years, but now it's possible (in some cases) to fill out a Web-based form, linked directly to the institution's registration office. Talk about virtual convenience!

Advantages of Online Education Before we look at some examples, you should know a bit about the advantages and drawbacks to these methods. It's mostly a trade-off: convenience versus face-to-face human contact. In fact, the upside of electronic learning is heavily weighted toward convenience. Here's what I mean:

- In many cases, you can learn about what you want, when you want to—without ever having to leave your home.
- The selection of courses and degree programs is expanding all the time.

- You often have the freedom to go at your own pace. That means you can learn at your natural speed, instead of the tempo dictated by a teacher.
- Often you can start at any time of the year. So you may not have to wait until the normal back-to-school periods.
- A growing number of distance education courses qualify for credits or certification. These range from high school diplomas and college certificates all the way to university degrees.

Drawbacks to Online Education As with just about every new technology, there are some downsides, too. With distance education you don't get the benefits of live group interaction that you'd find in a classroom. This can have a pretty strong effect. Many people thrive in a classroom setting. The ability to exchange ideas and interact with others directly (and throw little crunched-up wads of paper at a teacher whose back is turned) can greatly enhance the learning experience.

Some people argue that distance is no longer a barrier. They claim that video conferencing, phone tutoring and computer networking are starting to eliminate the perils of remoteness. No doubt there's some validity to this line of thinking. But you can't get around the fact that people are generally motivated and stimulated in the presence of other people. You just don't get that with your nifty laptop!

Reliance on technology may also mean that you have to spend a large chunk of change just to get the equipment. A computer, modem, software and ISP connection are the minimum requirements to take a course via the Internet. If you have to buy it all from scratch, the price can add up quickly. Not to mention that if your equipment breaks down, you're stranded.

Where to Find Courses Online For those of you who decide to take a course electronically, there are some excellent educational facilities in cyberspace. One is Athabasca University, which bills itself as Canada's open university. It's at **www.athabascau.ca**. The school offers full bachelor degree programs in arts, general studies, science, administrative studies, commerce and nursing. They even have master's programs in business administration (MBA) and distance education (MDE). A number of certificate programs are offered as well.

Another Canadian cyber-education institute is the Open Learning Agency (**www.ola.bc.ca**). This is a "fully-accredited, publicly funded facility providing a wide range of formal and informal educational and training opportunities for learners around the world." The Open Learning Agency is physically located in Burnaby, British Columbia, but you can see full course descriptions, prices and enrollment procedures at its Web site. Additional cyber-learning sites are:

- TeleEducation, from New Brunswick (**teleeducation.nb.ca**)
- Academic Technologies for Learning, from the University of Alberta (**www.atl.ualberta.ca**)
- Node Distance Education Resources, from Ontario (**node.on.ca**)
- Le Répertoire de distance en français, in French from Quebec (**redo.on.ca/refad**)
- International Centre for Distance Learning, from the United Kingdom (**www-icdl.open.ac.uk**)

Computer Based Training (CBT)

It's apparent that education is expanding into new territory. Take a stroll through the software department of your local computer or business equipment retailer. There are virtually hundreds of CD-ROMs and software titles that are designed to teach you something.

The range is incredible. From Mavis Beacon on typing to Canadian history, you can find pretty well anything that suits your fancy. Courses stretch from hard skills (such as basic computer skills) to edutainment (the combination of learning and entertainment), with almost anything else you can imagine. Want to learn how to teach adult learners? Itching to improve your math skills? What about gourmet cooking, losing weight or fixing your car? You can even learn a foreign language or view an entire encyclopedia via multimedia—all at your own pace, any time of the day or night. Lifelong learning has truly come of age!

III. WIRED WRAP-UP

A career consultant I used to know had a great system for motivating his clients. "Help them plan their work," he'd say, "then help them to work their plan." Sage advice, if you ask me. What he was advocating, in essence, was a strategic approach to career/life planning. That meant being proactive rather than reactive, looking inward before exploring external opportunities and always considering both the career and personal sides of the coin.

Perhaps this is no more relevant than today, when workplace stress has become the number one ailment in Canada, according to the Canadian Medical Association (**www.cma.ca**). Doesn't it make sense to at least try to re-define who we are, including the work we're best suited for and the lifestyle that allows us to be ourselves?

People often speak of "life balance" when it comes to this sort of thing. It's basically about getting your priorities straight. The key is to find a happy medium for you, by trading off the things you *must* have for things you'd *like* to have. All this can be expedited by putting a plan together, and then following the action steps as best you can. Not that I'm claiming to have found some sort of magical solution for myself or my clients. Far from it, actually. But I have seen my clients become more fulfilled and less stressed in many facets of life by striving for consistency based on being who they are. It's even started to work for me!

Part of this, of course, is ensuring that you maximize your marketability to enhance your employment prospects. Increasingly, this translates into upgrading your educational credentials. Many industries and employers now stipulate minimum standards in terms of degrees, professional certification or courses. Find out what is required as soon as you can, so you can fit educational upgrading into your action plan if you have to.

Need I remind you that just about all of the above can be done online? Creating a career/life plan, looking up schools and even taking a course via the Net—it's out there, available for you now! Test out a few sites and see which ones work for you.

CHAPTER 6 Create Superb Marketing Materials

Quick question. Why do you absolutely need a top-quality résumé? If you answered "to get a job offer," you're close, but no cigar. The primary goal of a résumé is to catch the interest of potential employers—when they're thinking of hiring someone in your field—so they'll contact you for an interview.

Here's a sad and sobering follow-up question. How long does the average résumé screener take to look over your résumé? Ten minutes? Maybe five? How about (and this is no joke) between 20 to 40 seconds. That's right: seconds.

Welcome to the wonderful world of job hunting in the 1990s. To prepare yourself, there are three main tools you need to market yourself effectively to employers. And no, they do not include:

- being close to a relative or friend who owns a large, successful company (who can hire you and pay big bucks),
- having an attractive face and nice hair (it's true this can't hurt, but it won't do much when your scannable résumé is read by a computer with no appreciation for your good looks), or
- possessing every possible academic degree known to humankind (to impress the heck out of your next boss, who may have never finished high school).

The truth is somewhat more mundane, but at least we all have a shot. The three basic tools you need to market yourself are a polished résumé, targeted cover letters and professional-looking business cards.

These are the things that you will learn about in this chapter. You will also be introduced to the new format for résumés, known as the keyword format. And, as always, we'll look at how the Internet can help us accomplish all of this more efficiently. Then, in Chapter 7, you'll learn how to adapt these age-old marketing tools to send them in a variety of ways electronically.

REAL LIFE What about having a personal homepage on the Web to help you secure work? I'm sorry to report that it's practically useless for work searchers, unless you're in a high tech field where you need to impress potential employers, or if you're self-employed and want to market your products and services online. For the most part, very few employers will take the time to look up your site. Why should they, when everything they need is in your résumé and cover letter?

I. THINKING LIKE AN EMPLOYER

There is an old adage among fox hunters about how to snare prey. "In order to catch a fox," it goes, "you must first think like a fox." And so it goes when you are trying to snare a job. In order to get employers interested in you, first put yourself in their shoes. It's not hard to do. Simply imagine that you're the one who needs to interview and hire a person to fill a specific role (such as the one you're capable of filling).

In other words, if you were the boss, what would you want to see? Probably a neat, professional-looking résumé with a dynamic cover letter, all contained in an attractive envelope (if sending by mail or courier). There would likely be clear, direct writing and useful details about the applicant's work experience, plus examples of his or her accomplishments and what that person can actually do for your company. You probably wouldn't want to see any grammatical errors. And would it be asking too much to see your own name and title spelled correctly, if only just once?

The Screening Process

What you really need to appreciate, if you're going to do this right, is how employers sift through all the résumés they get bombarded with.

The most common process is called screening. This is where some lucky sap gets to open and read the hundreds of application packages that are typically received in response to an ad posted in the newspaper, trade journals or online.

Do you know what the screener's objective is? I can tell you what it is not. Screeners are not necessarily there to find the best candidate for the job. What they're really looking for is a way to get rid of as many résumés as possible. The goal is to present whoever is making the hiring decision with a manageable short list of potential candidates—maybe 10 or 20 out of all the applications they received.

CYBER TIP If you really want to understand this process, read an article called "Writing a Résumé for Susie the Screener" (hey, I didn't make up the title). It's written by Douglas Richardson for the National Business Employment Weekly. Find it at **www.gsia.cmu.edu/afs/andrew/gsia/coc/student/screener.html.**

What Screeners Look For So what do these screeners look for? Well, it depends on how stringent they are. Many will chuck your résumé right off the bat if they find any of the following:

- a single, visible spelling or typographical error,
- incorrect title, name or company of the person you're writing to,
- an anonymous address such as "To whom it may concern" or "Dear Sir/Madam,"
- coffee or grape juice stains (or any other kind of dirt).

You might be wondering how these folks can be so cavalier. After all, you've spent so much time putting your application package together. Then, just because of one little careless act on your part, they toss it callously into the recycling bin (if they're progressive enough to have one).

When It's a Buyer's Market The answer, plain and simple, is that they can afford to. It goes right back to the economic times we find ourselves in. Employers are enjoying a buyer's market out there. The competition for posted work opportunities is huge (which is why Chapter

9 encourages you to network into the hidden job market, where your chances are much better). Odds are that if your résumé gets trashed, there are several hundred others for the employer to choose from.

Let's go back to our fox-hunting adage. You might now want to put yourself in the place of the screener. Imagine that it's 9:40 p.m., you've been at the office since 7:20 this morning, and your daughter is at home running a fever. Meanwhile, your boss has demanded a short list of candidates by the end of tomorrow's business day. You're just about to open the 213th application, with another 93 to go. If you saw obvious errors, wouldn't you question applicants' reliability and commitment? I mean, they haven't even taken the time to get their own résumés right!

I won't dwell further here on the weeding-out process. Suffice it to say that employers are looking for any way they can to send you a "thanks, but no thanks" letter. They ask themselves if your skills and work achievements match exactly what they're looking for. If not, out you go. They check if your cover letter is concise and targeted to the reader. If it's a form letter, out you go. The list of reasons to disqualify you goes on and on.

The Future of Screening Is Scanning Not to plunge you into further despair, but if you think the process is bad now, just wait. It's going to get worse (or better, depending on your point of view) very soon. What's coming down the pike, and is already here in some cases, is a process known as scanning. We're not talking about a pair of eyes skimming over your work of art, but a machine that reads electronically.

It works in a fairly straightforward way. You send your résumé to an employer and it gets scanned (electronically copied) into their database. An employer who wants to hire someone just has to search the database. The candidates with the most relevant qualifications are selected for interviews (talk about dehumanizing). Later in this chapter, I'll give you some hints on how to format your material for this type of process.

II. YOUR RÉSUMÉ

If you recall the opening paragraph of this chapter, I stated that the primary purpose of your résumé is to "catch the interest of potential employers—when they're thinking of hiring someone in your field—so that they'll contact you for an interview." Keep in mind that résumés serve a range of other related purposes, too, such as:

- showing an employer what you're capable of doing by describing your accomplishments, not just by listing your duties or responsibilities;
- providing a discussion guideline to help the employer who chooses to interview you;
- giving you something to hand out to your contacts as you network, to ensure they understand exactly what it is that you do and what areas you're searching in.

CYBER TIP Canadian author Gary Will has put together an excellent Web site that summarizes more than 50 résumé-writing articles on the Web. Gary deserves our thanks for providing direct links to—and ratings of—these Web-based articles. Check them out for yourself at **www.golden.net/~archeus/reswri.htm.**

Résumés Come in a Variety of Formats

There is no longer such a thing as a standard résumé. The standard I'm referring to here, of course, is the two-page version, with your work experience listed in reverse chronological order, preceded by a one-page cover letter. Now there are all sorts of variations, including résumé alternatives. Essentially, you need to select the style that will make it easier to achieve your goals. As Tom Jackson, a well-known job-hunting expert, says, "The perfect résumé is a written communication that clearly demonstrates your ability to produce results in an area of concern to selected employers, in a way that motivates them to meet you." Table 6.1 lists the more common types of résumés that you will now encounter.

REAL LIFE No matter which format you decide to go with, your résumé, cover letter and the package you send it in are the only things (in most cases) that a potential employer will know about you. In other words, your application, for all intents and purposes, is *you.* Thus, you should make sure that your materials represent you in the best possible light. Keep them neat and professional looking. Eliminate any spelling or grammar errors. Use wording that is interesting and easy to understand. And always, always keep in mind the needs of your reader.

Table 6.1 Résumé Variations

STYLE	NUMBER OF PAGES	WHEN IT'S MOST USEFUL
Traditional		
Chronological	2 max. + cover	When you have a lengthy, consistent work record
Functional	2 max. + cover	For recent grads or people changing careers
Combination	2 max. + cover	If you're somewhere between the above two
Keyword Format	3 max. + cover	When you think your résumé will be scanned by a computer
Résumé Alternatives		
Alternative One: Targeted Marketing Letter	1–2 max.	When you're trying to tap into the hidden job market
Alternative Two: Broadcast Letter	1–2 max.	When you're making initial contact with many companies in a variety of fields

Traditional Résumés The traditional résumé is the one that most of us are familiar with. It's usually a one- or two-page description of your work history and accomplishments. For specialized situations (e.g., academia, law, scientific research or very experienced workers), you might opt for a longer, more comprehensive résumé, which is often called a curriculum vitae (or CV). In either case, you start with a one-page cover letter aimed directly at your reader.

Most often you send a traditional résumé when responding to a published job advertisement, such as one you've seen in the classifieds section of your newspaper or on the Net. This type of résumé actually comes in four main varieties: *chronological, functional, combination* and *keyword.*

No matter which format you choose, certain elements are common in the traditional résumé. For instance, the résumé is divided into distinct sections. The headings are in bold or set apart to show clear demarcation points, and the language is very active and results-oriented. Take a look at Table 6.2 for a list of the sections usually found in a traditional résumé.

Table 6.2 Sections to Include in a Traditional Résumé

SECTION	PURPOSE
Career Objective	Explains what kind of position you're applying for
Personal Summary	Gives some highlights of your most relevant skills
Employment History	Shows where you've worked and what you accomplished
Education	Lists your degrees, diplomas, certificates and other courses
Additional Qualifications	Describes volunteer experience, awards, computer skills, etc.
Personal Information	Lists relevant hobbies and special interests or skills

Guidelines for Choosing a Traditional Résumé

The style you choose, and when you decide to use it, depends on your situation. In the next few paragraphs, I provide some guidelines for selecting the style of traditional résumé that is right for you. You will also find Web sites that show you numerous examples and offer tips in design and writing.

Chronological Résumé Format As I said before, the chronological résumé format is used most often, which can be good and not-so-good. On the positive side, employers are familiar with the layout, which tends to be easy to read. The drawback is that this kind of résumé may not stand out in a meaningful way from the rest of the pack. In terms of format, your jobs and achievements (not just duties) are listed in reverse order, starting with most recent. The emphasis here is on what you have already accomplished and where you have worked.

Chronological Résumés Are Best Used When:

- You plan to stay in a similar field to the one you're in now.
- There are no large gaps in your employment history.
- Your work history shows development and increasing responsibility.

CYBER TIP Want to get a professional's opinion of your existing résumé—for free? Here are two Web sites that offer free résumé evaluations (of course, if changes are required, they'll be glad to assist you, for a fee). On-Line Career & Management Consulting Services is at **www.dnai.com/~career/form_qa.htm**. At the other Web site, **bakosgroup.com**, you can fill in the online form to inquire about the free assessment by The Bakos Group. They accept Canadian calls toll free.

Notice that in this type of résumé, it's your work history that really stands out. It shows movement from one level to the next. In fact, it can demonstrate to the reader that you're reliable, progressive and ready to take on the very role that they are offering. Some online sources to visit regarding chronological résumés include:

- Sample Chronological Résumé (**jobsmart.org/tools/resume/res-chr1.htm**)
- Writing a Chronological Résumé (**jobsmart.org/tools/resume/res-chro.htm**)
- Put a Free Sample in Your Résumé (**www.asktheheadhunter.com/FreeSample.htm**)
- Writing a Winning Résumé (**amsquare.com/america/advantag/winning.html**)

Functional Résumé Format The functional format is really just a variation on the chronological résumé. It's particularly effective when you're a freelancer (that is, you have many jobs or contracts instead of a steady employment history), or when making a career change. It's also a good format when you're just starting out. It focuses the reader on the things you can do, rather than where you've worked.

You actually use most of the same information that you would in the chronological version; however, it's arranged in a different way. The functional format uses special headings to emphasize your skills and accomplishments, instead of your work experience. It's less common than the chronological type, but, in the right situation, can be extremely potent.

Functional Résumés Are Best Used When:

- You are changing industries or are making a significant career change.

- There are substantial gaps in your employment history.
- You have held a series of short-term jobs or contract positions.
- You do not have much work experience.
- Your work history shows little development or increase in responsibility.

You can find examples of functional résumés at the following sites:

- Sample Functional Résumé (**jobsmart.org/tools/resume/res-fu1.htm**)
- Writing a Functional Résumé (**jobsmart.org/tools/resume/res-func.htm**)
- Defeat the 5 Most Common Resume Myths (**www.nbew.com/archive/960421-001.html**)

Keyword Résumé Format In the first edition of this book, I only mentioned keyword résumés briefly in the final chapter, "A Glimpse into the

REAL LIFE I've successfully used a functional résumé myself. Twice, actually. The first time was when I switched from that management job in a corporation to a university teaching position. The second was after working part time on my master's degree in education, when I applied to become a career consultant. In each case, I gathered my information and achievements in sub-headings such as Training Experience or Individual Counselling to highlight the qualities that were most important to my potential employers.

CYBER TIP The combination résumé is a mixture of the chronological and functional approaches. It's handy when you don't fit precisely into either of these two categories. Check out the following URLs for more details and examples: the UBC Career Centre (**www.student-services.ubc.ca/careers/info/sample3.htm**) and About Work (**www.aboutwork.com/rescov/resinfo**).

Future." This time I'm including them among the traditional types. There are two reasons for this: 1) a growing number of employers in Canada are using "scanning and tracking" systems for which keyword résumés are ideal, and 2) they are basically a simple variation on the traditional résumé.

Fundamentally, a keyword résumé is a traditional chronological or functional résumé with one major addition: a section that uses words, not phrases to describe your skills and experience. This is in contrast to the rest of your résumé, which is written with strong action verbs and sentence-long descriptions of your accomplishments. According to U.S. résumé expert Jeremy Shapiro, you should add a "keword summary" section either near the top or bottom of your traditional résumé. The words and phrases you use should be *different* from those you've used in the other parts of your résumé, in order to increase the number of "hits" (more about this below).

In order to appreciate what's involved here, let me state for the record that keyword résumés have already become the rage in the U.S., especially with the Fortune 500 companies there. Keyword résumés can substantially reduce recruiting costs while enlarging the company's capacity to accept, process and screen applications. Mind you, it does tend to negate what we used to call the "human factor." Despite this, here are two parts of the process that you should know about:

- *Résumé scanning*. For companies that require a keyword résumé, your résumé itself is run through a scanning system, which usually uses Optical Character Recognition (OCR) software. You'll read more about this in Chapter 7. Suffice it to say for now that your résumé is first scanned in as an image and then turned back into electronic text. This text is then stored on a database. The employer can search the database using keywords, and the higher your score (the more "hits" registered on your résumé), the higher your odds are of reaching the top of the pile.
- *Applicant tracking*. As your résumé gets turned into electronic text, it is automatically sorted into the appropriate category for storage and retrieval in the database. This avoids duplicate applications and allows the employer to categorize you into a neat little box.

For some examples of—and instructions on preparing—a keyword résumé, check out the following:

- Format Your Résumé to Be Scanned by a Computer, by Jeremy Shapiro (**www.service.com/cm/crc/crc35.html**)

CYBER TIP To learn more about optical scanning and tracking, check out two of the most commonly used systems: Resumix at **www.resumix.com** and Restrac at **www.restrac.com**. Both sites provide suggestions and templates for you. But be forewarned that they appeal to the U.S. market, which is far ahead of us in the electronic résumé game. Not everything you see applies to the Canadian market.

- How to Build and Submit Your Resume in ASCII Text (**www.careermosaic.com/cm/rwc/rwc13.html**)
- Key Word Resumes by James Gunyen (**www.on-trac.com/resart1.htm**)
- The Online Job Application: Preparing Your Résumé for the Internet (Riley Guide) (**www.dbm.com/jobguide/eresume.html**)

Keyword Résumés Are Best Used When:

- You know the recipient is going to scan your résumé for use in a searchable database.
- The employer has stipulated that you send in your application via e-mail, in ASCII or Plain Text.
- You are responding to an ad placed by a large company that is likely to have a huge response (and is therefore more likely to use electronic means to screen applicants).

Résumé Alternatives

If you're doing your job search right, you won't be spending a whole lot of time replying to positions that you've seen advertised. In Chapter 9 I explain that advertised jobs account for only 5 to 20 percent of all the available vacancies today. To make things worse, since everyone else gets to see the ads at the same time, competition can be ferocious. In fact, I'm frequently asked about the best time to use an alternative to the traditional résumé.

The bulk of employment opportunities are buried somewhere in the hidden job market. This is where a traditional résumé might not meet your needs or those of your reader. As it turns out, there are two popular options to consider. One is the *targeted marketing letter*, and the other is the *broadcast letter*.

Microsoft Word - Sample key word resume

LARITA E. JANVERS, B.A.

456 Maple Leaf Street
Anytown, Nova Scotia N7X K9Q

E-Mail: laritaj@email.com, Phone (222) 333-4444

KEYWORD SUMMARY
Results oriented Administrative Manager, 12 years experience, professional, operations, management experience with small to mid-sized companies in start-up, reorganization, expansion, downsizing, growth

Supervise administration, operations, managing staff, accounting, accounts receivable, accounts payable, payroll, budgeting, forecasting, collections, facilities management, employee development, marketing, customer support, planning

Computer Literate: Wordprocessing, Word, WordPerfect, Spreadsheet, Lotus, Excel, Presentations, PowerPoint, Harvard Graphics

WORK EXPERIENCE

1996 – Present

Alternative One: Targeted Marketing For this approach, you produce a one-page, customized selling letter. Your goal is to capture the interest of a specific reader at a particular company—namely, the person who you think can hire you at the place you'd like to work. You become the product, and the letter serves as a brief brochure outlining your features.

The targeted approach takes a skillful hand at letter writing. It also requires quite a bit of preparation. You must immediately show the reader what you can do for his or her company. And you have to do so in one page, without an accompanying résumé. This is no small feat, considering that in most cases the person you're writing to hasn't even advertised an open position.

Targeted Marketing Letters Are Best Used When:

- You're trying to tap into the hidden job market (e.g., you're not aware of any advertised position).
- You've done some initial research on the needs of the company, as well as the person who might be in a position to hire you.

- You're going after the top 10 or 15 companies on your target list—they appear to be good prospects—and you want to customize your message.
- You've been unsuccessful at contacting a key person by phone.

Alternative Two: Broadcast Letters In an ideal world, you'd have the time to customize your letters for every single company in each industry where you might want to work. The reality? Looking for work is a game of percentages. You can't afford to spend too much time chasing too few opportunities. As part of your overall strategy, you might also want to consider a mass mailing. This allows you to contact a whole lot of companies at the same time, but the odds of getting a response are greatly reduced.

Enter the broadcast letter. This one-pager is similar in format to the targeted marketing letter. The big differences are in the content and the number of copies that you send out. A targeted letter is customized to each particular reader, whereas the broadcast letter is generic. You can use a single version only (instead of individually targeted letters) aimed at the human resources manager. All you really change is the address. Your broadcast letter might go to 50 or even 200 different companies. It might even go to organizations in a variety of industries, depending on your career objectives. Compare this to the 10 or 20 targeted letters that you might prepare.

Broadcast Letters Are Best Used When:

- You're trying to tap into the hidden job market, but don't really care what company you work for.
- You want to contact as many potential employers as you can in a short period of time.
- You're seeking a job as an administrative assistant or secretary, or service person in the food/hospitality sector.

Things to Leave Out of Your Résumé

Whether you choose a traditional format or résumé alternative, there's a definite art to knowing what to put in your résumé. Remember that your main goal is to grab the interest of your reader. You don't want to overwhelm the person, yet you want to prevent your résumé from being screened out in the initial stages. Here's a rule to keep in mind: Put as

REAL LIFE To make your campaign less stressful, try sending out your letters in manageable waves. If you're going the targeted route, you could mail out four or five at a time. For broadcasting, you could mail out maybe 20 or 30 at a time. This way, you'll be able to follow each one up with a phone call (or an e-mail message) within a week of sending it. This can definitely increase your chances for success.

much in as you need to pique the reader's interest, then use the face-to-face job interview to close the sale. Just as there are sections that you must include in your résumé, there's information that you should think about leaving out, including:

- salary expectations and history (unless absolutely demanded by the employer);
- personal details such as your age, height, weight, marital status, country of origin, criminal record or state of health;
- details unrelated to the position that you're applying for;
- jargon or technical terminology that your reader will not understand;
- the names of any references (you can give these once you're asked for them, so that you keep a semblance of control over this process); and
- outright lies (there's a fine line between exaggeration and fibbing—don't cross it, because it can be grounds for firing, among other things).

Résumé Software

If I had to create my résumé from scratch today, I might just run right out and buy a special software package to assist me. There are numerous résumé and cover letter kits available at your software store (mostly on CD-ROM, as diskettes are becoming old hat, and almost all are from the U.S.). These programs give you just about everything you need to design and produce an excellent résumé. For about $25 to $70 Can., you get exercises that transform your list of skills and accomplishments into a usable résumé. You're also given a selection of templates with various styles. Choose the one you like, cut and paste your text where appropriate, then view it on screen and print a copy to proofread carefully before you send it.

Résumé software tends to work well enough. Watch out, however, for the U.S. bias (e.g., a one-page résumé is preferred by American employers, but the two-pager is more popular in Canada). And try not to make your résumé look too prefabricated. If it looks like it was assembled by a cookie-cutter (like a professional wrote it, not you), it could turn some screeners and employers off. Try to have it reflect your personality and way of speaking, if possible.

There are other offerings of this type available at your software store. Look for a program that will make it easiest for you to create a résumé that fits your style. Some examples of software programs (and locations to learn more about them) are:

- Tom Jackson's The Perfect Résumé program, Davidson and Associates (**www.davd.com/products/resume.html**)
- Résumé Maker Deluxe, Individual Software Inc. (**www.individualsoftware.com/**)
- WinWay Résumé, Winway Corp. (**www.winway.com,** then "Products")
- Résumé Writer, Expert Software Inc. (**www.expertsoftware.com/resume.htm**)

REAL LIFE Feel free to use your word processor's spell-checker and grammar functions, but never rely on them exclusively. They may not catch everything (especially if you have the dictionary set to U.S. English, instead of Canadian). Read your documents thoroughly yourself. You should then get someone whose opinion and language skills you trust (maybe a friend, colleague or career practitioner) to give them a thorough review.

By the way, you may also be able to use built-in templates from your word processor to design your résumé. In recent versions of Word, for example, go to "File," "New," "Other Documents," then "Professional Résumé." With WordPerfect, try "File," "New," "Business," then "Résumé." Input your information, save the file and you're set. Be sure to buy good-quality specialty paper to run through your printer. Unless you're going into an artsy field, where colour and creativity are essential, try to keep the design of your paper stock simple (e.g., a plain blue border around the edges is nice). Pre-printed, résumé-quality paper is available at your business supply store.

III. LETTER WRITING

Wouldn't it be nice if the toughest part was over, now that you've slaved away to create the ultimate résumé? You knew there'd be a catch though, didn't you? It's called letter writing. In the work search, writing letters is as critical as creating a résumé. A specialized letter is one used in specific situations to achieve particular objectives. There are two basic types that you will run across in your self-marketing campaign:

- cover letters (sent with your résumé before the interview), and
- thank-you letters (after interviews and networking meetings).

Cover Letters

Who needs a cover letter? Just about everyone who sends out a résumé. It is important to include a covering page to introduce your résumé.

The purpose of a cover letter is to impress the potential employer right off the mark. If you get that attention (in a positive way), the reader may actually decide to skim over your résumé. If not, consider yourself screened.

Because it's often the first glimpse that an employer gets of you, your cover letter is critical. Done right, it gives you the chance to summarize your potential worth to the company and keeps you in the running.

Helpful Hints for Making an Effective Cover Letter

- Create personalized stationery with a word processing program. It should include your name, academic credentials (if appropriate), address and contact numbers (phone, fax and e-mail). Try to make it look as professional as possible.
- Tailor the letter to the person who makes the hiring decisions at the company where you want to work. Show that you know something about the company and the industry. This is where the research you learn how to do in Chapter 8 comes in. No need to go crazy—just make it clear that you didn't pick this company randomly from the phone book.

- Write in your own words so that it sounds like you—not like something out of a book. This is a good chance to let the best of your personality show through.
- Use terms and phrases that are meaningful to the employer. (This is where your industry research, networking and thorough review of the company's employment ad and Web site come in.)
- Keep it to one page. If you overload it, you just might frighten the reader off (who may have to read hundreds of other letters and résumés, too).

More info on cover letters, and some design templates, can be found at:

- Sample Cover Letter from Expert Software (**www.expertsoftware.com/resumelt.htm**)
- Archeus Cover Letter Articles (**www.student-services.ubc.ca/careers/info/cover1.htm**)

REAL LIFE Consider test-marketing your application package before you use it for real. Send your cover letter, résumé and envelope to a friend or colleague whose opinion you value. Then get honest feedback from them. How did the package look? Did it grab the reader's attention when they opened it? Are you missing anything?

Thank-You Notes

One of the most overlooked components of an effective self-marketing campaign is the thank-you letter. Ironically, it's also one of the quickest steps to do. You should always send out a brief thank-you immediately after any of the following:

- meeting someone for an information interview (as part of your networking);
- completing a job interview, whether it's a first, second or final one; or
- speaking to someone who has helped you with your work search.

Cyber-Version or Hard Copy? Thank-you letters are a nice touch. In your continued quest to differentiate yourself in meaningful ways, why not try a more personalized approach? Send a homemade, customized paper card, or send an electronic greeting card. The idea behind using a card instead of a letter is simple. If you send a basic letter, it may be appreciated for a few moments before it's tucked away in some file or maybe even tossed out. A card, on the other hand, is something that may get displayed. If the recipient puts your card somewhere where it can be seen—by that person as well as others—you've secured yourself some free advertising.

Hard-Copy: Do-It-Yourself Software Let's say you have access to a computer and a good-quality printer (either black and white laser or 600 dpi inkjet). You could create a thank-you card using any one of the following software programs:

- Stationery Shop or Greeting Card Maker, Expert Software (**www.expertsoftware.com/soho.htm**)
- Print Shop, Broderbund Software Inc. (**www.broderbund.com**, then "Printshop Deluxe")

Cyber-Version: Electronic Greeting Cards This is the newest (and some would say funkiest) way to send a message to someone you've met during your work search. It's literally a customizable electronic note with graphics—or even animation and sounds—that you send via e-mail. Cool as this is, I personally think that it may not be the way to go just yet. That's because, in most cases, the recipient doesn't get the actual note right away. They receive notification in their e-mail box that they have a note from you and then they must go to a special site with a password they're given to retrieve your note.

This cumbersome two-stage approach makes this technology less appealing. If you do decide to use it, make sure that you have the correct e-mail address of the person you want to reach. If it's not on the business card they gave you when you met with them, try searching WhoWhere at **www.whowhere.com**. (Hint: try the "Advanced" feature to look up a person's e-mail address by name, province and city.) Examples of free electronic cards are at:

- Canada Yellow Pages, picture post cards (**www.canadayellowpages.com/canada/postcards.html**)
- IVillage iGreeting post cards (**www.ivillage.com/postcards**)

IV. BUSINESS CARDS

A simple, relatively inexpensive way to remind folks of who you are is with your business card. You can use it when you meet new people while networking, as an introductory or concluding piece at an interview, as part of your mailing package or as a way of advertising your new business. This handy tool is useful whether you're employed or unemployed, and especially useful if you're self-employed. Also, collecting and sorting the business cards you receive from your contacts helps you to manage your work search.

Below is the type of information that you can consider including on your card. Choose only the points that will make the strongest impact on your intended audiences (feel free to substitute any others that are appropriate).

- Your name and any relevant credentials. This can include your degree (BA) or professional designation (CHRP).
- Area of specialty (e.g., finance, marketing, plumbing).
- The name of your company and your title, if you're self-employed.
- A full address where any correspondence can be sent to you.
- A phone number where you can easily be reached (preferably one hooked up to some sort of answering system, so that you can retrieve your messages regularly).
- A fax number. Note that it doesn't have to be your own fax machine. For instance, a friend might have access to a fax machine you can use while you're looking for work. Or you could rent a number from one of the many business service companies that have sprung up recently.
- Your personal e-mail address. You'll need this to send and receive messages with potential employers, and to take part in newsgroups for networking and work searching.
- The address of your personal Web site on the World Wide Web, if you've got one.

For some sample layouts of business cards, visit "World's Easiest" online business forms (**www.easiest.com**), and click on "Raised Print Business Cards."

Do It Yourself or Outsource?

Whenever I speak at a conference, people approach me to exchange ideas (and business cards). I can always tell when someone has prepared a homemade version. In my humble opinion, I have never seen one that remotely approaches similarly priced, professionally printed cards (in terms of feel or quality). This is one of those instances where the homemade version doesn't yet rival that of the printing services. Don't misunderstand me—you can get some very creative and professional-looking business cards from a variety of software packages. It's just that they tend to feel, well, inferior.

Why They Look and Feel Homemade What makes it so obvious that a card is homemade? The card stock (that is, the grade of paper) supplied in the software kit is usually substantially thinner than the stock a printer would use. This is because most home printers aren't equipped for heavier card stock that might cause paper jams. The second clue involves the edges of the card. Printing services use huge cutters to make cards come out with sharp, even edges. The software-produced version can't do this. Instead, it provides perforated sheets, which you carefully tear apart once the cards have been printed.

What you end up with are serrated, rough edges and thin paper instead of clean-cut edges and firm, heavy stock. I'm not saying that this is the end of the world. But when so much is riding on the impressions you make in your work search, you might want to take this into account.

Creating a Business Card Using Software You may not share my lack of enthusiasm for doing it yourself, and may still want to try making your own cards. What you'll need is a computer and printer (preferably 600 dpi laser or high-quality colour), plus software designed to produce business cards. There are some programs that enable you to create customized business cards, usually offering templates, design tips, graphics and font choices, plus sheets of perforated paper. All you have to do is fill in the blanks with the information you want. Here are a few examples:

- MyBusinessCards, MySoftware (**www.mysoftware.com/mybusinesscards/index.htm**)
- Business Card Designer Plus (**www.camdevelopment.com/bcdp.htm**)

If you don't want to buy extra software, you can always use templates from your word processor to design business cards. In recent versions of WordPerfect, for example, go to "File," "New," "Business," then "Business Card." Fill it out, select a graphic from your image files and you're set. You'll have to buy perforated sheets of card stock to run through your printer (available at your local business supplies store).

REAL LIFE Colour can provide an impressive effect. However, it's not critical to have it on your business card, if you're seeking employment. A clean, clear black and white version is fine for most purposes. If you are self-employed, however, definitely consider a splash of colour. Your card represents you in the eye of the beholder, so don't be afraid to spend more than the $15 or $20 extra it costs for the basic version at your local business supplies store.

V. WIRED WRAP-UP

I cringe when I think back to how I applied for one of my first "real" summer jobs. The previous summer (after my last year of high school), I had worked—on a volunteer basis—at a small ad agency run by a gem of a man named Reid Bell. He was kind enough to refer me to a friend who held a very senior position at the biggest ad company in Canada. Talk about networking heaven. All I had to do was write to Reid's friend and set up a meeting. What could be more simple, right?

So guess who blew it—big time! I figured I was in, so I didn't take it seriously. I waited until the last minute, hastily typed up a letter without bothering to proofread it, then sent it (typos and all) in a wrinkled envelope with an actual footprint on it. I even spelled the contact person's name wrong and didn't take the time to find out her title. Can you picture the reaction of this unsuspecting communications professional? I needn't tell you that I didn't get the job. However, Reid and I did have a good laugh over this years later.

You can avoid the spectacular mistakes that *I* made in my misbegotten youth. With a word processor and some basic advice that you can get for free on the Web, you can create first-class self-marketing materials. In fact, it's become so easy that employers now demand a very high standard, as a baseline. Just keep in mind the way that employers typically hire when they've advertised a position. Once you understand the screening process and that the needs of the employer are paramount, the rest is simply a matter of tailoring your material to your audience. If you (and the person who you get to review your material) are happy with your results, then you're ready to consider sending your materials electronically.

CHAPTER 7

Know How to Send Your Material Electronically

I. WHAT YOU DON'T KNOW CAN HURT YOU

The previous chapter was all about preparing your work-search marketing tools (e.g., a résumé and cover letter). Now we move on to the part that makes many people nervous. Yes, it's time to find out how to send your materials the *wired* way. Be forewarned: if you're used to sending out your résumé only by regular mail or courier, some of the concepts in this chapter may shock you. Yet they really aren't difficult to master. It's mostly a matter of knowing when to use which format, what the techno-speak really means and how to satisfy the new recruitment tactics.

What you'll find here are ways to send your cover letter and résumé via:

- fax (by regular fax machine and by your computer's fax program),
- e-mail (within the body of the message and as an attachment), and
- the World Wide Web (by way of Internet form).

You will also learn how to modify your material so it best fits the mode of transport, depending on the needs of the employer.

It's Not the "Same Old Same Old" Anymore

Have you noticed anything different about employment ads lately? One obvious change is that almost half of the postings are geared toward techies (in computer and engineering fields). Another is that even employment ads for traditional fields increasingly include a Web site and e-mail address. So what does all this mean to you? Plenty, if you want to gain a competitive advantage.

The message here is loud and clear. Organizations are slowly but surely shifting their recruiting techniques. They are moving to electronic media. The pressure is on you to keep up and meet the needs of these employers, not the other way around. In other words, you're better off learning how to adjust your materials now, rather than later.

Anyone Can Adapt For starters, don't be put off by a company's ad that gives only a fax number, or only a fax number and e-mail address. (Look at those high tech ads—they often have nothing but an e-mail address and an Internet address with no phone number or company location at all!) No need to panic. Just follow the instructions below and you'll soon be sending off your application as a professional-quality fax or a correctly configured e-mail message.

But Not Everyone Will What's incredible to me is how many people are not embracing these new techniques and don't realize what this means. It shows up in the numbers. An employment ad that offers only the option of sending in your application via e-mail, for example, may only receive 10 to 15 percent of responses this way. Everyone else will fax, mail, courier or hand-deliver their packages. Not that 10 to 15 percent is a bad thing, necessarily. It's just that 85 percent of applicants are not taking the opportunity to show off their computer skills! Wouldn't it be great if you could be among the few who send in their résumé via e-mail? Wouldn't that give you a bit of a leg up over your competition? And what happens when we turn the statistics around so it's 85 percent who are responding via e-mail, while you're not?

Fortunately, you don't have to reinvent your marketing materials completely to play in this game. That résumé and cover letter we worked so hard on in Chapter 6 are still useful. However, be prepared to move things around a bit and to learn a few new techniques.

II. SENDING YOUR RÉSUMÉ VIA FAX

Let's start with a device that most of us are already familiar with: the fax. By far, this is still the most common form of electronic carrier for résumés. No wonder—it's a fast, relatively cheap way to send material to potential employers. Did you know, though, that there's a science to sending the perfect fax?

Like many people, I used to think that all you had to do was drop a copy of your cover letter and résumé into the fax machine, dial in the recipient's number, press "Send" and wait for the receiving company to call you for an interview. Unfortunately, it's a bit more involved than that. There are all sorts of subtleties that you should consider. Things like layout and design, print quality and accuracy. Things like making sure it's received by the right person. Ignoring any one of these could scuttle even the best-laid faxing plans.

Plus you have the option of faxing directly from your computer or scanner without even using a fax machine. Let's start with the known, however, and that is with a typical fax machine. Then we'll move on to computer fax and home scanning equipment.

REAL LIFE Your fax cover page should reflect the type of position that you are applying for. If you're sending material to a bank, make sure that it looks dignified and conservative. But what if you're applying to an ad agency? Let your creativity (and courage) be your guide. Of course, these aren't hard and fast rules. The crux of this advice is to know your audience.

Layout and Design

If you're going to send an employment application by fax, you need three components: a fax cover page, your cover letter and your résumé. All should be faxed together, as one set of documents. Bear in mind that the fax cover page will be the first thing that the recipient sees. It must be attractive, professional-looking and error-free. Furthermore, it should resemble the other material in your package, in terms of layout and font of the text.

The fax cover page gives the recipient the basic information needed to process your application. It tells the recipient who the fax is from, and who it's for. You will likely want to include some of these details:

- The name and title of your intended recipient.
- Who the fax is from (include your title and company, if appropriate).
- Your phone and fax numbers.
- Your e-mail address.

- A brief description of the subject or purpose of the fax (e.g., Application for Position A345: Sales Clerk at National Shoes, Inc.).
- The number of pages being sent, including the cover sheet.
- The date that the fax is being sent (your machine may print the time automatically).
- Who else is receiving copies (if applicable).

For more details and examples of fax cover pages, go to:

- Enable Designs, for professionally crafted fax cover sheets (**www.enabledesigns.com:81/ed3fxcvs.htm**)
- Guidelines for the Secure Transmission of Personal Information by Fax, from the office of the British Columbia Information and privacy commissioner (**www.oipcbc.org/publications/advice/faxguide.html**)

Obtaining the Best Image from a Standard Fax Machine

All you need to know about the mechanics of a fax is that it converts the image of your message into electronic data, which is transmitted at the rate

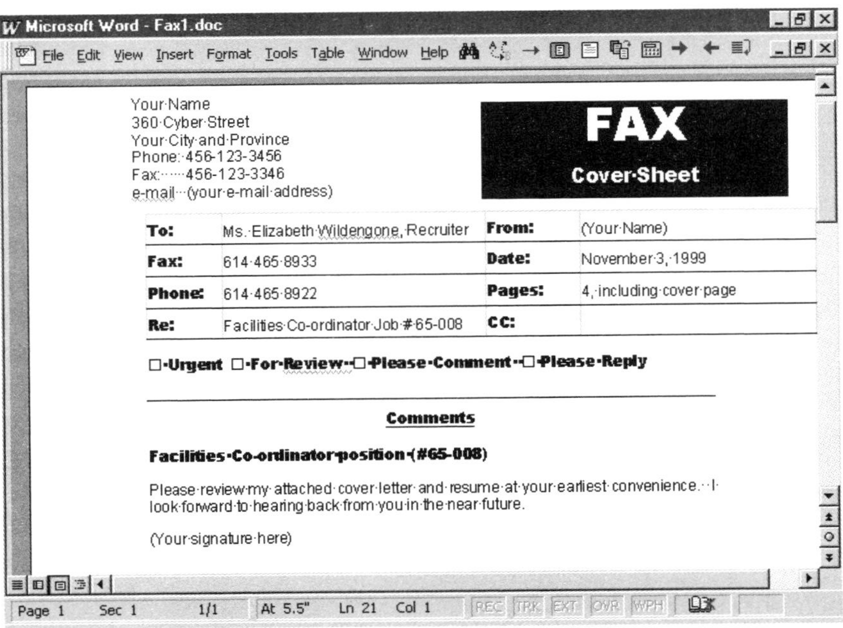
Microsoft Word - Fax1.doc

Your Name
360 Cyber Street
Your City and Province
Phone: 456-123-3456
Fax: 456-123-3346
e-mail (your e-mail address)

FAX
Cover Sheet

To:	Ms. Elizabeth Wildengone, Recruiter	**From:**	(Your Name)
Fax:	614 465 8933	**Date:**	November 3, 1999
Phone:	614 465 8922	**Pages:**	4, including cover page
Re:	Facilities Co-ordinator Job # 65-008	**CC:**	

☐ Urgent ☐ For Review ☐ Please Comment ☐ Please Reply

Comments

Facilities Co-ordinator position (#65-008)

Please review my attached cover letter and resume at your earliest convenience. I look forward to hearing back from you in the near future.

(Your signature here)

Page 1 Sec 1 1/1 At 5.5" Ln 21 Col 1

of your fax's modem. The printer output varies widely and depends on a number of factors, such as:

- whether the image your machine sends is at 300 dpi (dots per inch) or 600 dpi;
- whether the receiver's machine reads at 300 or 600 dpi (the higher the better);
- whether the receiving machine uses thermal, inkjet or laser technology for printing documents; and
- how recently you've cleaned your fax machine.

Improving Your Output Before you send your fax, you can do several things to enhance the image that your recipient will see. First, use high-quality, white paper only. Coloured paper can cause the image to come out dark grey. Next, check your original for any marks or blotches (known as hickeys in printing jargon). You may be able to cover these up with correction fluid or correction tape, instead of reprinting the whole thing. But if you leave the hickeys as they are, they are guaranteed to be there when the person at the other end starts reading.

You can also fiddle with the resolution of your transmission. Many fax machines (especially those for home office use) give you the option of standard, fine, super fine or photo transmission quality. I advise you to go for the super fine, which is the highest resolution possible for text. This increases the number of dots per square inch of your image, resulting in a sharper version of the final output. Note that it may take longer for your message to be sent, and you might have to play a bit with your fax machine's settings, but it's worth it. (Make sure to read the manufacturer's instructions first.)

Something as simple as cleaning your fax machine regularly can also make a huge difference. In particular, make sure that the scanning bar (the part that reads your documents) is free of dust and streaks. Check the owner's manual of the machine you're using to see how to clean it properly.

Check for Shrinkage There's one more thing to watch for, and you may not have any control over it. I'm referring to the "shrinkage effect" (this has nothing to do with a certain Seinfeld episode). Sometimes when you send a fax, it arrives looking smaller than the original. Suddenly the 12-point type that you chose so carefully looks to your recipient like scrunched-up, hard-to-read, 8-point type. Unfortunately, there's not

REAL LIFE If you think it's appropriate, don't just send your application to the human resources department. Take the time to find out who is doing the actual hiring and consider sending that person a copy, too. Make sure you spell names and titles properly. This may help you to stand out from the competition. Keep in mind, though, that some recipients might not like having their screening process circumvented. The bottom line? Use your best judgement to get an edge.

much you can do about this from your end—unless you know beforehand how your image will appear on your recipient's machine.

To get around this, you could speak to the person who will first receive your fax (e.g., an administrative assistant or someone in the mail room) and enlist his or her aid. After the fax goes through, call and ask—politely—if he or she could quickly view your résumé *before* passing it on to your intended recipient. You want to ensure that the quality is the best possible. If it's not, ask for suggestions on how to improve it, then re-format and re-send.

On Time, to the Right Person

When sending out any résumé or letter, make sure that you know exactly who to send it to. Get the correct name, spelling and title of that person. You can do this by calling the company directly and asking the recep-

REAL LIFE What if you're sending out applications across the country, or internationally? A long-distance fax costs the same as any other long-distance phone call. Charges can rack up pretty quickly, unless you do it a smarter way. I suggest that you get a long-distance saving plan for your fax line. Try Sprint Canada for The Most, at **www.sprintcanada.ca** (go to "For Home"). Bell Canada's First Rate plan is at **www.bell.ca** (go to "Residential," then "Products and Services For Your Home"). AT&T's Canada's True Choice is at **www.attcanada.com** (go to "Residential Services").

tionist or administrative staff. At the same time, ask for the right fax number for the person you're trying to reach. Some larger companies have several fax machines on their premises, and you want the one that your target recipient uses.

Making Sure It Gets to Your Intended Recipient

There's a problem with faxing that can slow you down. Can you ever be sure that your intended recipient actually gets your message? Sure, your fax machine can notify you that the message went through and was received by the machine at the other end. But once there, how does it actually get to the actual recipient? Does it arrive on that person's desk quickly, or after several days of lying around somewhere? If the recipient works in a large office, the fax probably gets routed through a delivery system that might not be very direct. When timing is critical, this could slow things down dangerously.

The Follow-Up Factor Just because your fax machine says "Transmission OK" doesn't mean that it will arrive in the hands of the recipient quickly and safely. Ever heard of an in-basket? That's where every piece of correspondence and documentation gets dumped on someone's desk. It's easy for your fax to get lost (or buried) in this ever mounting pile of messages and files.

Consequently, it can be useful to call the receptionist or administrative assistant at the company soon after you've sent your fax to make sure that it has been received. Note the time, date and name of the person you're speaking to, and keep it in your files. That way if things don't go according to plan, you have a confirmed record that your application was indeed given to the right person.

CYBER TIP Do *not* send your résumé via fax machine if you know for a fact that it will be fed into an employer's "scanning and tracking" system. Instead, send it by mail, e-mail, or Web form as determined by the employer, or else it may not be scanned correctly.

REAL LIFE Since a follow-up call isn't always an option, I strongly recommend that you also send a hard copy of your application by regular mail ("snail mail") or courier. That way, you get two hits at the same target. By doing this, your recipient still gets your information immediately by fax. This puts you in the running when responding to a published ad (as long as you meet the deadline!). Then your recipient can also see the high-quality paper version when it arrives in an envelope several days later. By the way, this suggestion applies whether you're using a fax, e-mail or Internet form.

Faxing Directly from a Computer or Scanner

Faxing a document directly by computer used to be my favourite way to send out material. It's fast, cheap and accurate (and hey, let's not forget it's cool, too, as my daughter says). The quality of the image stays high, since you don't print the document onto paper before you send it. But—and this is a big consideration—you should still print out a hard copy so you can keep it in your file folder for quick access.

CYBER TIP Set the modem command in your fax program to match the top speed of your modem (e.g., a 56.6 kbps modem should be set to 56,600 baud in your fax program). This allows your faxes to be sent as fast as the receiving machine can load them. Note that this still tends to be at a rate of 9,600 baud, since many people are using older or inexpensive fax machines. The maximum receiving speed today is still 14,400 on a conventional fax machine, but watch for this to increase.

What You Need All you require is a computer or stand-alone scanner, a modem and some fax software. You don't have to be hooked up to the Internet to make this work. Your modem must, of course, be plugged into your phone line (or cable outlet, if that is what your ISP uses). You'll also need to set up the fax program as one of your available printers.

(Read the manufacturer's instructions for specific set-up procedures. It's a cinch once you've tried it six or seven times!)

Take the fax program that is built into Windows 95, for example. If you're using Word, you can call up "File," "New," "Letters and Faxes" and then choose "Fax Wizard." This takes you through the fax creation process. Once you've built the template, you can customize it however you want. It's usually sufficient for introducing yourself quickly by referring to the job and your attached cover letter. Then proofread it carefully, print it out to look it over (if that increases your comfort level) and click on "File," "Send To" and "Fax Recipient."

Other Software You Can Use There are several popular fax programs on the market. They generally allow you to convert files from your other programs (e.g., software for word processing, spread sheets, presentations, etc.) directly into a fax image. You can also store your faxes in specific categories and view their status, such as time and date sent, if they were transmitted without error, size of file, plus other relevant details. Here are some products you can view (and even sample) via the Web:

- WinFax, from Symantec (**www.symantec.com**)
- FaxMail, by ElectraSoft (**www.electrasoft.com**)

Make a Hard Copy, Too Don't forget to print yourself a hard copy of any fax you send by computer. You may want to file it for later reference. If you're relying on your computer to store all your fax images, keep in mind that they can take up lots of valuable space on your hard drive, so you should purge these regularly (or else zip them into a compression package)—not to mention the sad fact that you would lose them all if the unthinkable happens to your hard drive. I realize that paper is uncool for some people, but if you think we've reached the era of the paperless office, take a look around.

CYBER TIP Why shop retail? Fax programs range in price from zero (freeware) to between $10–$30 (shareware) and as much as $200 for full-featured, bundled communication packages. Here's a software Web site to search through for information and demo versions: **www.download.com**. Once there, enter "Fax" in the search box. Then look for a program that meets your requirements, download it for free and test it out.

III. USING E-MAIL TO SEND YOUR MATERIAL

The newest way to send your application package is by e-mail. There are quite a few reasons for considering this option seriously:

- You will likely stand out from your competition, because most people are not bothering to apply to jobs via e-mail (yet), even when given the option to do so.
- You may not be given a choice. If the employer is using a "scanning and tracking" system, they may insist on receiving your application via e-mail in Plain Text, within the body of your e-mail message (more about this soon).
- You can demonstrate immediately to potential employers that you have the computer skills needed to use e-mail properly. This alone can give you a competitive advantage.
- The version you send by fax or mail will probably be pre-screened and sorted into a pile somewhere. The e-mail version, however, might actually get to the decision maker faster—without being screened.
- An e-mailed résumé remains in the recipient's private mailbox until that person decides to open it. If privacy is a concern, an e-mail to an individual's address beats a fax, which may lie around in the fax tray for prying eyes to see once you've sent it.
- There are no long-distance charges for sending e-mail anywhere in the world.
- The transmission speed is quick, ranging from instantaneous to several hours, depending on routing and other related factors.

REAL LIFE As with sending any e-mail, always check your e-mail inbox a few minutes after pressing the send button, or a few hours later, to see if your message has been returned as "unsendable" or "undeliverable." If not, your message arrived safely. But if your mail bounces back, double-check the e-mail address and re-send it.

Knowing What Format to Use Can Be Critical

When sending information by e-mail, you need to decide which method of transmission to use. (I know, I know...why can't everyone just use one standardized format?) You've basically got two main choices:

1. When your application will be "scanned" by the employer: You can put your cover letter and résumé directly *into the body of the e-mail message,* by typing it in or by cutting and pasting it from an existing file, or
2. When your application will be printed out by the employer: You can affix your existing word-processed document containing your cover letter and résumé as an *attached file.*

Solving the Mystery If there's any uncertainty at all about how your recipient will view your application package, *I recommend that you include both a plain text version and an attached version whenever you e-mail a potential employer.* That means sending an ASCII keyword résumé in the body of your message as well as a fully formatted version as an attached file. According to Canadian online recruiting expert James Fehrenbach of the CEO Group (**www.ceogroup.com**), this reduces the risk of your material being "unreadable" at the other end. Mention in your opening words that you've provided a plain text version for scanning and fully formatted version for their convenience, should they want to print it out. As always, state that they should contact you immediately if they need more information. Be sure to include your phone number where it can be easily seen! Of course, if you know exactly what format your recipient uses, there is no mystery—go that route.

CYBER TIP Employers who ask for an e-mailed version of your résumé (and cover letter) may just be testing to see if you can do it properly. On the other hand, they may be using a scanning system. Thus, I recommend that you use a *keyword* version of your résumé in Plain Text whenever you send it in the body of your e-mail message.

Option 1: In the Body of Your Message

As I mentioned, you can put your cover letter and résumé information directly into the body of your e-mail message. In fact, this is the way that most employers want you to do it, unless they specify otherwise. You should also take this approach when:

- the person you're sending e-mail has a different or lower version of the word-processing program you're using, or
- you have no idea what kind of e-mail or word-processing program your recipient is using and want to make sure that your message is readable in any event.

Upsides and Downsides of "In the Body" Method The upside of this option is that it virtually ensures your message is viewable by your recipient, regardless of the e-mail application or word-processing program at that end. In fact, it eliminates the need for opening the file into a word-processing program altogether. Your message can be read directly in the e-mail message you've sent. This increases your chances of having your material read quickly.

There is some not-so-good news, though. By putting your text into the body of your message, you can only send it as plain text (ASCII). The result? Say goodbye to all your fancy formatting (bold, italic, underline) and attractive layout (indenting, bullet points, graphics). Your application might as well have come out of a 1940s typewriter. Not exactly cutting edge on the visual side, but it does make it easy to scan, if needed.

Inputting the Text Manually in the Body of Your Message This is where you type in, word by word, your complete text into your e-mail message. It can be laborious and time consuming, especially if you are creating a long document each time you e-mail an employer. But if your message is short, sometimes this is the method to choose.

Maybe you want to start off with a relatively brief personalized message to the employer. Since this will be the first thing the recipient sees when opening your e-mail, it doesn't hurt to make your message as relevant as possible. Or perhaps you don't have access to a word-processed version of your cover letter and résumé. This being the case, you would have to input all of this from scratch. Note that this should be an emergency procedure only!

In all other instances, you are better off to use the cut-and-paste method described later in the chapter. For now, though, the following steps will guide you with inputting text manually into the body of your message.

1. Call up your e-mail program onto your screen (refer to Chapter 1 for more details on basic e-mail procedures, if necessary).
2. Click on the "New Mail" or "Compose Message" icon (or whatever your program uses to create a new message).
3. Put in the recipient's e-mail address (from your e-mail program's address book, if it's stored there).
4. Type in the topic of your message in the "Subject" line. It should be short, and should mention the job you're after.
5. Type in your message. Include a keyword summary in your résumé.
6. Review your document for errors, using the e-mail's spell-checker (if available). Then proofread it again yourself, or have someone else read it over, as an extra precaution. (Consider printing out a copy—it's often easier to proofread on paper than on screen.)
7. When you're satisfied that everything is OK, click on "Send" to send your message to your recipient.
8. Remember to check your e-mail inbox later to see if your message has bounced back.

Cutting and Pasting Text into the Body of Your Message This method is more efficient than rewriting your entire application package every time you respond to an ad. All you need do is insert the existing word-processed version of your cover letter and *keyword* résumé, having first saved them in one file. You can then customize the covering letter to your recipient, and off you go.

Mind you, there is the little glitch of first converting your text to ASCII (plain text). I suggest that you do so within your word-processing program before pasting it into your e-mail. This way, you have a better chance of not having to readjust your material after you transfer it. And whenever you save an ASCII file, it's a good idea to put ".txt" at the end of the file name (as in, "Application for Company X.txt"). This lets you know that the text can be opened in any program.

How to Create an ASCII Version of Your File

1. Using your word-processing program, open the file that has your cover letter and résumé saved together as one document (the cover letter should come first).
2. Make a plain text (ASCII) version of the file. In Word, start by selecting "File," then "Save As." Click on "Don't use suggested format" and then move your cursor to the "File Name" box and type in the file name (e.g., "Application for Company X.txt"). Click on the drop-down box called "Save as type" and point to "text only." Finally, click on "Save." For WordPerfect, click on "File" and then "Save." In the "As Type" box, choose "ASCII DOS TEXT." Be sure that the name you give your file refers to the particular company you are mailing to.

How to Cut and Paste an ASCII File into Your E-mail

1. Once you've got your ASCII file open, use the "Edit" command to choose "Select All." This highlights all the text. Select the "Copy" command to pick up and store all the text.
2. Call up your e-mail program (refer to Chapter 1 for more details on basic e-mail procedures, if necessary).
3. Click on the "New Mail" or "Compose Message" icon (or whatever your program uses to create a new message).
4. Point your cursor to the uppermost, left-hand corner of your message area. Press the "Enter" key once to anchor the text, then select "Paste" from the "Edit" menu to insert the text from your word-processed file into the body of your e-mail message.
5. Make any adjustments that are needed to customize the layout or wording of your text or make it look right (but don't add anything fancy, or it could throw things off).
6. Review your document for errors, using the e-mail's spell-checker (if available). Then proofread it again yourself, or have someone else read it over, as an extra precaution. (Consider printing out a copy to proofread.)
7. Put in the recipient's e-mail address (from your e-mail program's address book, if it's stored there).
8. Type in the topic of your message in the "Subject" line. It should be short, and should mention the job you're after.

9. When you're satisfied that everything is OK, click on "Send" to send your message to your recipient.
10. Remember to check your e-mail inbox later to see if your message has bounced back.

CYBER TIP With most e-mail programs, you can create your message off-line (that is, when you're not connected to the Internet). Then, when you're ready, you can dial up your ISP and quickly send your completed message, using up very little of your online time. This can save you money (if you're paying for your Internet connection by the minute), and it frees up your phone line (for potential employers to call in!).

Option 2: Sending an Attached File

This is the second most common option. And oh, how sweet it is. In my opinion, it's like sending a fax from your computer, only better. If you can send your attachment in its original format (that is, without having to convert it first into plain text), you have a fast, efficient way of getting your material anywhere across the globe—with the full layout intact. When are you most likely to use this approach?

- When you want the recipient to receive a fully formatted version of your word-processed cover letter and résumé, complete with fancy layout (in other words, as it appears in your Word or WordPerfect file), rather than a stripped down "scannable" version.
- When you are certain that your recipient will be able to convert and print your attachment properly, because he or she uses a similar word-processing program with the same version number as yours (or higher).

If you're not sure about this, do yourself a favour—call the company and ask what type and version of word-processing program the receiving computer uses. If no one can tell you, then revert to my earlier advice: insert your application in the body of your e-mail package, plus include it as a formatted attachment.

How to Send a Fully Formatted Attachment:

1. As always, review the word-processed file containing your cover letter and résumé to ensure that it's exactly as you want it, with no mistakes.
2. Call up your e-mail program and click on the "New Mail" icon (or whatever your program uses to create a new message).
3. Put in the recipient's e-mail address (use your e-mail program's address book, if you've stored it there), and type the topic of your message in the "Subject" line.
4. Type in a brief message, mentioning the purpose of your e-mail and that you've attached your cover letter and résumé (mention the file type and format). Also state the reference number and title of the job you're applying for. This, in effect, becomes your cover page—it's the first thing the recipient sees before opening your attached file—so try to make it accurate and professional.
5. Click on the "Attachment" icon to select the file you want to send (or look for "Attach file" in the "Message" menu). Browse through your files and select the proper one.
6. After checking over what you wrote in Step 4 one more time, send your message to your recipient.
7. Don't forget to check later to make sure your message hasn't bounced back.

CYBER TIP On rare occasions, you may be asked to send an attached file that you've already converted into plain text. If so, follow the steps outlined in Option 2, taking care to save the file first as a text-only or ASCII version before you do the attaching.

Do a Test (Just in Case) Regardless of which option you choose, here's a neat idea. To preview how your message will appear, send your e-mail to yourself first. This won't guarantee that your recipient will see it exactly the same way, because different e-mail packages may have slight variations in formatting. You will, however, be able to catch most major glitches. Simply type your own e-mail address into the "To" box of your message, send it and open it when it arrives (hopefully shortly thereafter).

CYBER TIP Think about using a free, third-party e-mail provider when sending out job applications. Ponder this: your ISP gives you an e-mail address with its name in it (like yourname@sympatico.ca). If you switch providers, you lose access to replies being sent to that address. Using a third-party e-mail provider eliminates dependency on a particular ISP, as we discussed in Chapter 1, plus it gives you easier access to your mail from any Internet-enabled computer in the world. Some providers to consider include Microsoft's Hotmail (**www.hotmail.com**), Yahoo (**www.yahoo.ca**) or Excite (**www.excite.com**). Watch out for "premium" fees on special services you might not need.

IV. APPLYING USING AN ONLINE FORM

A growing number of companies are trying to make the electronic transmission of your application as painless as possible (for both parties). They have set up automated forms on their Web site that you fill in to apply for employment. In general, not only can you see the company's posted jobs but you can also apply immediately by completing the required information and clicking on the "Submit" icon.

These Web forms usually come in two varieties: "fill in the blanks" or "cut and paste." In either case, the objective is to standardize the application package to make it easier to read and store once you've sent it in. Here's a quick look at each type.

Fill in the Blanks

With some companies, you're asked to fill out a form online, field by field. Usually they want the "tombstone" information first, such as your name, address, phone number and e-mail address, etc. Then you are asked a whole series of questions, such as "employment history," "education attained," "special skills," and so on. In other words, you get to type in your entire résumé and history letter by letter. You can see an example of an online recruiting form at the Toronto Dominion Bank's Web site at **www.tdbank.ca/tdbank/hresource/ccgetresume.html**.

Some Fill-in-the-Blank Tips Typing in all your information is just the beginning of your application. Here's some advice to make your material more readable:

- Complete every single question. If you leave empty boxes, the company may not accept your application.
- Try to avoid using the hard return. Instead, let your words wrap according to the employer's settings.
- If the form asks for your computer skills, list each program you know how to use separately (e.g., Word, Lotus 123, Harvard Graphics).
- If the form asks for "start" and "end" dates of your previous work experience, consider supplying only the years (e.g., 1996 to 1998) rather than the years and months (e.g., April 3, 1996, to December 1998). In no case, however, should you ever lie about your current employment status.
- When the form asks you to describe your previous position(s), try to include your accomplishments (such as sales you generated, savings you created or the number of people you managed). Quantify these as best you can without revealing confidential information.

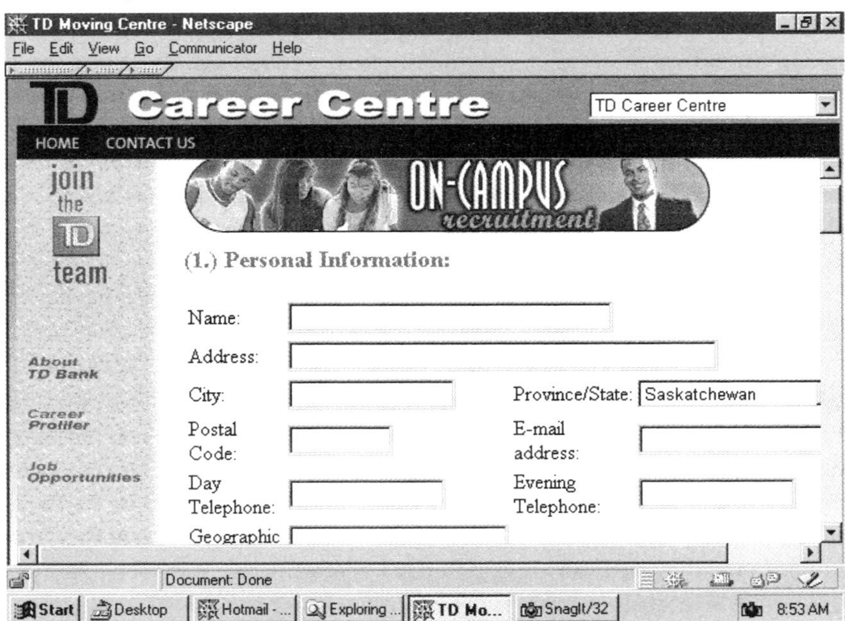

- If the form asks for a "salary range," see if it will accept "to be discussed" or "depends on the position" as an answer so you don't have to state a fixed amount that might be used to screen you out early in the game.
- If there is a button that allows you to preview your responses before sending them, use it! It's always better to double-check now than to find out you made a typo later.

Cut and Paste

More often than not, companies that provide online employment forms give you the option of cutting and pasting your résumé onto their page. Imagine how much easier this is than filling in the blanks. You'll find a few variations on this theme, including:

- part form, part cut and paste,
- e-mail only, and
- some combination of the two.

Part Form, Part Cut and Paste In this instance, you are asked to complete some personal information by filling in the blanks. In addition, there is a blank space provided so you can cut and paste in your cover letter and résumé. You do this the same way as described earlier in this chapter (see "Cutting and Pasting the Text into the Body of Your Message"). An example of this approach may be found at Canadian Tire online application for employment (**www.canadiantire.ca/CTenglish/hridx.html**, click "Application").

E-mail Only Some organizations ask you to apply via online form, when what they really mean is by e-mail. You'll discover this when you click on the button that says something like "post your résumé here." If it immediately calls up your e-mail program, you know what you have to do. First, see if it says somewhere on the Web site whether they want your application as a fully formatted attachment or as an ASCII cut-and-paste. Then follow the detailed instructions I described above. An example of this is at Toronto Dominion Bank, e-mail application (**www.tdbank.ca/tdbank/hresource/insert.html**, then click "Attach ASCII Resume").

REAL LIFE Whenever you send your résumé electronically, it never hurts to send a "snail mail" (regular mail) copy as a follow-up. Note that you can state on your electronic version that you've also sent a hard copy. Likewise, with the paper version you send—state in the cover letter that you've sent an electronic version as well. Mention the format you used, the time and date you sent it, and the name and Internet address of the recipient. Consider following up with a phone call after a few business days have passed, too, to express your continued interest and to make sure that your application was received. (Caution: if you overdo it here you could be perceived as obnoxious, desperate or both!)

By the way, you should always include your customized cover letter first when you're given the e-mail option. It will set you apart from other applicants!

V. SUBMITTING YOUR MATERIAL FOR SCANNING

We've talked a lot about scanning throughout this chapter. The word itself chills me to my very core. Isn't this what the aliens did to the humans in that flick *Independence Day*? Well, maybe not. But like I said in Chapter 6, it is something that most of us need to know about if we're looking for work. It has already become extremely popular in the United States for processing résumés (almost every Fortune 500 company is using it). Now our very own Canadian firms are starting to hop on board.

It's easy to see why scanning is becoming so popular. It enables human resources departments to manage massive numbers of paper résumés easily. That's because the text itself can be stored in an electronic database, which employers can search using specific criteria (keywords). Although it's expensive for companies to have their own complete system, there are services in Canada that are starting to act as affordable, third-party résumé handlers.

The Joys of OCR

You say you haven't heard of optical character recognition (OCR) before? It sounds more intimidating than it really is. OCR is the part of scanning that converts your paper résumé into electronically readable text. This way, the employer can retrieve résumés on the basis of "keywords," as described in the section on Keyword Résumés in Chapter 6. Note that you'll need to format your documents using the guidelines outlined in Table 7.1.

Table 7.1 Formatting for Scanning with Optical Character Recognition (OCR)

FORMATTING REQUIREMENTS	OCR (TEXT)
Recommended Fonts	Plain fonts only (e.g., Helvetica, Univers, Optima, Futura). In other words, no fancy stuff.
Text Features	No bullet points, underlines, italics, bolding, tables or tabs. Also, minimal use of hard returns, shading or solid lines.
Text Size Guidelines	Minimum 10-point type, maximum 14-point type, so that the OCR software can read it properly (try 12-point type if it will be read by a human, too).
Images or Graphics	Don't use 'em.
How to Send a Hard Copy	Send original by regular mail or courier. Fax is not a good idea, because it will degrade print quality. Use good-quality, white paper with print on one side only. Do not use staples.
How to Send an Electronic Copy	Send by e-mail in plain, ASCII text only or Internet form (if available).

Hints to Make Plain Text Stand Out

Imagine that you're heading out for an important interview. When you arrive, you realize—to your horror—that you've been stripped of all your clothes, shoes and hair-grooming gunk. Now you know what it's like to be a plain text résumé. Because you must eliminate all the formatting, it's almost as if you are sending in your application stark naked (nowhere

CYBER TIP When you know your résumé is going to be scanned and you've been given the option of sending it via regular mail or courier, always make sure that it's the highest possible quality. Use plain white paper (not too thick); provide an original, not a photocopy (otherwise you start to get text degradation, which scanners hate); print on one side only; and don't use staples. Make sure you use a good printer—try for at least an inkjet of 600 dpi, although laser printers are definitely preferred. And check to see that there are no errors or hickeys (or the scanner will choke).

near as embarrassing, I'm happy to say, as showing up that way yourself for the interview).

To compensate for the stripped down look of ASCII, there are ways to make your application stand out. Here are a couple of tips:

- Use dashes instead of horizontal lines to separate portions of your résumé.
- Substitute capital letters for fancy formatting (e.g., bold, underlines, shading).
- Replace bullets with asterisks (*).
- To indent text, use the space bar instead of the tab key; don't bother trying to centre text, as you don't know the width of the page at the other end.
- Include as much white space (using carriage returns) as possible for that "open" look.

REAL LIFE Try not to feel too de-humanized by electronic screening techniques. Even when you're sending your résumé to an electronic database, consider including a customized cover page. It will be scanned along with your résumé. Let your expertise and personality show through. It just might be the thing that differentiates you from the other applicants.

VI. WIRED WRAP-UP

When my five-year-old son sits down to cut and paste, we give him some scissors and non-toxic glue. When you do it, odds are you'll be using a mouse, a word processor and an e-mail program. Oh, how times have changed! I can barely remember the last time that I licked a stamp or placed a letter into an envelope. Between faxing, e-mail and the Web, I can reach virtually all of my business contacts (and pay most of my bills)—whenever I need to.

The same holds true for your work search. Now that an increasing number of employers request materials to be sent electronically, it falls directly on your shoulders to respond accordingly. If you do it properly, you can give yourself a competitive advantage. If you ignore the trends, you do so at your peril.

Points to Remember

- You should know how to fax your information in its best format, e-mail it when asked to, put it in a Web form when required, and design it for scanning when need be.
- You can significantly improve the image of your fax by following a few simple instructions.
- When e-mailing your application, include both an ASCII version in the body and a fully formatted version as an attachment (to cover all bases if you're unsure of the required format).
- OCR-scannable résumés should include a keyword summary at the top of the first page. Use mainly nouns to describe your skills, experience and credentials.

PART 3

SEARCH FOR WORK — THE *WIRED* WAY!

CHAPTER 8 Research Before You Search

Not long ago, one of my clients burst into my office full of excitement. "Here," she proclaimed as she threw some papers onto my desk. "This is the best damned résumé that you will ever see!" As she pointed to it triumphantly, she said, "Now I'll get that dream job for sure!" Then she paused for a moment and added, somewhat hesitantly, "There is one thing I'm having trouble with, though. Who exactly should I send this to?"

As it turns out, I had a few ideas to get my client moving ahead. And she came up with a few creative ones of her own. In fact, we worked together to generate a list of companies and people for her to target. Thus, she discovered the first law of seeking employment effectively: *be strategic*. In other words, don't just blindly send out your résumé in the magical hope that someone, somewhere, must have a job for you. Instead, try to select target companies that you would like to work for. And how do you find out who these firms are? Quite simply, by doing your research.

I. DIGGING FOR GOLD

In this stage of your job hunt, information-gathering skills become critical. If knowledge is pure gold, research is your tool to pan for it. You'll want to know things such as:

- which companies are offering work in your particular field,
- where they are located and what kind of people they are looking for,

- whether there are certain companies you should definitely consider,
- what kinds of products and services they offer,
- who their primary target audiences are,
- what makes these particular companies special, and
- who does the hiring in your specific department.

You'll learn how to answer these questions, and so much more, in this chapter.

The Four Golden Rules of Work-Related Research

I'm intrigued by the recent spate of best-selling books proclaiming to know the answers to everything. Their titles invariably start with "The Five Laws Of..." or "The Seven Habits Of...," and my personal favourite, "226 Immutable Principles Of..." Thus, I offer you my very own Four Golden Rules for research. They're not really rules, but they *are* suggestions based on my personal experience, on that of my clients and on conversations with professional researchers. Here they are:

1. *Expand your awareness of the economy and current events.* Keep on top of our economy and stay informed of major happenings.
2. *Learn more about your industry.* Discover the trends and statistics that affect your chosen field.
3. *Develop a workable list of potential employers.* Establish an initial roster of all the organizations for which you might work, then narrow it down to a manageable number of "hot prospects" to focus on first.
4. *Prepare to market yourself to your hot prospects.* Find crucial information that will help you stand out and make solid decisions when it comes to the prospects on your hot list.

REAL LIFE I'm the first to admit that the approach I've just described may not suit everyone's needs. But even if you're in a situation where you must find work—any work—as soon as possible, you'll still need to do a bit of research and targeting. So don't worry. I won't be offended if you only use the parts of this chapter that will help you immediately.

Some Starting Points

Note that these rules don't have to follow the sequence I describe. They are merely guidelines for you to construct your own career research path. To assist you with this, each rule is discussed in detail later in this chapter. For now, let's look at some of the general options available for finding useful data.

Real Live Libraries Have you walked into your local library recently? There are books on career-related topics, as well as newspapers, magazines and trade journals to browse through at your leisure. Ask to speak to the reference librarian. This person is a highly trained info-seeker who can sniff out an industry publication or specific article before you can say, "Gee, I looked everywhere for that online!" You can find a list of libraries by province on the Web at the Canadian Library Index (**www.lights.com/canlib**). Or try Sympatico's list of libraries at **www1.sympatico.ca/Contents/Reference/libraries.html**.

Virtual Libraries Can't get to a real library right now? Not a problem with today's online versions. An example is the Electric Library, at **www.elibrary.com/s/hotbot**. You can visit there day or night, pose questions that are answered by expert researchers, and view articles and other documents in your browser. Oh yeah, there is a fee involved. But you can usually get a 30-day trial for free. Other related sources:

- E-Journal (**www.edoc.com/ejournal**), a collection of electronic reading material sorted by subject.
- PathFinder Article Search (**www.pathfinder.com/search/altavista**), from Time Warner. Lots of their magazine stuff here.
- LookSmart Virtual Library (**www.looksmart.com**), where you can search for info by category and sub-category.

REAL LIFE Not all the information you need will be found in published form. Don't forget about the human touch. You can often get better intelligence from your colleagues and networking contacts than you will ever find in published sources, be they traditional or online.

The Free-Versus-Fee Debate

Almost everyone is out to make a buck online, except perhaps for some government agencies and other not-for-profit organizations. Is the free stuff any good? Is it worthwhile paying for information? Read on and decide for yourself.

Free Can Be Good I'm astounded by the amount of free stuff on the Internet. I used to wonder how all these people and firms could afford to put up detailed information without charging for it. Now I know better. If the material you're using is free, it may just be another form of marketing. By this I mean that the Web site may give out only a sample or demo of the full version of the firm's product. The rationale is that if you have a taste without charge, you'll gladly fork over the bucks to get the real thing. At any rate, some good stuff free is better than no stuff at all (at least to my way of thinking).

On the other hand, many sites give you tons of detailed information and it won't cost you a cent (see the Canadian Business Top 500 site as an example, at **www.canbus.com/CB500/p500.htm**). What price do you pay then? (There's always a catch, ain't there?) Depending on the type of site, you may have to:

- look at advertising banners that others have paid for to get your attention,
- fill out a basic information form before entering, to be on their mailing list, and/or
- give even more details about yourself than you might feel comfortable doing, so that the company can market to you individually.

REAL LIFE When viewing "free" information online, always consider the source. Why is the source being so generous? Does it have a particular bias to be wary of? And just how accurate or timely is this information, anyway? One way to reduce the risk of using "bad" information is to double-check critical data in multiple sources—and this is also true for offline sources!

Paying for It The alternative to free online information is, of course, fee-based data services. A great example is Hoovers Online (**www.hoovers.com**), which offers both. This is a U.S. firm that gathers detailed information on key corporations. On the free side, you get Hoover's Company Capsules, which are a "source of basic information and useful links for all the companies we cover." For a mere $12.95 U.S. a month, however, you can have access to Hoover's Company Profiles, which "offer in-depth information on over 3,000 companies. They cover each company's strategy, history, products and operations, competitors, and financial performance."

What are the benefits of shelling out some bucks for information like this?

- It's easy to search for and find exactly what you need.
- The level of detail is often far better than the free versions.
- You can usually get online assistance with your searches.
- The information tends to be more current and accurate.

You'll find more about fee-based resources later on in this chapter.

Taking a Strategic Approach

Whether you're going to pay for advice or get it for free, search online or in magazines and newspapers, you probably want to get started right away. My advice? Whoa, cyber-cowboy. Before racing ahead, ask yourself three quick questions to make your search more efficient:

- Why am I looking for this specific piece of information?
- What will I do with it once I get it?
- Where will I find it?

In order to do your research strategically, you must establish clear objectives before you gallop off. Any information you gather must be "actionable." By that I mean you should be able to use it some way to move you forward in your search for employment. Otherwise, you might just be wearing down your hooves needlessly.

II. RULE 1: EXPAND YOUR AWARENESS OF THE ECONOMY AND CURRENT EVENTS

A Real-World Example

I'd like to personalize this chapter a bit by showing how research and targeting worked for me, and how it can definitely work for you. As you know, not too many years ago, I made a significant shift into the career management field. Although I had networked extensively and had upgraded my education, I now had to find an organization that would hire me and—gasp!—pay me money to do what I enjoyed doing. I already knew that career counselling was offered in the private, public, academic and not-for-profit sectors (as I outlined in Chapter 3). But now I had to find out where I'd really fit in. So I followed those four golden rules I mentioned earlier.

The first thing I did was to brush up on my knowledge of what was happening in general, locally and nationally. This helped me enormously in several ways, by alerting me to:

- important stories and trends that employers might expect me to know about,
- employment opportunities (and things to avoid) in specific sectors,
- government employment initiatives that could help me find work, and
- general business news, such as company start-ups or plant closings.

The Local Scene

Your best bet for local news coverage is, you guessed it, your local or regional newspaper. Here's where you can find links to all your favourites, many of which offer story coverage online, for free.

- Canadian Newspaper Association (**www.cna-acj.ca/english/newsonline.html#seven**). Links to most local newspapers across Canada.
- NewsLink from American Journalism Online (**www.newslink.org/nonusn.html**). Links to all Canadian papers, searchable by province and type of paper.
- Canadian Community Newspapers Association (**www.ccna.ca/regions.html**). Web sites for community papers across the nation.

If it's information about local employment trends you're seeking, check out the labour market information sites provided by Human Resources Development Canada. These gems can be searched by locality within provinces and can show you what types of jobs are in the area, what those jobs involve and what type of people are in them. Start at **lmi-imt.hrdc-drhc.gc.ca/lmi.html**, click on your province of choice, and choose the locality you want to learn more about.

Another great route to follow is looking up local business information. You can do this through municipal boards of trade, chambers of commerce and economic development councils. Use a search engine to find them in the city of your choice.

Oh, Canada

You can also get purely Canadian info from many sites on the Web. National news stories, for example, can be found at *The Globe and Mail* (**www.theglobeandmail.com**). Or check out Canadian Online Explorer (Canoe), a Web site developed by Maclean Hunter (**www.canoe.ca**). It's got 24-hour news, with articles that can be easily downloaded. You can also link to *Maclean's, The Financial Post, Chatelaine* and all the Sun newspapers. For the latest updates, visit the Toronto Star (**www.thestar.com**, then "Updates").

When you're looking for Canadian economic data, head straight to the Strategis site. Their Microeconomic Monitor is a detailed review of economic activity, produced on a quarterly basis, plus sector-specific information (see **strategis.ic.gc.ca/sc_ecnmy/engdoc/homepage.html**). You can also try their provincial industrial overviews at **strategis.ic.gc.ca/scdt/bizmap/nav.html** (choose "Provincial and Territorial Information"). Then there's Statistics Canada's look at our economy. StatsCan has gone to great lengths to produce some extremely useful information on its Web site (**www.statcan.ca/english/Pgdb/Economy/econom.htm**). This particular portion includes general economic conditions, the international trade picture and industry performance.

Going Global

I'd be remiss if I ignored the fact that many Canadians look beyond our borders today for employment. For news from around the world, visit the CBC's Newsworld Web site at **www.newsworld.cbc.ca** or CNN's Web site at **cnn.com/WORLD/index.html**. Both give you headlines and stories from Canada, the U.S. and around the world, which are frequently updated. You can click on the headlines to get the details on stories that interest you most.

When it comes to international economic information, consider viewing Industry Canada's multicultural information advisor. It's on their International Business Information Network site, at **strategis.ic.gc.ca/SSG/bi18087e.html**. Strategis is just about the best site on the Internet for finding international business and economic information from a Canadian perspective.

III. RULE 2: LEARN MORE ABOUT YOUR INDUSTRY

Getting back to my story, the next stage for me was getting a solid grasp of the career counselling industry itself. I was looking for such information as:

- the different kinds of organizations in this field, and the variety of products and services they offer to their target markets,
- the names and profiles of key people in the industry,
- contact details for associations representing the industry, and
- the main issues and trends relating to the industry.

Visit Your Association Web Site

As it turns out, getting the lowdown on the career management field was a snap. I started with one of the industry associations, the International Association of Career Management Professionals (IACMP). Their Web site was (and still is) at **www.iacmp.org**.

There I beheld a wealth of information. There were articles on how the industry was changing, along with lists of member companies. There were even interviews with some of the top people in the field, plus lots of articles about future trends, key issues and important past events. Not to mention an interactive forum to learn about what's going on right now. You can find industry and professional associations that are relevant to you, by visiting the following Web sites:

- Career Internetworking (**www.careerkey.com/ass.htm**). Links to numerous Canadian associations in the areas of engineering, communications, manufacturing, scientific organizations, architecture, finance and human resources.
- Job Futures, from Human Resources Development Canada (**www.hrdc-drhc.gc.ca/JobFutures/english/volume1/assoc.htm**). You've gotta love this resource. It has sorted all industries by National Occupation Code, with direct links to relevant associations.
- Canadian Associations Online, Canadian Almanac's Canada Info (**www.canadainfo.com/associations.html**). A fine list of links to assorted Canadian associations.
- Strategis Business Map (**strategis.ic.gc.ca/scdt/bizmap/nav.html**). Nicely laid-out list of national and international associations, by

Standard Industrial Code (a common way of categorizing companies). Select "Industry and Professional Associations" from the menu.

CYBER TIP Finding information on your specific occupation is easier when you know its National Occupation Code (NOC). You can locate yours at the Job Futures site. To search alphabetically by occupation, go to **www.hrdc-drhc.gc.ca/JobFutures/english/volume1/alpha_a.htm**. For NOC information by category, try the labour market information site at **hamilton.london.hrdc-drhc.gc.ca/english/lmi/noclist.html**.

Tap into Industry Trends

Looking for economic overviews, predictions and news about your chosen field? Try the following sites:

- Maclean Hunter Biz Link (**www.mhbizlink.com**). Trade journals galore from Maclean Hunter, with something for everybody.
- Industry Link (**www.industrylink.com**). A good source of data geared toward electronics and heavy industry.
- Strategis Business Map, yet again (**strategis.ic.gc.ca/scdt/bizmap/nav.html**, then go to "Sector Analysis and Statistics," then "Sector Analysis," then select yours). You'll find all sorts of articles and papers written about your specific sector. Also, once you've clicked "Sector Analysis and Statistics," try clicking on "Canadian Industry Statistics," then either "Industry Overview" (for trends in employment and trade) or "CIS Classic" (for detailed overviews of specific industries).

REAL LIFE If you're thinking of using your skills and talents in the not-for-profit sector, go directly to the Charity Village Web site (**www.charityvillage.com**). It has links to many Canadian and international not-for-profit organizations. There are discussion forums to exchange ideas and make contact with others in this field. Even if you're not thinking of a job in this field, you can consider doing volunteer work. It can be a great way to expand your experience and increase your marketability.

IV. RULE 3: DEVELOP A WORKABLE LIST OF POTENTIAL EMPLOYERS

Once you're comfortable with what's happening in your industry, it's time to think about who you might want to work for. There are two basic tasks at this stage: first create a list of all the organizations in your chosen industry, and then narrow it down to the 10 to 20 hot prospects to target in your initial marketing campaign.

Breaking it down into these two steps gives you an understanding of how large or small your employment market is. Plus it allows you to identify the key players, so you can focus your efforts where they will pay off.

Task 1: Make a Broad List of Relevant Organizations

Why not start with a complete list of all the companies in your field, like I did. Where did I turn first? To my trusty online Canada Yellow Pages, of course (**www.canadayellowpages.com**, then "Search Canada"). In the alphabetical Business category I chose Career Counselling, then chose Toronto from the City list. To my delight there were more than 50 companies listed. I also looked under Outplacement Counselling, where I found another 20 companies. This was great! I now had 70 potential employers to choose from, along with their addresses, phone and fax numbers, plus e-mail addresses and URLs (where available).

Other sites that enable you to search for companies and organizations by industry and location:

- InfoSpace's "Business in a City: Canada" (**206.129.166.101/categ/cancategory.html**) or "Canada: Business By Category" (**in-128.infospace.com/_1_159603627_info/canyellow.htm**).
- The U.S. "Big Yellow" site (**s18.bigyellow.com**), with 16 million listings in the United States.

Task 2: Narrow Down the List to Your Hot Prospects

My next step was to find out a little bit about as many of these 70 organizations as I could. My goal? To get a feel for what types of companies, in which sectors, might be a good fit for me and my skills. Obviously I didn't have time to personally approach each one of my 70 prospects. So first I crossed off my list all the places I knew something about and felt there wouldn't be a fit. Then off to the Web I went.

Visit Each Organization's Web Site I knew that I could find out all sorts of basic information at each company's Web site. Things like company background, products and services provided, bios on the key people in the firm and links to related sites. What I did not know, however, was how to find every single site quickly.

So I decided to use a shortcut. Over at the Yahoo Canada search directory (**www.yahoo.ca**), I did a category search starting with "Business and Economy" (also clicking on "Canadian Sites Only"). From there I clicked on "Corporate Services," then "Human Resources," then "Outplacement Services."

Many of the companies I wanted (and a few I hadn't thought of, too) were listed here, but not all. So it was off to the AltaVista Canada search engine (**www.altavista.ca**), where I did keyword searches on each company's name. For example, in the "Search" box I typed in the name of one of the companies I'd found in Task 1, "verity filion" (quotes included, to force all words to appear together in any documents located). This brought up 30 separate hits, and I chose the one with Verity in its root (i.e., **www.verityintl.com**). Other ways to find links to a company's Web site:

- Yahoo Canada's search categories, to search by industry type (**www.yahoo.ca/Regional/Countries/Canada/Business_and_Economy/Companies**).
- Maple Square Search Engine (**www.maplesquare.com**).
- Canada 411 from Sympatico (**canada411.sympatico.ca/english/business.html**), to search by company name or location.
- Canada.Com from Hollinger (**www.canada.com**).
- Yahoo's U.S. and international search directory (**www.yahoo.com**). The U.S. version of Yahoo has links to more than 150,000 companies. You'll find it at **www.yahoo.com/text/Business_and_Economy/Companies**.

Other Useful Details Are in "Company Capsules" The World Wide Web is full of free information on companies and organizations. The most popular form of data is a "capsule." Typically, this is a very brief summary that includes the company's address, line of business, annual sales, main contact numbers and the like. Hoover's Online, as mentioned earlier, gives you information capsules on more than 10,000 companies worldwide for free. Try going to **www.hoovers.com** where you can search by industry, location and annual sales. In many cases there is also a hyperlink directly to the company's Web site, and to online news services that automatically search for articles on that company (but don't expect too much, since it's free).

Other company capsule sites include:

- The Thomas Registry (**www.thomasregister.com.html**). Details on nearly 55,000 industrial products and services, as well as information on thousands of manufacturers. In all, more than 1,500,000 individual product and service sources are included for companies in the U.S. and Canada (and enrolling is free).
- Strategis Canada (**strategis.ic.gc.ca/sc_coinf/engdoc/homepage.html**). They've put together a series of links on their Canadian Company Capabilities site. Basically, it's a searchable grouping of Canadian companies. By clicking on the company's name, you are magically transported to each company's homepage.

REAL LIFE Many Canadian companies are subsidiaries or divisions of larger conglomerates. How do you find out if the head office is outside of Canada? You could start with the main Web site. If it's a U.S. or international site, there may be a section with links to individual offices in different countries. Otherwise, off to the library you go to view the Inter-Corporate Ownership CD-ROM, which lists more than 75,000 corporations. Published by Statistics Canada, this resource basically tells you who owns who.

Where This Left Me

Doing the above was admittedly a tedious process. By the end of it though, I had reduced my broad list of 70 organizations down to 20 or so firms that seemed like my best prospects. It helped, of course, that I was also meeting with people in the field to get their opinions (more about networking in the next chapter). I knew from my career counselling training that this would truly enable me to be proactive. That is, I could start going after these 20 companies directly, instead of scattering my efforts over all 70 prospects. That's where the next section comes in.

V. RULE 4: PREPARE TO MARKET YOURSELF TO YOUR HOT PROSPECTS

Once you have an idea of who you want to target, you can spend time finding out some critical details about the organization, such as:

- the location of branches, plants, corporate parents and subsidiaries;
- the financial status of the company (including profit history and future forecasts);
- the operating style and corporate culture (will you fit in?);
- the names, titles, contact information and background on the people who are in a position to hire you;
- who the main competition is, and how each company differentiates itself; and
- which target markets each firm specializes in.

CYBER TIP You can get automatic updates on all your favourite topics. *News gathering agents* collect the information on subjects that you select. They travel all over the Internet and bring it directly to your computer. An example is the Pointcast Network at **www.pointcast.com/whatis.html**.

These details can help you to secure networking sessions with targeted individuals, customize your cover letters and prepare for job interviews. In fact, the more you know about the company and people you're dealing with, the better your chances are—to impress potential employers with your knowledge, demonstrate your initiative and seriousness about working with that particular firm, understand the realities of what you're getting into and stand out from your competitors. Here are some of the tools I found most helpful.

"Top Company" Profiles

- Profit 100 (**www.profit100.com**)
- Financial Post Top 50 (**canoe2.canoe.ca/FP_Top50**)
- Canadian Business 500 (**www.canbus.com/CB500/p500.htm**)
- Report on Business Top 1000 (**www.robmagazine.com/top1000**)

REAL LIFE Many of the more detailed information sites on the Web are starting to charge fees. To avoid paying these, consider using CD-ROM–based resources and old-fashioned books at your library. A great advice piece on which guides, directories and CD-ROMs to use is available at the York University Library site (**www.library.yorku.ca/depts/gdas/resinfo.htm**).

Other Company Profiles

- Canadian Company Capabilities (**strategis.ic.gc.ca/sc_coinf/ccc/engdoc/homepage.html**)
- SEDAR Canadian Public Companies (**www.sedar.com**)
- EDGAR U.S. Public Companies (**edgar.sec.gov**)
- Canadian Stock Prices (**www.canada-stockwatch.com**)
- Carlson Canada Online Services (**www.fin-info.com**)

Press Releases

- Canada News Wire (**www.newswire.ca/htmindex/organization.html**)
- Canadian Corporate News (**www.cdn-news.com/cgi-bin/company-search2.cgi**)
- Business Wire's Corporate News Releases (U.S.) (**www.businesswire.com/cnn**)

Info on Government Departments and Agencies

- Federal government search directory (**direct.srv.gc.ca/cgi-bin/wgweng**)
- Government of Canada Primary Site (**canada.gc.ca/main_e.html**)

REAL LIFE Although research is important, so is taking action. Try not to spend so much time gathering information that you ignore other parts of your work search. Find only as much data as you need to help you make an informed decision. Meanwhile, keep up your networking, letter writing and interviews.

- Provincial government links (**www1.sympatico.ca/Contents/Government/provgov.html**)
- Provincial and Municipal On-Line Information Kiosk (**www.intergov.gc.ca/prov/index.html**)
- Directory of Diplomatic Representatives in Canada (**www.arraydev.com/commerce/embassy/english/directory.htm**)
- Web sites of foreign governments (**www.ipu.org/english/parlweb.htm**)

REAL LIFE A word of warning: you might want to double-check your cyber-data to make sure nothing's changed. For instance, don't rely exclusively on Web-based telephone numbers and addresses. Although this information may be up-to-date, you can never really be sure. People get shifted around, and companies move or close down. When in doubt, pick up the phone and call the company to verify your contact person's name, title and location.

Specialized Search Engines

- Finding e-mail addresses (**www.Four11.com**)
- Finding fax numbers (**www.555-1212.com/fax_ca.htm**)
- Finding area codes (**decoder.AmeriCom.com**)
- Finding Toll-Free numbers (**canadatollfree.sympatico.ca/search**)
- Doing reverse look-ups (e.g., you have a phone number or e-mail address and want to see who it belongs to) (**pic1.infospace.com/_1_205849552__info/reverse_ca.htm**)
- Finding Internet Phone users (**www.whowhere.com/iphone/search.html**)

Annual Reports

- Order one alphabetically from the Globe and Mail's Web site (**www.theglobeandmail.com/**, then "Annual Reports" under the Report on Business heading).
- The Public Register's Annual Report Service (**www.prars.com**)
- The Investor Relations Information Network (**nt1.irin.com/**)

Fee-Based Services

Most people will find more than they need for free using the Web and CD-ROMs (and by talking with other people, of course). For those of you seeking the ultimate in convenience and more specific details, however, they are definitely available online—for a fee.

Cheap and Cheerful—At a Flat Rate For the budget minded, there are pay-per-use information services that focus on basic company data. Quote.com (**www.quote.com**), for example, lets you track specific companies in terms of stock prices and investor reports. At $9.95 per month (Cdn) you also get access to Nelson Reports for greater detail. View their free "Company of the Day" to see what I mean.

Another relatively affordable route is Hoover's Company Reports, mentioned earlier in this chapter. For $12.95 U.S. per month you can get up to 100 reports. Here you can quickly look up detailed profiles on more than 3,000 major companies.

Pay Per Report Dun & Bradstreet (**www.telebase.com/dbcanada.htm**) offers Canadian Company Profiles on a cost per use basis. They currently charge $6.00 to search up to five headings, and $6.00 for each individual record that you order. A free sample is available on their site.

Watch Those Fees Climb Higher Let's move the scale up a notch in terms of price and depth of information. Now we're getting into databases that give you in-depth reviews of the company (or industry) of choice. One such service is called Vault Reports (**www.vaultreports.com**). Employer Profiles range from $9.50 to $25.00 (U.S.). These profiles can be up to 50 pages in length, and are available for more than 600 American companies. Industry overviews can be had for $35 each.

And Higher... For the info-junkies among us, there's even more. For instance, the Conference Board of Canada offers "Economic Intelligence on Canada, the Provinces and Metropolitan Areas" through its WEBlinx service (**www.conferenceboard.ca/Weblinx**). This *starts* at an annual fee of $595 (Cdn.). There is data galore to be had, but it really is getting beyond the realm of the typical user. Likewise the Fortune 500 database series (**www.ownthefortune500.com**). Previously free, it now costs $495 (U.S.) to subscribe to the Fortune 1000 or Global 500 online. Granted, you save $200 if you order both at the same time. However, my sense is that you have better ways to spend your hard-earned money.

Highest! If this isn't enough for you, it's time to seek professional help. No, not that kind (although you might want to ask yourself why you need all the information that you're gathering). What I mean is, you can hire the services of a trained researcher who will go online for you to sophisticated databases such as Lexis, InfoMart or Dialog. The detail that can be found here is mind-boggling. But heed my alert: you may get charged on more than one front. The database company may charge you simply to search each database, plus there may be an additional download fee per article chosen. Moreover, the researcher will definitely charge you in the range of $25 to $100 per hour of their time. My suggestion: Use this approach only in emergency situations, or if you have very little time and extremely deep pockets.

VI. WIRED WRAP-UP

Surprise...It Really Worked!

Ultimately, my combination of research and targeting started me on the road to a successful career change. I saved vast amounts of time by only pursuing the companies where there appeared to be a clear fit. I felt more in control, because I had taken the bull by the horns instead of lying back and waiting for something to "come up." Best of all, I knew that my competitors would soon be eating my dust, as they sent out their résumés indiscriminately in the hopes of getting a response.

How Much Is Enough?

There's no doubt, though, that we have entered an era of "information overload." When it comes to work-related research, you need to pick and choose which methods you'll use. Otherwise you could fall into that dreaded syndrome known as "analysis paralysis" (you get frozen by having too much data to sort through).

Having acknowledged this, one of the first decisions you must make is *how much time to devote to research* as part of your overall work search. There is no one-size-fits-all answer to this. It depends on what stage you're at in your employment search, how much (or little) you already know about your field, how much (or little) potential employers expect you to know, and your personal comfort level in terms of what "enough" means to you.

Take heart in the following. No matter how much effort you devote to researching and targeting, it's worth it—you have my word. There is no more effective way to find work than by actively pursuing companies that you've targeted. How to approach these companies is the subject of Chapter 9. For now, it's enough to know that relevant information is a critical part of your work search. And electronic resources can help put you in the driver's seat on the road to securing the work you really want.

Points to Remember

- Research builds the foundation for a targeted, proactive job hunt.
- The Four Golden Rules of Research are
  1. Expand your awareness of the economy and current events.
  2. Learn more about your industry.
  3. Develop a workable list of potential employers.
  4. Prepare to market yourself to your hot prospects.
- Try not to get caught in "analysis paralysis." Make sure that you devote only enough time to researching as you need, while continuing to be active in other parts of the overall process.
- Ensure that you pay for information only when it is absolutely necessary to do so. You may find that your needs are adequately met by the many free resources available.

CHAPTER 9 Network into the Hidden Job Market

I. HEY, WHO HID ALL THE JOBS?

Seen any good want ads lately? Whenever I searched for work in the pre-Internet days, I'd flip through the employment classified pages in my local paper every single day, hoping (OK, praying) to find the "right" job. Not that it never appeared. On those few occasions when I did see an opening that even remotely matched my skills and experience, guess what? That's right, thousands of other hopefuls were seeing it at the same time. So when my résumé finally landed on the desk of some overburdened human resources manager, it was often buried along with those from hundreds of other applicants.

So How Do Most People Find Jobs?

Let me clarify something up front. I'm in no way suggesting that you abandon the job ads in newspapers and trade publications. I've personally secured some excellent work (including permanent, part-time and even contract work) this way. Let's keep things in their proper perspective here:

Perhaps 10 percent of all work, on average, is found through posted advertisements in newspapers, trade journals, the Internet or anywhere else.

Note that this percentage varies widely by field. On the high side are techie jobs, of which maybe 50 percent or more are published in one form or another. If you need further evidence of this, simply open up your local newspaper's employment section. Then ruthlessly tear out every single ad that mentions computer and engineering jobs. Now, do the same for, say, vice-presidents of marketing in the financial services sector, which might have 0.1 percent or less advertised publicly. Notice a difference?

REAL LIFE Note that even high tech workers should do more than read the paper and surf for jobs online. They can attend virtual career fairs and get interviewed in person at job markets, to name but a few available avenues. Try the section in Chapter 11 devoted to high tech workers for more hints and advice, if you fall into this category.

What About Everyone Else? People often ask me what the "best" way to find work is. I explain, of course, that it depends on their level of seniority, the type of companies they've targeted, the general economic climate and their personality style. Still, it's a very good question. Recruitment firms, placement agencies and executive search companies account for a certain amount of success. Mass mailing your résumé and cold calling can produce results as well. Yet these methods completely ignore the main way to secure employment: by networking in the "hidden job market." A quick look at Table 9.1 tells the story clearly.

Does this reveal an astonishing statistic or what! On average, 50 to 80 percent of all work is found through something called the *hidden job market*. What's the best way to access these jobs? By networking, for sure. But also by doing all the groundwork described in the earlier chapters, in particular:

- knowing who you are and what you have to offer (see Chapters 3 and 5),
- creating excellent marketing materials (see Chapter 6), and
- researching and targeting to draw up a hot list of potential employers (Chapter 8).

By combining the results of your efforts from Chapter 8 with the advice you're about to read, don't be surprised if you open up doors to potential employment that you might otherwise never have had access to. That raises some interesting and immediate issues. For example, what exactly is the hidden job market? How do you break into it? And, just as important, how can going online assist you to do that? That's what this chapter is all about.

Table 9.1 How People Find Work

TYPE OF APPROACH	% OF WORK FOUND THIS WAY*
Reading advertisements for posted positions (including newspapers, trade journals, the Internet and others)	5% to 20% (excluding techies —for them it can go high as 50%)
Sending out mass-mailed and broadcast letters	1% to 5%
Mailing out targeted marketing letters	1% to 5%
Working with recruiting firms to get permanent jobs	5% to 15%
Using a "temp" agency to find short-term employment	5% to 15%
Having a close relative hire you (nepotism)	.05%
Walking unannounced into an office with your résumé	.05%
Dressing up in funny costumes and handing out your résumé on street corners in major metropolitan areas	.0001% (It worked for the cow guy in Toronto.)
Posting your résumé online (including job and résumé sites, matching services and personal Web pages)	1% to 10%
Chanting ancient Latin spells and placing pins into miniature likenesses of your favourite human resource manager	0% (Well, it's never worked for me, yet.)
Researching, targeting and networking your way into the hidden job market	**50% to 80%**

* Figures are rough averages only, based on estimates provided by job seekers, recruitment firms and career consultants. The precise figure in your particular field will likely vary over time.

II. WHERE IS THE HIDDEN JOB MARKET?

The hidden job market refers mainly to upcoming vacancies, work postings and business opportunities that are known only to insiders. In many cases the vacancy doesn't even exist yet. For instance, a position may be about to become available, but the company doesn't want to let anyone know about it just yet. Or maybe an employee suddenly leaves the company, creating an unplanned vacancy.

It's Hidden Because It May Not Be Real Yet Perhaps an example will clarify this. I once knew of a pharmaceutical company in Moncton that was unhappy with the performance of its finance manager. The company decided that it was going to fire this manager. That put management in a bit of a catch 22. The finance department was very busy, so it would need to fill the position immediately after this manager was let go. The problem was, the company couldn't openly advertise the position yet because, technically, there was no vacancy.

How did the company deal with this? In several ways. First management worked with a confidential executive search firm to canvass potential candidates discreetly, without revealing the name of the company. Senior managers also reviewed their files for anyone who had recently shown interest in this position from within the company. Then they asked their colleagues if they knew anyone who might be interested in such a position. Best of all for you, the job seeker, they also looked for outside people who had shown interest in that company, and specifically in the finance manager's position, through networking.

CYBER TIP To get a better understanding of the hidden work market, you can read more about it online. There are some very good articles at the Archeus site (**www.golden.net/~archeus/othres.htm**), as well as "How to Find a Position in the Hidden Job Market," from the National Business Employment Weekly (**www.nbew.com/archive/sackett**).

When Else Do Hidden Opportunities Appear? Not every hidden vacancy comes about because some unfortunate soul was let go. Vacancies can also arise when a company is about to launch into a growth phase. As a company opens up new areas, it needs more staff—but it may not want to advertise this to its competitors. Or maybe someone is going on maternity leave and the company needs someone to fill in for five or six months. (I landed one of these early in my career, and the five months turned into three and a half years!)

In addition, we're not just dealing with openings for jobs or contracts here. If you're starting a business, there are also hidden opportunities and hidden customers. These, too, can be accessible by the networking process that's discussed in the following section.

III. NETWORKING THE TRADITIONAL WAY

With all the changes that companies experience on an ongoing basis, staff turnover is almost inevitable. The trick is to take advantage of these changes, by being at the right place at the right time, with the right mixture of skills and experience. That's where networking works best.

The Basics of Networking

You've all heard that old work-search maxim, "It's not what you know, it's who you know." There's no denying that this statement holds a lot of truth. The full reality is a bit more involved. What you know (your skills and experience) are critical in marketing yourself to employers. Who you know—and more important, who you can get to know—may determine your success in the job hunt.

At its most fundamental level, networking is about making contact with a variety of people who can assist you in your search for work. By creating a critical mass of contacts, you eventually get known by the people who are in a position to make hiring decisions. Then, when one of these hidden openings springs up, guess whose name is forefront in their minds? Yours!

REAL LIFE Even when a position has been widely advertised, networking can be your magic key. Try to get a referral to see the decision maker by someone he or she already knows and trusts. (Back in my social psychology days, we called this the "halo effect." Today it's referred to as "gaining a competitive advantage.")

I won't spend the entire chapter on basic networking techniques. There are plenty of books and articles around that cover this process in great detail (I point you to some of these online later in the chapter). Still, if you're not used to formal networking as it pertains to the work search, it's important to know what it's all about. Hence I've provided some highlights of how it works in the traditional sense, before moving on to cyber-networking.

Stages of Traditional Networking

1. You start by writing down the names of just about everyone you know. This could include friends, relatives, colleagues, former employers, professionals, members of your social and religious groups, and the like.
2. From these, you make a short list of people you want to meet with first. These are your warm and fuzzy contacts, the ones you know well and who won't intimidate you too much during your practice sessions.
3. You can call or write the folks on your short list to secure an initial meeting. Explain that you're not asking them for a job: you just want to share some ideas about your work search and get their advice.
4. When you meet with them, you exchange information and make a positive impression. Then you ask for a couple of referrals to other people who might offer similar assistance. Soon you'll have a broad range of contacts in a variety of companies.
5. Use those research and targeting techniques from Chapter 8 to focus your networking on your "hot list" of companies. Keep this up over a period of time and you're sure to expand your chances of being there at the right time.

CYBER TIP To find out (in elaborate detail) how to build and nurture a successful network, try the following articles: "Grooming Your Granfaloon," from the National Business Employment Weekly (**server1.pa.hodes.com/cm/cm29.html**) and "Networks That Work" (**www.hrdc-drhc.gc.ca/hrib/ocd/prospects/tools/networks.html**).

Are There Different Types of Networking?

The way some people describe it, networking is this all-encompassing term that includes any contacts you make during your work search. Do not be fooled by this oversimplification. I firmly believe that you should know exactly what your goals are well before you approach a contact. It helps if you understand that there are three distinct kinds of networking:

1. *Information Gathering.* This is where your main objective is to gather first-hand information about an industry or occupation.
2. *Contact Prospecting.* Here you are focusing on increasing your contact base through referrals, with an eye on securing employment.
3. *Meetings with Decision Makers.* Now you're meeting with the hiring person at a company you'd like to work for, before a job has been widely posted. It's like having a relatively informal job interview, but neither one of you wants to admit that openly.

Realistically, there is likely to be some overlap in goals at each session you have. It will, however, help both you and your contact if you're clear about your objectives in advance. Here are some more details on the three different types of networking.

REAL LIFE When getting ready for a networking session, keep in mind that the only thing you should really leave behind is an impression. These meetings, as informal as they appear to be, are your professional route to finding work, so come prepared. Do some research on the company, as well as on the person you'll be meeting with. Bring along a list of well-considered questions to ask. Hand out your business card as a reference point. Have a hard copy of your résumé ready, but give it only if asked. You can always send it afterward with that personalized thank-you note you're going to send.

Information Gathering This first type of networking is most appropriate for people who are switching industries, just coming out of school or making a significant career change. You're looking for honest information that will help you decide what path to take. One of the best ways to do this is to speak informally with people already working in your field of interest, to get their candid opinions. Note that you do not expect this person to hire you, or even refer you to someone who can. All that comes later.

Many of my clients feel reduced pressure in these types of discussions. After all, you're not there to impress anyone with your brilliance, nor do you expect to get a job offer out of it. This allows you to be your natural self. You're simply doing research that you happen to be conducting with a live resource. You're hoping to find details such as:

CYBER TIP There are some very good articles and instruction manuals for information interviewing that can be found on the Web. Here are two sites to consider: **www.adm.uwaterloo.ca/infocecs/CRC/manual/informationinterview.html** at the University of Waterloo Career Resource Centre and **danenet.wicip.org/jets/jet–9407–p.html** at Dane County Community Information, which also lists 20 questions you can pose to your contact.

- What's it really like to work in this industry?
- Is the field on an upswing or facing a downturn?
- How do people typically get their start in this field?
- What types of skills, experience and attitude are employers in this area looking for? Are they having trouble finding good people, or is the market swamped?
- What are the best and worst things about working in this particular industry? How about in a company like this?

While you're gathering information, you also want to confirm the research you've previously done in terms of who the key players are, what the nature of their target markets is, what their reputation in the industry is and what your prospects are of fitting in. You can also try to get a feel for the level you'd be qualified to start at (e.g., entry or intermediate), and the positions of people who might hire someone like you.

CYBER TIP To get a sense of the jobs a company advertises for, and what qualities it is looking for in its employees, try visiting the firm's Web site. Look for links to the "Hiring," "Employment" or "Human Resources" page. Read about the positions and the minimum qualifications. This should give you some indication of how the human resource folks are thinking.

Contact Prospecting The second type of networking is all about expanding your contact base. You've already done your preliminary research and are ready to start meeting with people who are in a position to hire you. One way to get to them indirectly is to meet first with others who may know people who are about to hire.

This approach is very important. You are looking for solid referrals to more contacts here—either to people your contact knows who may be able to hire someone like you, or to people who may know someone else who could hire someone like you. It now becomes essential for you to arrive armed and ready for action. The impression you make will either encourage this contact to pass you on to the decision makers, or will stop you in your tracks.

The content of the meeting can build on the things you've learned during your information-gathering discussions (and preliminary research). For example, rather than asking, "What are the key trends in this industry?" you can start to bring your knowledge in to play by saying, "I understand that the two major issues facing this industry are [insert the two pressing trends here]. If that's true, what sort of impact do you expect these to have long term?"

REAL LIFE Networking is a great tool for job hunting, but it's not the only one. Make an effort to used a *balanced approach.* This could mean spending 20 hours a week on networking, six on looking at and responding to job postings (in newspapers and on the Internet), four on targeted marketing letters, three on follow-up phone calls, three on keeping things organized, two on working with recruiters, and two on planning next week's strategy. Does this add up to a 40-hour week? Yes! Is finding work a full-time job? If you want to stay ahead of the pack, it sure is!

Meetings with Decision Makers I like this third stage. What you're actually doing is interviewing for work, although you don't come right out and say so. Instead, you meet with your contact and do things like share your ideas on how the industry is evolving. You make observations on the company itself with regard to policies and new directions. In other words, you use all the tricks you learned in Chapter 8, plus the new information you uncovered in the first two types of networking, to blow the socks off the employer before (hopefully) he or she has a chance to open up a potential job to a full competition.

Careful—This Could Be You Many of my clients are understandably skeptical about networking when we first discuss it. But consider the alternative. You can sleep in until as late as you want every morning (no boss to hound you, for now). Around 11:30 a.m. or so, you rummage hungrily through the want ads. Then you spend two or three hours on the Internet looking for any other posted vacancies. Your phone's ringer is adjusted to "high" so that you'll never miss a (rare) call from the search firms you've sent your résumé to. When the afternoon comes, you sit back and watch your favourite talk show, congratulating yourself on being in your pyjamas and out of the rat race for a while.

Suddenly, you realize time is passing. Slowly at first, but soon with alarming speed. You experience your first pang of anxiety. "Will anyone ever hire me again?" you say to yourself out loud. You buy an amplifier for your phone, but still it stays hauntingly silent. The newspaper ads have all begun to blur. You've sent out more than 30 replies to ads and have only heard back from one—an opportunity to sell an "amazing new product" if you'd just invest $25,000 up front. Eventually you sink into a state of hopelessness and utter despair. You begin watching re-runs of talk shows, and take to hanging out at the mall dressed only in your underwear and carrying a briefcase.

Or *This* Could Be You You rise bright and early, enjoy a healthy breakfast, then attack the target list of employers you've generated. You're feeling pretty confident because you're working your plan. Today you're meeting with your 15th new contact in less than four weeks. You've already answered about 10 ads that appeared to fit, and have followed up with phone calls and e-mails. What a difference this makes. Not only can you now begin to choose the companies and people to network with, but you're starting to get some call-backs. Meanwhile, you're active every day, either meeting new people or working on the other aspects of your search.

The Downsides of Traditional Networking

Of course, every silver lining has its dark exterior. Networking is no exception. A full-fledged networking campaign can be time-consuming and exhausting. You have lists to write up, people to call, visits to schedule, research to prepare, meetings to attend and thank-you notes to send. Plus you have to do all the other stuff in your work-search campaign!

Just travelling to and from people's places of work alone can take its toll, not to mention the expense of attending dinner meetings, breakfast sessions, parking, transit fares, etc. On top of this, you should be keeping track of all those people you've seen, what they've said and what you plan to do next. It's easy to burn out if you're not careful. Not surprisingly, this is where online resources can make a real difference.

IV. INTRODUCTION TO NETWORKING ONLINE

Going online to do a portion of your networking is a great way to increase your efficiency. If you have even minimal keyboarding skills, you can take part in electronic *discussion groups*. These enable you to exchange information with people locally, nationally and all around the world. The idea here is to make contacts that you might not otherwise be able to make. Since you're not limited by time, geography or expense, vast new realms become available to you.

Let's look back at Chapter 8. I began my networking armed with a detailed overview of the industry. Then I started contacting some people in the field. It was a lot less difficult than I'd imagined. My first step was to e-mail a few of the people who'd been quoted in the articles I'd collected. If their e-mail address wasn't included in the article, I called their company to ask what it was. If I still couldn't find it, I tried to look it up on a search engine like Four11, which specializes in finding e-mail addresses (**www.four11.com**).

Networking for the Inside Scoop Once I reached these folks, they were almost unanimously thrilled that someone had taken the time to follow up. Of course, there was the one jerk who flamed me with a scorching e-mail reply about violating his privacy and taking up his time. Sheesh! At any rate, soon I was meeting with some of these industry insiders at their offices. They graciously spoke with me about their perspectives on the field. Their information was invaluable, and I always followed up with a thank-you note.

Each time I met with someone new, I asked very specific questions:

- What are the best companies in this field?
- Are certain companies known for their work in particular areas?
- Where do you think someone with my skills and interests would do well?

- Can you give me the names of a few people to contact at companies that you would recommend?

By the time I'd met with a dozen or so people, I had a pretty clear idea of the kinds of companies that were out there, and where I might fit in best. This enabled me to revise my primary target list to 10 companies. My task had now become much more manageable, although no less difficult. Now I could focus my efforts on these top prospects.

A Quick Review of Discussion Groups

You'll recall from Chapter 1 that discussion groups come in many formats. They can be located on Usenet (where they're known as newsgroups) or on the Web (where they're called forums).

Different Types of Discussion Groups Discussion groups can be very large, involving tens or even hundreds of people. They can also be small and private—just you and one other person. In some you correspond by e-mail messages. Others use chat, which allows you to hold real-time conversations (via keyboard). You even have a choice of how to post your messages. You can send a private message to a single person at a time or you can broadcast to an entire discussion group.

What to Expect There are many things that you can do in these groups. From a career standpoint, you can swap strategies about writing your résumé and get yours critiqued by people in your field. Or ask advice about changing careers, interviewing or work searching. Sometimes you can just share your joys or frustrations with a sympathetic ear. (Or is that pair of eyes when it comes to keyboarding?) Essentially, you can learn some valuable information while making new contacts. Details on careers, industries, companies and people that interest you can all be exchanged online.

Making the Internet Work for You

Electronic networking differs from the traditional methods. You don't approach your targeted companies or specific people directly. Instead, you identify discussion groups that focus on your field of interest. Then you make contact, exchange information and gradually develop individual relationships. Table 9.2 breaks down the key steps.

Table 9.2 Steps to Networking Electronically

KEY STEPS	ACTIONS INVOLVED
1. Identify relevant discussion groups.	Use the methods outlined later in this chapter.
2. Get a feel for the group. What are the key topics and what is the tone?	Sign on and monitor discussions for a while (don't post a message immediately).
3. Decide if this group truly meets your needs.	See if discussion threads and level of detail are relevant to what it is you want to know.
4. Check to see if the questions you're considering have been answered in earlier postings.	Review the forum's stored conversations (discussion archives or FAQ—"frequently asked questions") or use a search engine to find specific topics.
5. Make your first contact.	Post a private message to a group member who seems particularly approachable.
6. Respond promptly if contacted.	Answer in a timely and professional manner.

CYBER TIP Paul Agre, from the University of California, San Diego, has written an excellent article on electronic networking. He states that "electronic mail is part of a larger ecology of communication media and genres—telephone conversations, archival journals and newsletters, professional meetings, paper mail, voice mail, chatting in the hallway...job interviews...visits to other research sites, and so forth—each with its own attributes and strengths." See the full article at **communication.ucsd.edu/pagre/network.html**.

The Good and the Not-So-Good of Electronic Networking

The online world can definitely broaden your reach; however, it doesn't completely replace the meet-and-greet networking that most of us are used to. Keep this in mind while you consider the following.

The Main Benefits of Electronic Networking

- Electronic networking allows you to contact people from a wider variety of fields and industries than you might normally have access to.
- Electronic networking can be a quick, inexpensive way to meet new people and get advice.
- Geography poses no limits: you can speak to anyone, anywhere (if they're online).
- The relative anonymity of e-mail may allow people to give you their honest opinions.

  Sounds wonderful, doesn't it? But there are limitations.

The Drawbacks to Electronic Networking

- The intimacy of face-to-face contact just isn't there. Even when video-conferencing becomes widespread, the human element will still be missing.
- You can't see the other person's body language or hear voice intonations through a keyboard, thus you can sometimes miss a person's real message or intended tone.
- Whatever you say in cyberspace can leave a permanent record. Even private conversations aren't 100 percent secure.
- If you happen to make a mistake when posting to the newsgroups in general, all subscribers get to see it!

A Word about Netiquette

Discussion groups are really just small communities of people. To help groups run smoothly, informal rules of conduct have begun to evolve. Collectively these are known as *netiquette* ("Net etiquette").

CYBER TIP Newsgroups are notorious for the viruses they can harbour. However, it's important to remember that ordinary e-mail messages—which are transmitted as ASCII—cannot contain a virus. Viruses can be hidden in attachments, though, and you might get unsolicited e-mail with an attachment, so make sure you're using effective protection software that works with your e-mail, too. Scan your files often to ensure that they're not infected. And never download any attachment you didn't ask for! To get trial versions of two of the most popular products, go to Macafee's Virus Scan (**www.mcafee.com**) or Symantec's Norton AntiVirus (**www.symantec.com/trialware/index.html**). Both Web sites have useful information about real viruses and hoaxes, as do the folks at the Computer Incident Advisory Capability site (**ciac.llnl.gov/ciac**). And remember to update your virus software regularly via the Net!

Think of It as "Business Casual" Just as with any form of business communication, you always want to be as professional as possible. For instance, don't just barge in on a discussion group. Hang back at first. Get to know the main topics and the frequent contributors. Then approach people individually (that's how any networking relationship is built).

Try not to post a message to the entire group unless you have something specific to contribute. Throwing out something to the group like "Hi, can you help me find a job?" is considered poor form. That's not to say that you shouldn't occasionally ask for advice from the group. First, though, follow all the steps outlined in Table 9.2. If you still haven't received a satisfactory response, then you can try a general post.

Other Informal Guidelines for Discussion Groups Following up is also extremely important. If someone helps you out, send them an individualized thank-you note by e-mail. And don't forget the law of reciprocity. When someone asks you for information, try your best to respond. Otherwise you could earn a reputation as an info-hog. This is a sure way to get frozen out of a group.

One final note about discussion group decorum. On a rare occasion, you might unintentionally (or intentionally) annoy or offend someone. If this happens and someone sends you a scathing e-mail (known as a *flame*), show some restraint. If you whip off an emotional reply, you could fall victim to a flame war. That's when everyone gangs up on you and floods your mailbox with nasty e-mail. You can't win a flame war. It's likely that you'll just end up looking hot-headed—not the professional image that you want to convey.

V. FINDING THE RIGHT DISCUSSION GROUPS

It's not hard to find a discussion group online. There are virtually thousands of them, covering practically every subject you can think of (yes, even those subjects). The trick is to locate the groups that will help you to further your work search.

The Technology Differs

The variety of technologies that you can use complicates matters (review Chapter 2). Usenet newsgroups and Web-based discussion groups use e-mail; whereas chat groups (discussed later in this chapter) use Internet Relay Chat (IRC). This allows you to hold virtual conversations with one or more people, just as you would on the telephone (except you're using your keyboard). And listservs are like mail robots that you can subscribe to so you can receive participants' postings by e-mail on your favourite newsgroup topics.

Keep It Simple For most people, I'd suggest staying with discussion groups that are based on e-mail. They tend to be easier to use than chat. You also have more time to consider your questions and responses. Plus the depth of the discussions is generally better. In the next part of this section, you'll find a sampling of Canadian career-related groups you can take part in.

Where to Begin?

New Usenet and Web forums are opening up (and closing down) every day. One site I highly recommend is WorkPlace, hosted across Canada by Sympatico. You can access it at **workplace.sympatico.ca**, then choose your province. Or go directly to **www1.sympatico.ca/forums**, and look under "Money and Careers." Select from JobQuest, Gripevine, HomeBase and Manager's Corner.

Exploring Association Discussion Groups Another way to start is to go to the Web site of the association that represents the industry you're interested in. Often these areas include a forum, where you'd find people in the industry exchanging e-mail messages back and forth. The better forums are broken into categories (e.g., Job Search or the Economy), allowing you to choose the themes that suit your needs.

There are many new association-based forums, although quite a few of them are password protected. That means you have to be a member to join in (you get a password that gives you access to the forum). An example of an open forum that does not require a password is the Canadian Real Estate Association (**realtors.mls.ca/crea/newsgroup.htm**). A protected forum can be found on the Canadian Direct Marketing Association's Web site at **www.cdma.org**. In order to see if your industry or professional group has a forum or listserv, you should visit its site directly. Refer back to Chapter 8 for directions on how to do this efficiently.

Career-Related Forums on the Web

There are many other places where career-related discussions take place online. For Canadian content, go to the On-line Discussion Forums at B.C.'s Work Net (**workinfonet.bc.ca/forum/discussion.cfm**). Topics include traditional and electronic job-hunting techniques, and the site is part of the CanWorkNet portfolio. A great U.S. equivalent site is called Hard At Work. Their forums can be found at **www.hardatwork/cooler/cooler.html**.

Talk to Your Magazine and Connect with Your Newspaper Some of the best forums for employment networking are located on the Web sites of Canadian magazines and newspapers. This makes sense when you realize that these are the most likely media in which to find career-related topics. *Chatelaine*, for example, has created discussion areas geared toward Canadian women. Its work category is at **www.chatelaine.com/chatelaine/sources/work/home.html**.

Maclean's also has forums that can be accessed for free. Try **www.macleans.ca**, then "Forum," then "Business and Finance."

Going Commercial

A number of well-structured discussion groups can be found on the commercial online providers such as CompuServe (**www.compuserve.com**) or Prodigy (**www.prodigy.com**). They have put together special interest groups that focus specifically on work. It's easy to find a discussion in your field. Of course, you have to subscribe to that service first if you want access to its information.

Locating an Appropriate Group

As I said before, finding a discussion group is a cinch; finding one that's right for you is another story. My suggestion is to try the general career-related groups described earlier in this section. Then try to find those that are directly related to your field of interest. That's where you can do your most effective networking.

Thankfully, other people have created comprehensive search engines for just this purpose. All you have to do is check specific ones to find relevant groups. These search engines are updated regularly (some even daily). They are divided into several categories, based on the type of Internet technology that they use. Table 9.3 provides a brief description to help you sort things out.

Chatting Your Way to the Top

Man and woman do not live by e-mail alone. Sometimes you get the urge to converse with someone else in real time. In the online world, that translates into the realm of chat. The principal advantage of chat over e-mail is that it's instantaneous. As soon as you type in your message, the person (or people) you're connected to see what you've written. They can then respond immediately, as they would in a real conversation.

Think Before You Press "Enter" Ironically, speed is also the main drawback of chat. You often don't have time to think carefully about what you want to say. You're expected to respond quickly, as in a normal conversation. This is a real barrier if you don't type well.

Table 9.3 Search Engines for Exploring Discussion Groups

Search Engine Name	DejaNews	Forum One	Liszt
Type of Discussion Group	Usenet newsgroups	Web forums	Listservs
Search method	Searches by topic	Searches by keyword	Searches by subject
URL	**www.dejanews.com**	**www.forumone.com**	**www.liszt.com**

CYBER TIP There's a great new feature at the Usenet search engine DejaNews (**www.dejanews.com**). It's called "My DejaNews." You register for free, and it allows you to access newsgroups directly from the Web, instead of using a newsreader.

And as for spell check? Forget about it. What you type in goes out right away—no chance for proofreading or revisions after you've pressed the enter key. This can be frustrating when dealing one on one. In a group chat with many participants, it can be mayhem!

Now you know why I recommend chat for advanced Internet users only. As always, this doesn't mean you shouldn't at least try it. I'll even give you a tip for finding some groups to check out. On the Web, go to **www.yahoo.ca**, and click on "Options" beside the word "Search." This will take you into the advanced search page. In the space to the left of Search, enter "chat and career" (without the quotes). You'll get tons of the most recent groups to choose from.

A Final Cautionary Note on Chat If you are going to use chat to network, my advice is to stick to one-on-one conversations as much as possible. You can follow the same steps as outlined in Table 9.2. You can invite someone to chat directly with you. Don't be put off if your first efforts are rebuffed. Chatting is not for novices. But used effectively, it can be helpful.

VI. WIRED WRAP-UP

Networking could very well be the most important tool of your work search. With the rapid changes in today's workplace, it's more important than ever to create and maintain professional contacts. Career experts agree that it will continue to be the most effective way to find jobs at every level in the economy.

The process of networking takes practice. It also requires finesse, plus a thorough understanding of your goals. Your objective is to put yourself in the forefront of the hiring person's mind. The secret is to focus your energy on the companies and people where you really want to work. It will probably take some initial, unrelated meetings. In the end, however, you'll be much farther ahead.

Electronic resources can definitely make your path easier and faster; however, you should not rely on them to the exclusion of face-to-face meetings and phone sessions. Instead, use online forums to broaden the scope of your traditional networking. Sharing information and building relationships are also your objectives. Remember, too, that behind the fancy e-mail addresses and electronically transmitted messages are people just like you and me. Treat them with respect, and they may just help you to find your next work opportunity.

Points to Remember

- Networking is the key to entering into the hidden job market, which accounts for as much as 80 percent of all work opportunities.
- It's important to try your hand at traditional networking first, to get accustomed to the process.
- Keep in mind that there are three distinctive types of networking:
  - information gathering,
  - contact prospecting, and
  - meetings with decision makers.
- Online networking can be a powerful tool. Remember to observe the rules of netiquette, and to incorporate it as part of your overall networking strategy.

CHAPTER 10

Look for Jobs and Post Your Résumé Online

I. THERE'S NO QUICK FIX

Let's start this chapter off with a quick show of hands. How many of you have actually read all of Part 2, as well as Chapters 8 and 9, before jumping to this page? Come on, let's see those arms go up. If you're sitting there with your hand in the air, congratulations! Unless you're lying to me (and I have ways of tracking you electronically), it's likely that you're very close to finding the work you really want by now.

If not, please read the next few sentences carefully. You may be thinking that online job hunting is the quick, easy solution to securing work. Not so. Here's why:

- Approximately 75 percent of the vacancies posted online are explicitly for computer or engineering folks. If you are fortunate enough to fall into these categories, you still have to compete with other applicants and interview with a decision maker before getting hired.
- The remaining 25 percent of postings are likely the same ones you see advertised in your newspaper's classifieds section or in some other widely published source. Therefore, your only real advantage of seeing them online is the convenience of searching a wide range of sources relatively quickly.
- Posting your résumé online can be a passive and highly inefficient way to find work. Services that claim to match your résumé to existing jobs have a relatively low success rate. Meanwhile,

employers are swamped as it is with applicants and are unlikely to go searching for your résumé somewhere in cyberspace. Never mind the risks of potentially revealing your personal information to the wrong person (discussed later in this chapter).

- The "fragmentation thing." It's not like you can visit three or four Web sites and have all your angles covered. In Canada alone, there are hundreds of job banks, résumé sites, matching services, Usenet groups and others to consider. Take my word for it—this does not make for a simple or direct process.

It's Best When You Combine It Alright, so I ain't exactly Mr. Sunshine. I realize that I'm starting off on a pretty negative note here. That's because I don't want you to ignore the other steps in your work search. In fact, it seems to me that we're about due for a brief review. If you've read the previous chapters and completed some of the recommended exercises, you should now be able to do the following:

- Describe your interests, skills and accomplishments with clarity.
- Create a professional quality résumé and cover letter.
- Send your application material in a variety of ways—including online.
- Pinpoint the exact companies and organizations where you'd fit in best.
- Network your way into the hidden job market where as much as 80 percent of opportunities are found.

These are among the key skills that you need to assist you in locating work, be it a full-time job or contract-based employment. Job postings online are simply another way of finding advertised positions—nothing more, nothing less.

For Those of You Who Didn't Raise Your Hands Please, please go back and read Chapters 3 through 9! I know, you've got places to go and things to do—just like all the other job seekers that you are competing against. Let me just reiterate: *you are very unlikely to find work just by reading this chapter alone.* Matching yourself to job openings via the Internet can be like looking for a needle in a haystack. Both you and the employer must dig through an enormous amount of hay to find something remotely worthwhile (if indeed it was ever even there).

Of course, none of this means that you should shun online job postings or avoid putting your résumé into some of the better résumé banks. It's really a matter of being selective and spending time on more productive approaches.

What to Expect in This Chapter So with these cautions firmly in mind, we can now look at a variety of job-searching techniques using the Internet. They basically break down into two distinct, yet related, categories:

- Sites Where You Can View Jobs and Post Your Résumé. By far the most common, this breaks down further into two sub-categories: Sites Where You Actively Search and Sites That Perform Automated Matching.
- Sites Where You Can Make Jobs Come to You. These are harder to come by. You can input the specifics of the job you'd like and receive e-mail notification whenever something close comes up.

II. SEARCHING FOR JOBS AND POSTING YOUR RÉSUMÉ

I have this fantasy (well, several actually, but there's only one I can discuss in this book). Wouldn't it be great if you could turn on your computer, press a few buttons and find the job you've always wanted? You'd boot up your computer, use voice dictation to input all the things you want from your next position, then press "Enter." Up would come a list of brand-new vacancies that precisely fit your specifications. Then, by clicking on "Submit," your customized video résumé would be automatically beamed to the employers you've chosen. Within a week, you'd be hired and happy, tooling along in your new Porsche.

Job-Search Reality

Sound pretty good? Well, we're not quite there yet, my friends. On the plus side, though, you can use the Internet to locate a growing number of advertised positions. This includes everything from entry-level postings right up to those for presidents and CEOs. There are full-time, part-time and contract jobs available. Many industries and occupations are covered, too. Unfortunately, you must visit these sites often and search repeatedly to see if there are any close matches. We'll look at six different areas to visit in your quest to job hunt online.

A. Web sites of specific companies and organizations

B. Job and résumé banks

C. Web sites of industry associations and professional groups

D. Web sites of employment agencies, recruiters and search firms

E. Classified ads online

F. Usenet newsgroups

Résumé-Posting Realities

Posting your résumé online today can be summed up in the following way: You pays your money and you takes your chances. What you're basically doing is uploading your résumé to the places you think are most likely to be visited by the type of employers you'd like to work for. This could be a Web-based résumé bank, job-related newsgroup, job-matching service or even a response to an advertised position electronically.

Then...you wait.

If your résumé happens to be spotted by the appropriate person, it's possible that it will get into the pile of potential candidates. Of course, that's not the end of it. The employer has probably seen a number of competing résumés by this time. Some will be on the Internet, like yours; others will have come from the employer's ad, which is being advertised in traditional media. At this point, things proceed in a normal fashion. The employer screens all the applications. If you're lucky, you might just get invited for an interview.

To Be (Online) or Not to Be (Online) As mentioned previously, this one approach alone is very unlikely to find you a job (unless you're a high tech worker). So why bother investigating it? Because you could use it as yet another arrow in your job-hunt quiver. If that's the case, there are a few reasons to consider putting your résumé online. Here are several:

- You can market your credentials 24 hours a day, seven days a week.
- It can give you inexpensive national and international exposure.
- Not everyone is doing it yet, so it gives you a chance to stand out.

- You may just impress a potential employer with your ability to post online.

Tread Carefully Once again there are some downsides that you should keep in mind. The biggest concern is the risk factor. Posting your résumé on the Internet can put you in a potentially vulnerable position, unless you take certain precautions (outlined later). You are basically tossing your private, personal information into the air, where anyone can get hold of it.

Ponder these possibilities:

- A recruiter or employment firm could find your résumé, duplicate it and start sending it out to all sorts of companies without your knowledge or consent.
- If a troubled individual happens to be lurking on the Internet and gets hold of your résumé, he or she could make undesirable changes to it and re-post it widely.
- That same troubled person now has your phone number, address and other private information about you. Need I say more?

REAL LIFE Paying to have your résumé posted online is no guarantee whatsoever that you'll receive a response. That's right. Many sites will charge you between $20 to $65 for the privilege of uploading your résumé to their (supposedly private) database. Does this mean that you'll fare better than with the sites that allow you to put up your résumé for free? At present, the answer is a resounding "no." I therefore advise you to spend your money cautiously, and use *privacy-protected*, secure, free sites if you do post online.

No Focus, No Results Other negatives include the relatively low success rate of online résumé postings for non-techies. The situation today is that if you're in a traditional field, don't bet on this option. Remember that the most effective job seekers take a targeted approach. Moreover, employers in Canada don't really expect people from every walk of life to be online yet. They're in the experimental phase, as are the job seekers.

Putting your résumé online can be considered the electronic equivalent of the broadcast letter. You can't really have a cover page attached, since you have no idea who's going to be viewing your file. Remember that the cover letter lets you customize your message to a specific employer. Without it, you're just shooting for whoever stops by.

And don't believe for a minute that employers will go out of their way to find you. They'll be looking only where they expect to find other candidates in your field. This assumes, of course, that they are bothering to look online at all. A recent study indicated that relatively few Canadian employers actively search the Internet for résumés.

REAL LIFE The truth about privacy on the Web is that it is almost nonexistent. Practically anyone can search résumé banks and view what you've posted. Insist on minimal protection at least. Use code numbers or box numbers instead of your real name and address, and insist on finding out who the company is before releasing your identity. It may cost a little extra effort, but it could save you some hassles. Also, make sure you can restrict access to your résumé by employers you're avoiding—like your current company (assuming you're still working and don't want your boss to know you're looking!).

A. Web Sites of Specific Companies and Organizations

As good a place as any to begin is with the firms that you targeted back in Chapter 8. An increasing number of companies are listing some job openings on their Web site. Note that I used the word "some" deliberately. Even large companies that may have many openings tend to place only a few on their Web site.

See for Yourself As an example, visit the Royal Bank's homepage at **www.royalbank.com** (pre-merger!). You might expect to see lots of positions advertised, along with a prominent link on the bank's homepage. Instead, the career pages are buried under a heading called "About Royal Bank Financial Group." Clicking here gives you a sub-list of eight categories, of which "Career Opportunities" is one. Then look for the

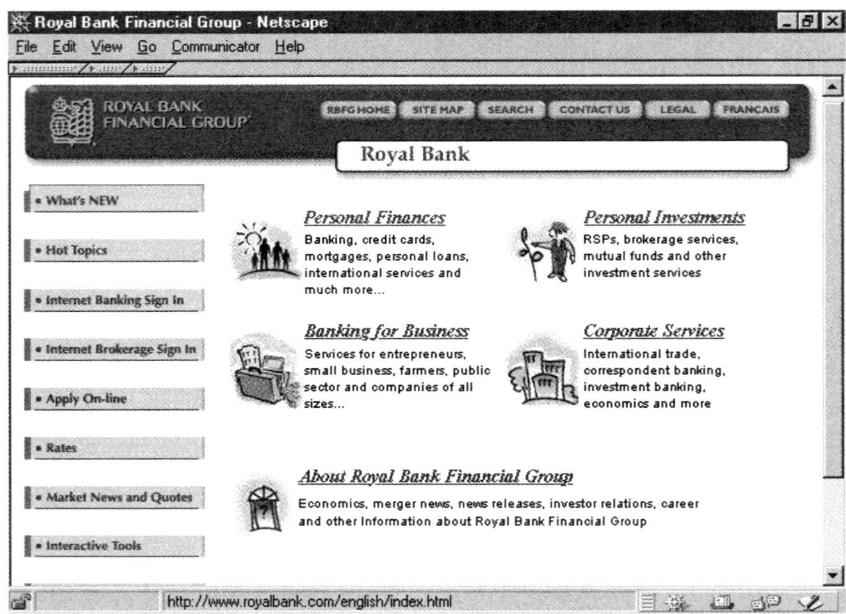

"Opportunities Heading," which further breaks down into "Immediate Opportunities" and "Career Programs." Under "Immediate Opportunities," you get to choose from techie jobs ("Systems and Technology") or traditional positions ("General"). I chose "General" and found that, in all of Canada, a total of 12 types of positions were being advertised. Not exactly overwhelming, considering how big this employer is.

REAL LIFE Note that companies that post jobs on their sites might use terms other than "careers" or "jobs." Watch for hyperlinks labelled "Employment," "We're Hiring," "Positions Available," etc.

Why Go This Route? Even though the odds of finding work this way are low, there are some compelling reasons to investigate it:

- You have a (very remote) chance of finding an opening at the precise company you want to work for. Used in combination with your networking, it's worth a shot.

- The postings tend to be current, unlike at some other places on the Internet.
- Postings are usually accompanied by very detailed job descriptions. You can get a real feel for what the company is looking for.
- Often your résumé can be e-mailed directly to the company (see Chapter 7).
- You can review the rest of the Web site immediately and get useful information on the company (e.g., products and services, history and press releases, for starters). You could even use some of this in your cover letter when replying to the advertised position.

Remember that there are four main ways to find a company's homepage. To begin with, the Web site's URL is often listed in the published ad you'll find in the newspaper. If not, you can search for specific companies by using a search engine and entering the company's name (the keyword approach). Or else you can use the search engine's categories to scan companies by type of industry. Or you can take an educated guess and type the company's name with a www. before it and a.com after it (**www.companyname.com**) into your browser. Refer back to Chapter 8 for more detailed instructions on the various techniques.

B. Job and Résumé Banks

If you don't feel like surfing from one company to another, you can always try a centralized job site. These are Web-based pages that advertise a variety of jobs or contract positions from all sorts of different companies. The best thing about these sites is the convenience that they offer. You can often use a specialized on-site search engine to look for a position by province, city, industry, type of job or company (or some combination thereof). In many cases you can also post your résumé for employers to see, should they happen to be looking in job and résumé banks.

Although this sounds wonderful in theory, the practical aspects can be disappointing. Once again, most of the jobs that you will find are already on the open market. Moreover, many sites charge the employer for each job that they post. Hence, the number of jobs in your specific field tends to be fairly low. Employers are wary of spending money until the site proves itself to be viable. At the same time, so many of these job sites have sprung up lately that the market is highly fragmented. Now that you know all of this, here's where to look.

Finding General Job Sites These are the ones to go to when you're looking for a wide variety of jobs listed in one place. You can find them via search engines at:

- Yahoo Canada search directory (**www.yahoo.ca**). Go to "Business and Economy," then "Companies," then "Employment," then "Canada only" and "Jobs."
- Maple Square search directory (**maplesquare.com**). Go to "Business and Money," then "Employment."

Another excellent starting point for job and résumé banks is Canada WorkInfoNet at **www.workinfonet.ca/cwn/english/main.html**. Click on "Links," then "Jobs and Recruiting," then "Job Matching Services."

CYBER TIP Some résumé banks ask you to upload your résumé electronically, while others will take your paper version and input it manually or through scanning. Make sure you find out what format they want (e.g., ready for scanning, e-mail or Web form, fully formatted or ASCII).

Examples of Canadian Job Sites Here are just some of the many Canadian sites you'll encounter when using the search techniques listed above. Note that almost all job sites allow you to view their open positions for free. When it comes to uploading your résumé, however, it may be a different story. This sample list is sorted alphabetically, and is broken down into free or fee-based résumé posting:

Free Services

- ActiJob (**www.actijob.com**)
- Atlantic Canada Careers (**atl-can-careers.com**)
- CanadaJobs (**www.canadajobs.com**)
- Canadian Career Page (**www.canadiancareers.com**)
- CareerConnect from *The Globe and Mail* (**www.theglobeandmail.com/careerconnect/**)
- CareerMagazine (**www.careermag.com**, then click on "Job Openings")
- CareerMosaic Canada (**canada.careermosaic.com,** then "Jobs")

Fee-Based Services

- Canadian Employment Weekly (**www.mediacorp2.com**).
- JobSat (**www.jobsat.com**). Job postings from across Canada, and some in the U.S.
- MonsterBoard Canada (**www.monster.ca**)
- NetJobs (**www.netjobs.com**). National database of job openings.
- Résumé Canada (**www.bconnex.net/~résumé/index.html**). Job openings by category across Canada. Search by country, skills and type of position.
- WORKaccess (**www.workaccess.com**). Some Canadian jobs, but still in the building phase of operation.
- WorkInk (**www.workink.com**). Focus on jobs for people with disabilities, but everyone welcome.
- Worknet (**www.worknet.ca**). National job database brought to you by Electronic Access Systems Inc.

CYBER TIP To determine if a résumé bank will attract the employers you're looking for, do a simple test. Surf the site. Go into the résumé area (if you're allowed to) and see if any other people have put résumés in the categories that apply to you. Contrary to popular thinking, in this case the more, the better. That's because employers are drawn to pools of candidates, not just single candidate postings.

Job Searching via Human Resources Development Canada (HRDC) The following government-sponsored job banks can be useful places to seek employment openings, particularly for less senior jobs (as opposed to those appealing to vice-presidents and CEOs). Begin your journey at the Canada WorkInfoNet site (**www.workinfonet.ca/cwn/english/main.html**, then choose "Links," then "Jobs and Recruiting," then "Job Searching via Human Resources Development Canada (HRDC)"). Some of the sites you'll find are:

- HRDC Job Bank—Database of employment opportunities found at Human Resource Centres across all of Canada. Searchable by province, city, type of work, etc., and updated daily.

Table 9.2 Questions to Ask a Résumé Bank Before Signing Up

QUESTIONS TO ASK	HOW THEY SHOULD ANSWER
What is the going rate for posting my résumé?	Free, or up to $40 for 3 –12 months of online exposure is the average.
What is your success rate in finding jobs for candidates?	There's no accurate way to track this data yet. (If they do give you a figure, ask for documentation.)
Are there any hidden costs?	No. (Make sure you read the fine print.)
What about additional options that you might charge me for?	You may be charged extra to have the service design your résumé for you, or to input it online (instead of you e-mailing it), or for a privacy option.
Can I make periodic changes to update my résumé?	Yes. (Usually you can update it once every month or two —for free.)
Do you automatically match my credentials to jobs that are posted on your system?	No. Employers can view your résumé and select it if they like. (See the job-matching section for more details.)
Are recruiters or search agencies allowed to view or download my résumé with my name on it?	No. We do not release your name and number unless you agree to it first.
If you post the résumés by job category, can mine go into more than one (e.g., marketing and sales as well as management)?	Yes. (You should be able to put your résumé in at least two or three categories at no extra charge.)

- Human Resource Centres of Canada—List of links to the centres in your area, which may provide additional or more detailed information on this subject.
- Selected Job Openings by Province—Local job postings broken down by sector, for a quick and comparatively easy search.

REAL LIFE For job sites geared toward specific groups (e.g., women, people with disabilities, Aboriginal people, students, etc.) see Chapter 11. A great example for students is Campus WorkLink (**ngr.schoolnet.ca/jp/stu_login.html**), which lets registered users view jobs listings at over 70 post-secondary institutions across Canada.

Sector-Specific Job Sites

- Charity Village (**www.charityvillage.com/charityvillage/career.html**). All sorts of listings for work at non-profit agencies.
- Public Service Jobs (**www.psc-cfp.gc.ca/recruit/sitemape.htm**). Federal government job listing, by category.
- Canadian Jobs Catalogue, Keneva Corp. (**www.kenevacorp.mb.ca**). Free demo of up to 250 sites. Join for $10 and get access to more than 2,000 sites with direct links to industry hiring locations.
- Canada WorkInfoNet (**www.workinfonet.ca**, then "Links," "Jobs and Recruiting" and "Sector Specific Jobs"). A good starting list of industry-specific job sites.

U.S. and International Job-Search Sites

- CareerMagazine (**www.careermag.com**)
- CareerMosaic (**www.careermosaic.com**)
- CareerPath (**www.careerpath.com**)
- e-span (**www.espan.com**)
- Monster Board (**www.monster.com**)

CYBER TIP Don't forget those commercial online providers as another source for job postings. America Online Canada (**www.aol.ca**) has several areas where jobs for Canadians are posted. If you are a subscriber, type in "jobs canada" in the search box and see what comes up.

C. Web Sites of Industry Associations and Professional Groups

Are you a plumber? Lawyer? Nurse? Salesperson? Armadillo cleaner? Do you work in the aerospace, timber or pharmaceutical industries? I mentioned in Chapters 8 and 9 that the association representing your profession or industry can be an excellent source for networking (particularly for armadillo cleaners in aerospace!). Some professional groups have also started to act as online job intermediaries. They list positions from member companies as a service to their clients. They may also allow you to post your résumé to a special part of their site.

So how do you find the Web site that's right for you? One thing you can do is search for your particular industry group, using the Strategis BizMap Web site (**strategis.ic.gc.ca/scdt/bizmap/nav.html**, then click on "Industry and Professional Associations"). Or else follow the detailed instructions provided in Chapter 8. Either way, there's no guarantee that you'll find job listings. On the other hand, you might just run into some other information that will assist you in your search for work.

REAL LIFE When submitting an application electronically, consider sending a hard copy as a back-up (by mail, courier or, if pressed, fax). Mention on the electronic version that you've also sent a hard copy. Note on the hard copy that you've also sent an electronic version. That way you can be sure that it gets noticed and processed properly.

D. Web Sites of Employment Agencies, Recruiters and Search Firms

Employment agencies and recruiting firms have now discovered the power of the Internet. The high tech recruiters were the first to market positions online and accept e-mailed résumés. This is filtering through to some of the more generalized search companies. Note that jobs posted by recruiters are often disguised. That is, the employer's name is left out so that you'll have to contact the agency directly if you want more information.

To find Canadian employment agencies online, you can start by typing in the name of a firm that you already know of at a search engine such as AltaVista Canada (**www.altavista.ca**). Sure, you could also type in some keywords, such as "placement agencies," but you'll end up with more than 1,000 somewhat random hits. To narrow this down, try one of our national search directories, then drill down by heading using the following instructions:

- Yahoo Canada search directory (**www.yahoo.ca**). Go to "Business and Economy," then "Companies," then "Employment," then "Recruiting and Placement." Here you can choose from "Temporary," then "Source Services Corporation/Regional."
- Maple Square Canadian search directory (**maplesquare.com**). Go to "Business and Money."
- Canada.com search engine (**www.canada.com**). Go to "Business and Finance," then "Jobs and Careers," then "Find a Job."

Three other excellent starting points for search firm lists are:

- Canada WorkInfoNet (**www.workinfonet.ca/cwn/english/main.html**). Click on "Links," then "Jobs and Recruiting," then "Job Matching Services."
- Association of Professional Placement Agencies and Consultants (APPAC) (**strategis.ic.gc.ca/SSG/mi01177e.html**). A list searchable by industry type and location in Canada.
- Directory of Canadian Recruiters (**www.gocontinental.com/candir.htm**). The directory itself is a book that you can purchase (or browse through at your local reference library), but you can do some sample searching online for free.

E. Classified Ads Online

Has this ever happened to you: You're anxiously awaiting the arrival of your morning newspaper, eager to check out the latest career ads, when you notice something at the bottom of your bird cage. Turns out the Employment section has already been used by your significant other—as a cage liner for your little budgie.

Fret no more, fellow Web meisters. You can now find almost all of the help wanted and employment ads from your city's paper online. Better yet, most of these sites provide a search engine, so you can locate recent job ads by criteria such as job category and location. Remember,

REAL LIFE Employment agencies, recruiters and search firms may operate in different ways. Some charge the employer a fee only if they find a suitable candidate. These are called "contingency" firms. Others are paid a flat fee whether they find someone or not. These are the "retainer firms." It is also important to know that many firms specialize in placing people within specific industries or levels of jobs.

though, that this service is a convenience only. Your competition may be pulling the pages from their bird cages (or cat-litter boxes) and responding to the same ads at the same time as you.

There are many large, medium and small newspaper Web sites across Canada that carry their employment advertisements in a searchable format. This ranges from *The Globe and Mail* to the *Halifax Herald*, all the way to the *Peace River Record Gazette*. Here's where to locate them quickly:

- Close to 20 major newspaper classified sites in Canada (**www.worldchat.com/public/stcharle/jobform.html**). Brought to you by the St. Charles Adult Education Centres (Hamilton).
- Canadian newspaper classifieds by region (**www.onestep.on.ca/online/newspaperlist.htm**). Hosted by OneStep, Ontario Network of Employment Skills Training Projects.
- Nearly 50 large, medium and small newspaper employment section links (**www.ns.hrdc-drhc.gc.ca/english/cbreton/workp/wantad.htm**). Sponsored by HRDC's "The WorkPlace" site, out of Cape Breton.

As OneStep describes it, in most cases you're linked directly to the classified section or the employment section of the newspaper. If the site uses frames, you are linked directly to the most appropriate frame for

CYBER TIP Job postings also appear in specialized industry publications, known as trade journals. You can now check out many of these online. Maclean Hunter offers perhaps the broadest range of such publications in Canada. Visit their site at **www.mhbizlink.com** and look for titles such as *Marketing Magazine, Modern Purchasing, Canadian Grocer* and many others.

convenient bookmarking and faster loading. Newspapers that don't post classified ads online do have useful contact and research potential, so they are included as well.

F. Usenet Newsgroups

The Usenet, you'll recall, is the part of the Net where messages are exchanged in newsgroups via e-mail. There are a number of Canadian newsgroups dedicated to jobs. These are places where people have e-mailed in positions for you to review. And it's also where some people post their résumés.

Such Nice Technology, So Primitively Deployed I must admit that I was deeply disappointed when I first ventured into a job-oriented newsgroup. Maybe I'd been spoiled by the attractiveness and graphics of the Web. Or perhaps I was just expecting...well, something better. After all, this is supposedly leading-edge technology we're dealing with here.

In my opinion, however, the set-up of these newsgroups and forums tends to be disorganized. Yes, there are jobs. Thousands of them, in fact. Jobs that are posted in an absolutely random order. Jobs for people who can program in C++ and solve the Y2K crisis (yes, the jobs here tend to be exclusively for techies). Plus, and this is where I just shake my head, you'll find untold opportunities to involve yourself in multi-level sales schemes and other such questionable practices. My advice on this? Any posting that promises you thousands of dollars a week just by working from home licking envelopes is to be studiously avoided!

To top things off, the vacancies here can remain online for an eternity. It's not like some official body monitors the content. Whatever goes on can stay on without being removed. So even if you do finally see something interesting (a glimpse of that elusive needle, perhaps), once you call it up it could be six months or even a year old.

Getting There Have I made it sound attractive? It's not that bad, I guess. I mean, some people in the high tech industry swear by newsgroups. As for me, most job hunters I've spoken to about newsgroups swear *at* them.

One great development: there are now Web sites that connect you directly with information that used to be accessible only via your Usenet reader. Moreover, some of these sites have search engines that dig into a variety of newsgroups at once. So you can input your criteria (e.g., city and type of work required) and get results from multiple sources—all at one site.

Here are some addresses of Usenet engines that search a number of newsgroups at once:

- Career Mosaic Canada's Usenet engine (**canada.careermosaic.com/cm/canada/canada17.html**). Search by province, using keywords (e.g., marketing, sales, finance, etc.).
- Deja News search engine's "power search" (**www.dejanews.com/home_ps.shtml**). Search by job newsgroups, specifying type of position and city.

For those of you who prefer to search newsgroups by city, try the linked Usenet resource at CanadaJobs (**www.canadajobs.com/news.htm**).

Some of you may be comfortable using your newsreader already, and may want to skip the Web altogether. If so, here are some newsgroups that you will find helpful:

National and Provincial

- ab.jobs (Alberta Jobs)
- bc.jobs (British Columbia Jobs)
- can.jobs (Canadian Jobs, National)
- nb.jobs (New Brunswick Jobs)
- ns.jobs (Nova Scotia Jobs)
- ont.jobs (Ontario Jobs)
- qc.jobs (Quebec Jobs)
- sk.jobs (Saskatchewan Jobs)

By City

- hamilton.jobs (Hamilton)
- island.jobs (Vancouver Island)
- kingston.jobs (Kingston)
- kw.jobs (Kitchener-Waterloo area)
- ott.jobs (Ottawa)
- mtl.jobs (Montreal)

- sudbury.jobs (Sudbury)
- tor.jobs (Toronto)
- van.jobs (Vancouver)
- uvic.jobs (Victoria)

International:

- alt.jobs
- biz.jobs
- biz.jobs.offered
- comp.jobs
- comp.jobs.offered
- misc.jobs
- misc.jobs.contract
- misc.jobs.misc
- misc.jobs.offered

III. MAKING THE JOBS COME LOOKING FOR YOU

Getting blisters yet from scrolling through all these sites? You're probably wondering if there's an easier way to see job postings on the Internet. The answer, happily, is yes. How would you like to have new job postings sent directly to your private e-mail account? It can be done, for free, using listserv technology.

The principle here is that you subscribe to mailing lists (listservs) or "Alert" services—as they're being called—that specialize in Canadian jobs. You specify the type of job you want (e.g., industry, level, location, etc.). If a job of that type gets posted, it will automatically be sent to your e-mail. All you have to do is check your in-basket on a regular basis and view any relevant files. The following are Canadian versions of this service:

- CareerConnect, offered by *The Globe and Mail* (**www.theglobeandmail.com/careerconnect**, then click on "Career Alert"). There are some good jobs on this database, and it's now free.
- JobShark (**www.jobshark.com**, then click on "Jaws"). Fill in the preformatted résumé to register for this national alert service.

- Employment News (**www.employmentnews.com**, then click on "Job Alert"). Most jobs are in the Toronto area.
- WorkSearch, from HRDC (**www.worksearch.gc.ca**, then click on the "WorkSearch" logo to enter, then "Tours," then look on the top toolbar and click "WorkLink," then "WorkLinks Automatic E-Mail"). As this service grows, it promises to be increasingly useful.
- Public Service Commission (**209.50.65.245/CareerAlert/psc/pscalerte.asp**). Enter your specifications in their "Career Alert" service for notification of government jobs.

REAL LIFE Other job sites offer alert services as well, sometimes under different names. When visiting such a site, look for a link such as "E-Mail Postings," "Job Alert," "Auto-Respond," etc.

IV. EMPLOYMENT-MATCHING SERVICES

Interested in a somewhat more direct job-search technique? "Employment matching" is when you upload your résumé to a specialized service that tries to match you automatically to specific jobs on its private database. You can think of it as kind of like a dating service (although in my opinion, less stimulating or rewarding). This is also where a *keyword scannable résumé* comes in handy, as described back in Chapters 6 and 7.

Employment Matching Versus Job Sites and Résumé Banks

Employment matching is significantly different from the techniques reviewed previously. When you surf a job site, you have to look at job listings individually. This means reading each ad, deciding if there's a fit and then sending in your application. Maybe the employer will contact you, and maybe it won't.

You might also post your résumé to these sites. Then you wait for the employer to visit and view these postings, choose yours (among others), decide to contact you and then do so (or not).

These connections are made automatically with employment matching. Once you send in your material, it goes into the database and gets compared to existing openings, and then you are notified if an employer wants to contact you.

Sound Too Good to Be True? Job matching sounds like a dream come true. All you need to do is send in your résumé and the rest is done for you. In some cases, you don't even have to know how to use the Internet (you can mail in your material by regular post). Theoretically, you then get automatically matched to every job on that database for which you qualify.

Here's the catch: "every" job means, in reality, only those vacancies that companies have posted on that particular database. Unfortunately, that currently translates into *not a huge number*. As for what "qualify" means, well, employers can run a keyword search. They can ask for specific experience, educational requirements and any skills that they want. If the computer doesn't find these on your résumé, you don't make the cut.

Job-Matching Sites

To get an idea of what's out there, I've provided you with the following list.

- CareerConnect (**careers.theglobeandmail.com**). Leave it to *The Globe and Mail* to come up with a wide-ranging career resource on the Web. Its CareerConnect site is more than just a matching system. It's also a place to find loads of information on job hunting, résumé preparation, even discussion groups with fellow career-seekers. It used to cost $24.95 for six months of this service—but now it's free. You can send them your material by Web form right on their site.
- Electronic Labour Exchange (ELE) (**ele.ingenia.com**). "The Electronic Labour Exchange is a computer-based service developed by Human Resources Development Canada to help job seekers identify employment opportunities suited to their qualifications and employers find appropriate candidates. The ELE automatically matches jobs to people and people to jobs." As I write this book, the ELE is focusing on the Ottawa area, although it is beginning to build a national representation.
- JCI JobMatch (**www.jcitech.com/jobmatch**). According to the company, the system uses state-of-the-art Web technology to bring job seekers and employers together. Job seekers enter an

electronic profile of their skills, along with a cover letter and contact information.

- JobNet (**www.jobnet.org**). As the Web site states, "JobNet matches Job Seeker skills and Employer recruiting needs by using Occupational Coding, Education, Geographic Location and Skills as primary Search Criteria. The database is secure and only registered companies have total system access." Registrants can opt for a confidential service where their approval is required before any file information is released.
- JobShark (**www.jobshark.com**). Uses JAWS, a search engine which "matches job seekers and recruiters according to specific criteria." Recruiters may list jobs under particular categories. Then, when they are posted, "JAWS actively searches the databank for résumés which match the criteria set out in the job posting. Job Seekers are notified instantly (via e-mail) of a possible match and recruiters can see responses in as little as five minutes to their posting."
- National Graduate Register (NGR) (**ngr.schoolnet.ca/ngr/home**). "An Internet searchable database funded by the Canadian Federal Government (Industry Canada)...designed to match recruiting employers with qualified graduates. The NGR provides anonymous résumés to inquirers, based on matches between the job skill requirements of employers and the skills of students and graduates as presented in the résumés registered in the system." Employers must go through NGR, which then contacts you to ask if you want to release your name and number. Also, you can electronically link with guidance, career and labour market information to assist in your job-search efforts.

Other free job-matching services tend to be localized. As such, they may be worth investigating. For example:

- SkillScape (**www.skillscape.com**). Vancouver-based.
- Alum-Net (**www.jobnet.org/alumnet**). Based in London, Ontario. Geared toward alumni of the University of Western Ontario.

V. WIRED WRAP-UP

The thought of searching for jobs in cyberspace is truly appealing. What better way could there be to look for work? From the comfort of your favourite chair, you could point and click your mouse to seek out every posted job in the world. Then, after grabbing some munchies, you could put your feet up while employers actively look for your résumé on the Internet. Soon the job offers would come pouring in.

Nice scenario, I grant you that. Unfortunately, the system doesn't quite work that way (at least, not yet). At best, it's a faint hope. Maybe someone will see your résumé online. Possibly that person will contact you (along with many others), if there is a vacancy that your qualifications seem to match. And perhaps you'll stumble upon a job that seems right for you somewhere on a job site or newsgroup. The fact that it's likely—though not always—the same posting that everyone is seeing at the same time in their newspaper means you don't necessarily get an edge.

On the downside, you could spend money unnecessarily or lose control of your most cherished personal marketing tool—your résumé—to a lunatic Internet surfer. What's worse, you could squander valuable time thinking that the online resources are doing your hard work for you, when you should also be out conducting a traditional work-search campaign.

The best advice I can give you here is to use the approaches outlined in this chapter sparingly. If you can find relevant sites to post your résumé on, if the right employers are looking at these sites, if your privacy can be guaranteed and if it doesn't cost too much, then go ahead and use the résumé-posting and job-matching sites. Remember that you need to balance this limited approach (searching for posted jobs) with an active strategy (networking into the hidden job market). Only then will you be maximizing all of your resources.

Points to Remember

- Posted jobs, including those found online, account for only 10 to 20 percent of all available opportunities. Job searching online should be practiced only as part of your overall work-search strategy.
- There are many different Canadian sites where job hunting takes place. Most sites include sections where you can view posted positions and upload your résumé for employers to find. There are also sites where you can only view jobs, or else only post your résumé.
- Job matching automatically compares your résumé to posted positions and notifies you if there is a potential fit. Few Canadian sites offer genuine matching engines. Those that do are still struggling to attract enough employers to meet the needs of job hunters.

CHAPTER 11

Find Special Resources for Specific Groups

I have a confession to make, now that you've read this far. It turns out that most of this book has been written with the "average" reader in mind. Trouble is, I don't believe that there is such a thing. I mean, do you consider yourself to be "average"? Obviously, there is no one-size-fits-all approach to finding work. So it is, too, with the online resources available to work searchers.

This chapter attempts to address this issue by focusing on the needs of some specific groups in Canada. Not that I could reasonably cover each and every distinct assemblage of persons from shore to shore. Instead, I've selected the following groups in that there is much available for them online:

- Post-secondary students and recent grads
- Workers age 45 years or older
- High tech workers (computers and engineering)
- Canadians who want to work abroad
- The "designated" groups:
  - People with disabilities
  - Women
  - Aboriginal peoples
  - Visible minorities
- People who are unemployed
- Self-employed folks (or "wannabes")
- Career counsellors

My objective in the pages that follow is simple and straightforward. I want to provide useful Internet resources for each of these particular groups, in order to save people from surfing randomly (and perhaps endlessly) in cyberspace. The format I've used is one you're already familiar with if you've been online before: the FAQ (Frequently Asked Questions). However, there is some overlap of information—for example, I've included the site of the Canadian Human Rights Commission (**www.chrc.ca**) under the listings for visible minorities, but it may well be of interest to just about anyone. So it doesn't hurt to browse through the whole chapter.

At this point I would like to thank the people at Canada WorkInfoNet (**www.workinfonet.ca**). They've assembled a remarkable list of Canadian and International career links, organized into easy-to-find categories. This site, which has the backing of Human Resources Development Canada, is easily the best free online resource for finding descriptions of—and links to—career-related sites. They have graciously allowed me to borrow from their link descriptions.

I. POST-SECONDARY STUDENTS AND RECENT GRADS

If you're still in school, or you graduated within the last few years, you know only too well how tough the job market is. Youth unemployment and underemployment are major issues in Canada. Gone are the days when employers swarmed the campuses in a hiring frenzy. There are still career fairs going on today, but employers are far more selective. Plus the work they offer comes with no guarantee of longevity. That's because you control your own destiny now.

Sound like a challenge? There are, fortunately, many electronic tools to help give you that competitive edge. Here are some of them, according to the more popular questions asked by students and recent grads.

What Should I Do with My Life?

- Job Futures (**www.hrdc-drhc.gc.ca/JobFutures/english/index.htm**). What career should you choose? What kind of jobs will be available in the future? If you're looking for answers to these questions, click here. This government site includes "Occupational Outlooks" and "Career Outlooks for Graduates"—information about the current world of work and projections for the future.

- Self-Assessment via MazeMaster (**www.mazemaster.on.ca/eng/mod1**). For youth aged 16 to 29, three interactive exercises to discover your values, skills and interests.
- The C-Files via Human Resources Development Canada (HRDC) (**cfiles.hrdc.globalx.net/scr01.html-ssi**). Be a "career detective" and find out about all the career possibilities that exist for you. Fill up your "C-files" as you do your investigation, based on your unique skills and talents.

Where Is the Work?

- Labour Market Information via MazeMaster (**www.mazemaster.on.ca/eng/mod2**). Top occupational areas for people aged 16 to 29 and who want to check out company and personal profiles.
- Statistics Canada Provincial Data (Eastern Canada: **www.statcan.ca/english/Pgdb/People/Labour/labor07a.htm**; Central Canada: **www.statcan.ca/english/Pgdb/People/Labour/labor07b.htm**; Western Canada: **www.statcan.ca/english/Pgdb/People/Labour/labor07c.htm**). Details on labour force, numbers and rates on employed and unemployed, by gender.

Are There Job Programs Set Up for Students and Recent Grads?

- CACEE WorkWeb (Canadian Association of Career Educators and Employers) (**www.cacee.com**). A non-profit partnership between education and business, established to find students and graduates relevant work.
- Campus WorkLink (from CACEE) (**ngr.schoolnet.ca/worklink**). Job-posting service for advertising jobs on Canadian campuses and accessing students' résumé listings. More than 70 college and university career centres are already hooked up.
- Career Edge (**www.careeredge.org**). A Canadian, private-sector national youth internship program.
- National Graduate Register (**ngr.schoolnet.ca**). Free online services and database containing the profiles of recent post-secondary graduates that can be matched with employers instantly.

- Student Summer Job Action (**jeunesse.hrdc-drhc.gc.ca/ssja/emain.htm**). Sixteen initiatives for creating summer employment opportunities for secondary and post-secondary students.
- International Employment, Youth Resource Network of Canada (**www.youth.gc.ca/infojobs/intremp-e.shtml**). International job opportunities, tips and advice on working and living overseas.
- Work Experience Opportunities via Youth Link (**jeunesse.hrdc-drhc.gc.ca/ythlink/sc2ind_e.html**). Information about the many programs and organizations that can help youth find international work opportunities.

II. WORKERS AGE 45 YEARS OR OLDER

Fifteen years ago, looking for employment as an "older worker" was often a nightmare. Many companies were reluctant to hire displaced, experienced workers. Employers thought that people who were not employed must be damaged goods, or must be too set in their ways, having already worked 20 years somewhere else. Since then, of course, we've had two recessions, untold numbers of de-hiring, downsizing, merges and purges. The world of work has truly undergone a major transition.

So have things really changed that much today? They certainly have, but only if you choose to seek out contract work or a position in a small or start-up firm. In these cases, your odds of getting hired are better than ever. That's because your experience gives you an edge over younger competitors, especially when a company doesn't have to pay your benefits such as disability insurance, extended vacations and the like.

But what if you're only looking for a "permanent" job with an established, larger company? In this case, I'm sorry to say things haven't changed all that much. Companies are moving increasingly to outsourcing and "contingency staffing." So what all-encompassing question should you be asking?

Where Are Government Programs for Work Searchers Age 45 or Older?

- Program for Older Worker Adjustment (POWA) (**www.gov.on.ca/MBS/english/programs/LAB0845.html**). A federal/provincial program for financial assistance for people between 55 and 64 in Ontario who have been laid off.

- Quebec Government Programs and Services for People 55 and Over (**www.comm-qc.gouv.qc.ca/over55.htm)**. Access to 27 government services and programs covering income, health, housing and miscellaneous concerns. Also includes contact information.
- NB Job Corps (**www.gov.nb.ca/ael/empprog/english/jcorps.htm**). A pilot project undertaken jointly by the federal and provincial governments to provide unemployed older adults with opportunities to work at development projects in or near their communities. Unemployed participants between age 50 and 65 are guaranteed work placements of 26 weeks per year for a three-year period.
- Manitoba Senior Citizens Handbook, Employment Opportunities (**www.mbnet.mb.ca/crm/other/genmb/msch/msch10.html**). Job opportunities and counselling services geared for employees and job seekers, small business owners or the needs of immigrant women.
- Veterans Affairs Services and Benefits (**www.mbnet.mb.ca/crm/other/gencdn/vetaffsb.html**). Programs and services for veterans, civilians, their survivors and dependents, including disability pensions, allowances, health care, information and advice and links to other programs in your region.

III. HIGH TECH WORKERS (COMPUTERS AND ENGINEERING)

Unlike people in traditional fields, those of you in high tech positions will significantly increase your odds of finding work by looking at job postings on the Internet. The reason is simple: more and more employers who are looking for technical people are using the Internet as their primary recruitment tool. In fact, a growing number of high tech employers are posting technical jobs exclusively on the Internet. Here's what they're really saying: "If you're not knowledgeable enough to use the Internet to find our job openings, we don't want to deal with you."

This goes a step further when it's time to send in your application. You're often expected to know how to submit your résumé and cover letter via e-mail or Web form. So now what they're saying is: "Good, at least you found us. If you can figure out how to get your résumé to us electronically—in the exact format that we need—then maybe we'll contact you." (Read Chapters 6 and 7 again!)

This phenomenon applies to those of you in the computer field (information systems, information technology, programmers, administrators, etc.), as well as engineers and other high tech professionals. There are numerous job sites and resources set up online specifically for you. Some of them can be categorized in the following questions.

Where Can I Find Out About "Job Fairs"?

- HiTechCareer Centre (**www.hitechcareer.com**). Sponsored by the CEO Group for people in information technology, information services, computers and engineering. Here are direct links to employers who are hiring and places to post your résumé online. You'll also see something called a virtual job fair: online gatherings of companies looking to hire high tech workers. Plus there are listings of actual job fairs that take place in cities across Canada.
- The Lendman Group (**www.lendman.com**). Part of the Kaplan Education Centre's Career Services, this firm hosts over 300 career fairs annually. The bulk of these are in the U.S., with the remainder in Canada and Europe.

Who Are Some of the Key Hi-Tech Recruiters?

- PositionW@tch Internet Recruitment (**www.positionwatch.com**). Heavily skewed towards IT, this site offers a job post search engine for Canada and the U.S. You can also sign up for their Job@lert service. It sends an e-mail to you each time a job in your field is registered.
- Fleethouse IT and Engineering (**www.cncglobal.com**). This site is designed specifically for information technology professionals. You can search for jobs in five Canadian cities as well as the U.S. and abroad. Another excellent resource for Canadian techies, producing more 300 career fairs in 67 countries.

Which Sources Should I Check Out to Learn More About the Industry?

- Canadian Association of Advanced Technology (**www.cata.ca**)
- Information Technology Association of Canada (**www.itac.ca**)
- Canadian Information Processing Society (**www.cips.ca**)
- TechnoGate global technology gateway (**www.technogate.com**)
- The Canadian Engineering Network (**www.transenco.com**)
- The Institute of Electrical and Electronics Engineers, Inc. (**ieee.ca**)
- Ultimate list of Computer and Communication Companies (**www.cmpcmm.com/cc/companies.html**)
- Branham 200 top Canadian IT companies (**www.canoe.ca/FPTechnology_Top200/home.html**)

IV. CANADIANS WHO WANT TO WORK ABROAD

Most of us have been struck by wanderlust at some point in our lives. The urge to leave Canada and explore new realms is very appealing to many people. Those who act on it find themselves facing an assortment of issues, such as getting work permits, learning new cultural norms and finding employment at an appropriate level. The rewards can be high, in terms of increased pay and a chance to enjoy a different lifestyle among new people. Here are some questions asked frequently by those who yearn for other climes (resources for young people who want to work abroad are included in the section on post-secondary students and recent graduates).

Are the Careers Out There Different Than in Canada?

- O*NET, the Occupational Information Network, United States (**www.doleta.gov/programs/onet**). Access to a database of descriptions of occupations, worker skills and requirements for jobs across the U.S.

- Occupational Outlook Handbook (**www.jobtrak.com/outlook**). Descriptions of more than 300 U.S.-based occupations.

Who Offers Good Advice on Working Internationally?

- Bilingual-Jobs.com, Career Management for International Career Seekers (**www.bilingual-jobs.com/library/Career_97_02_21.htm**). Advice on managing and using the right tools to develop an international career.
- Immigration U.S.A. (**www.immigration-usa.com/immigration-usa_com.html**). A collection of resources, tips and software for Canadians (and others) who are thinking of working state-side.
- EscapeArtist (**www.escapeartist.com**). A directory for anyone seeking to live an international lifestyle.

What Job and Résumé Sites Should I Check Out?

- Career Net (**www.netcareer.com/index.html**). Matchmaking services for job seekers and employers/search firms throughout the U.S., U.K., Germany, Japan and New Zealand, including both mailing campaigns and online exposure of job-seeker credentials.
- CareerExchange (**www.careerexchange.com**). An international career search database. There are no fees for job applicants.
- CareerMosaic International Gateway (**www.careermosaic.com/cm/gateway**). U.S.-based employment services with many international links. Job seekers can post résumés, check current job listings and read employer profiles.
- Get a Job, International Job Matching Service (**www.getajob.com**). Searchable database of job openings, with links to other employment resources.
- Heart Career.com (**www.career.com/heart.html**). An interactive recruitment site that connects employers and candidates around the world.

- Interim® Career Consulting, Job Find (**www.interim.com/career/menu.htm**). Individuals can submit their résumé, search a database of international positions and access a detailed interview guide.

V. THE "DESIGNATED" GROUPS

A number of years ago the federal government identified groups that it deemed needed extra support. They concluded that four specific segments would be targeted: people with disabilities, Aboriginal people, women and visible minorities. Programs were set up to provide assistance to these groups, in particular to make sure members of these groups are given equal consideration when it comes time to hiring.

Today we see these programs becoming increasingly available online. This is good news, especially from an accessibility point of view. Still, there are many popular questions about these services, some of which are shown below.

What's Out There for People with Disabilities?

- Atlantic Centre of Support for Disabled Students (**www.stmarys.ca/administration/studentservices/atlcentr/atlantic.html**). Dedicated to improving accessibility for people with disabilities who want to obtain a post-secondary education leading to meaningful employment. Educational support services include everything from pre-admission advice and assistance with registration and course selection to alternative examination accommodation and assistance with finding tutors.
- Chrysalis (**www.chrysalis.ab.ca**). Vocational training, employment, alternatives to employment, outreach and crisis intervention services to a diverse range of people with disabilities, offered by this Alberta society.
- Indie, Integrated Network of Disability Information and Education (**indie.ca**). Products and services for the Canadian and world-wide disability communities: employment, education, transportation, recreation, advocacy.
- Links for the Blind (**www.seidata.com/~marriage/rblind.html**). Information for Canadians and Americans on topics such as adap-

tive technologies, advocacy groups, training and assistance, books and magazines, commercial sites and employment resources, all at this one stop.

- Ontario March of Dimes (**www.omod.org**). A range of employment programs focusing on placement through vocational assessment, computer skill training, supportive employment and job placement services. Pre-employment services include literacy training and life-skill training.
- Wide Area Employment Network (WAEN) via the Canadian Council on Rehabilitation and Work (**www.ccrw.org/waen.htm**). A free database of résumés tailored for the marketing and promotion of skilled Canadians with disabilities.
- WorkWire (**www.workwire.com**). Virtual employment recruiting for both job seekers and employers. Job seekers can create WorkWire résumés and place them directly into a database that is "constantly being searched" by employers.
- Canadian Council on Rehabilitation and Work (**www.ccrw.org/index.html**). Canada-wide network of organizations and individuals, promoting and supporting equal and equitable employment of people with disabilities.
- Job Accommodation Network, JANCANA (**www.ccrw.org/jan.htm**). Job accommodation means giving an employee with a disability the advantage of the most effective tools and working conditions with which to carry out the job's responsibilities.

What Career Resources Are There Specifically for Women?

- BizWomen, for Women in Business (**www.bizwomen.com**). Online interactive community for women in business to communicate, network, exchange ideas and provide support for one another. Free membership.
- Women's Information Networking Directory (WIN) (**edie.cprost.sfu.ca/~spiders**). If you're looking for a career mentor or want to become a mentor for someone just starting out, then start here. The mentorship program is dedicated to providing young women with access to advice, guidance and inspiration.

- Bridges for Women Society (**vvv.com/~careers/index.html**). A unique training program for women with a history of abuse.
- Dalhousie Women's Centre (**www.cfn.cs.dal.ca//Libraries/hcrl/communitydb/dalwc.html**). A resource library, referral services and regular meetings and workshops.
- Atlantic Virtual Women's Business Bureau (**www.bizbureau.com**). A complete resource for women in all stages of planning and developing a business, including a library of resource materials, business links, chat lines and a hot line for questions and comments.
- Canadian Coalition of Women in Engineering, Science and Technology (CCWEST) (**www.ccwest.org/english/ccwest.html**). Career information, job postings, newsletters, listserv access, speeches and statistics related to women in science, technology, engineering and math.
- Employment Projects for Women Inc. (**www.winnipeg.freenet.mb.ca/iphome/e/epw/index.html**). Free service that offers individual and group employment-related counselling for women.
- The Canadian Federation of Business and Professional Women's Clubs, better known as BPW Canada (**www.bpwcanada.com**). A national organization whose primary concern is "the education, employment and economic status of employed women."
- SCWIST Work Pathfinder (**www.harbour.sfu.ca/scwist/pathfinder/index.htm**). Support for women in science and technology on their journey into the new workplace economy.

Where Are the Specialized Sites for Aboriginal People?

- CareerPlace (**www.careerplace.com**). A database of career-oriented Aboriginal women and a program that provides employment services to them as well as providing specialized services to employers (matching and referring, setting up mentorship programs and cross-cultural training).
- Aboriginal Youth Network (**ayn-0.ayn.ca/default.htm**). Programs, services, youth news, bulletins, chat lines, e-mail hook-up and more, including health information for teens—all specially designed for Aboriginal youth.

- Aboriginal Business (**strategis.ic.gc.ca:80/sc_mangb/abc/engdoc/homepage.html**). Canada Business services and support to Indians, Inuit and Métis, including individuals, partnerships and associations.
- First People's Business and Services on SchoolNet (**www.schoolnet.ca/english/ext/aboriginal/business.html**). A huge resource that includes links to a variety of business-related sites as well as publications, First Nations profiles and a list of organizations and associations.
- Indian and Northern Affairs, Programs and Services (**www.inac.gc.ca/faqs/index.html#programs**). Information about income security, health, housing and education benefits available to status Indians.
- Native Counselling Services of Alberta (**www.compusmart.ab.ca/ncsa/home.html**). Non-profit, private and non-political organization that promotes holistic development of the individual, family and community through culturally sensitive programs and services.
- Spirit of Aboriginal Enterprise (**sae.ca**). Assistance, resources and information for business and entrepreneurship development among Canada's Aboriginal peoples.

How About Visible Minorities?

- Black Studies Centre, Montreal (**www.black-studies.org**). Services to the Montreal community and to its various institutions, with a list of online links to sites of interest to members of the black and Caribbean communities.
- Dalhousie Black Student Advising Centre (**is.dal.ca/~bsac/final/info.htm**). Mediation, advocacy, employment and scholarship information to students and prospective students.
- Canadian Human Rights Commission (**www.chrc.ca**). Information on the Commission, its annual report and a listing of the Commission's documents and brochures, plus the on-line *Human Rights Forum*, a Commission publication featuring articles and discussions on human rights issues, and links to other sources of human rights information.

- Public Service Alliance of Canada (**www.psac.com/comm/policy/policy.htm**). Policy and position papers on topics such as equal opportunity, human rights and equal pay for work of equal value.
- Public Service Commission of Canada, Diversity Management Directorate (**www.psc-cfp.gc.ca/dmde1.htm**). The centre of expertise for the Canadian Public Service on equity and diversity. It offers advice, information, and administers the Special Measures Initiatives Program for the Treasury Board Secretariat. The site also offers the Diversity Collection, a selection of print and video materials, best practices in federal government departments and agencies, and links to related sites.
- Diversity Hotwire (U.S.) (**www.diversityhotwire.com**). Resource reviews, readers' forum, signs of change, spotlight on what companies and organizations are doing, diversity challenges and a diversity bookstore catalogue. Annual subscription to *Cultural Diversity At Work,* a 20-page newsletter, includes the Diversity Networker, a source for networking and learning events.

VI. PEOPLE WHO ARE UNEMPLOYED

Being unemployed can be a heart-wrenching experience. I've personally been through it twice—both times coincidentally when my wife was pregnant! The hard days of cold-calling, researching, networking online and in person are not easily forgotten. Nor are those gentle-as-a-grenade "rejection letters" you invariably receive.

For me, one of the hardest things about being unemployed—aside from temporarily feeling like I was scum—was not even knowing where to begin. Who could I call to get started? Would my employment insurance cover me in the event I couldn't find good work quickly? And how do you fill out these #!@&?$ forms anyway? Fortunately, much of what you need to know today is online. Here are some of the questions you might ask.

What Trends Are Shaping the Marketplace?

- Canadian Business Map (from Strategis) (**strategis.ic.gc.ca/scdt/bizmap/index_js.html**). Access to company directories, industry and professional associations, legislation and regulations, business and financial management, research and development, and provincial and territorial information.

- HRDC's National Labour Market Information System (**lmi-imt.hrdc-drhc.gc.ca/lmi.html**). Current information on local labour markets anywhere in Canada.

Where Can I Get Information on Employment Insurance and Other Federal Programs?

- A Guide to Employment Insurance, HRDC (**www.hrdc-drhc.gc.ca/hrdc/ei/sc1236_e.html**). Information about the program, employment insurance, and explanations about eligibility and the various benefits offered.
- Canada Pension Plan (**www.hrdc-drhc.gc.ca/isp/common/cpptoc_e.shtml**). Links to frequently asked questions, current CPP payment rates and explanations of the program, including information on disability benefits, survivor benefits and credit splitting.

What About Provincial Programs?

- Department of Health and Social Services, Northwest Territories (**www.hlthss.gov.nt.ca**). Programs and services in family support, child protection, public health, independent living, community wellness, environmental health and insured services.
- New Brunswick Family and Community Social Services (**inter.gov.nb.ca/hcs/family.htm**). Divided by region across the province. Information about programs and services such as child welfare services, support services for people with disabilities and the elderly, and support services to education.
- Newfoundland Department of Human Resources and Employment, Frequently Asked Questions (**public.gov.nf.ca/hre/hre_faq.htm**). If you're not sure about your eligibility or if you are having problems receiving your cheque, start here to find answers.
- Prince Edward Island Department of Health and Social Services (**www.gov.pe.ca/hss/index.asp**). Information about the depart-

ment's responsibilities and direct links to publications and divisions.

- Quebec Ombudsman (**www.ombuds.gouv.qc.ca/anglais/prod/serv/index.htm**). Do you know what recourse you have if you feel you have been treated unjustly by a Quebec government department or agency?
- Saskatchewan Social Services, Programs and Services (**www.gov.sk.ca/govt/socserv/Default.htm**). One-stop source of information on social assistance and available resources.
- Welfare Assistance, Ontario (**www.gov.on.ca/MBS/english/programs/CSS0103.html**). If you or your family has experienced a loss of income and need short-term assistance, this program could help with basic or extended services.

CYBER TIP Many of the government resources listed in this section have similar counterparts in other provincial governments, such as the Quebec ombudsman service. Check out your provincial government's site and poke around to see what you find. Try Sympatico's Politically Speaking site (**www1.sympatico.ca/Contents/Government/provgov.html**) for direct links to all provincial governments.

How About Job Assistance?

- Onsite Employee Placements Canada (**www.epi.ca**). A co-venture with Human Resources Development Canada and the Alliance of Manufacturers and Exporters Canada. Helps EI recipients find work in a variety of fields.
- Saskatchewan New Careers Corporation (NCC) (**www.sncc.sk.ca**). Opportunities for Saskatchewan people receiving social assistance for increased independence through preparation for employment. Also, the Provincial Training Allowance (PTA), Saskatchewan Post-Secondary Education and Skills Training (**www.sasked.gov.sk.ca/careers/success/financial/sfa/pta.html**). Information about this grant to assist with the costs of living for low-income adults enrolled in basic education and bridging programs.

- Human Resource Centres of Canada (**www.hrdc-drhc.gc.ca/maps/national/canada.shtml**). List of links. The HRCC in your area may provide additional or more detailed information on this subject.
- Employment Now Program via Edmonton Personal Support and Development Network (PSDN) (**www.sasked.gov.sk.ca/careers/success/financial/sfa/pta.html**). A two-week program for unemployed Albertans who have applied for social assistance.
- Job Connect, Ministry of Education and Training (Ontario) (**www.edu.gov.on.ca/eng/training/cepp/cepp.html**). Services for unemployed people, especially youth: information and referral service, employment planning and preparation, on-the-job training.
- The HRDC Job Bank (**jb-ge.hrdc-drhc.gc.ca**). Try the "Quick Search" option for a fast look at job openings in your region.

VII. SELF-EMPLOYED FOLKS (OR "WANNABES")

Ever wondered what it would be like to give up your job and work for yourself? For a growing number of us, this is the new reality. In fact, the number of self-employed Canadians has risen steadily in the last decade to more than 2.5 million people!

Although some of us deliberately choose self-employment, many of us do so because we simply cannot find a steady, traditional job. This has led to a substantial increase in the number of consultants, contract and part-time employees, franchise owners and small-business people. The trend away from traditional jobs does not appear to be slowing. In 1998, more than 18 percent of all working Canadians were self-employed. This is up from 12 percent in 1981, and 14 percent in 1991. As it turns out, self-employment represents more than 75 percent of the net gain in employment between 1990 and 1995, according to the Canadian Labour Congress. Colin Campbell, author of *Where the Jobs Are in Canada,* states that fully half of Canadians expect to be self-employed within five years.

Author and career expert Janis Foord-Kirk summed up this trend well in the following headline to one of her *Toronto Star* columns: "The Jobs Won't Come Back But There Still Will Be Work." In other words, there are fewer traditional jobs (e.g., full-time positions with established companies, including a steady pay cheque and full benefits). Instead, companies are turning increasingly toward outsourcing, contractors and part-timers.

Table 11.1 Self-Employment Options

SELF-EMPLOYMENT OPTION	BRIEF DESCRIPTION
Consulting	• You provide your expertise and advice to clients. • Start-up costs can be relatively low. • Continual marketing is required to secure new contracts. • Working environment tends to be unstructured (you make your own rules).
Operating a Franchise	• You purchase an established business operation or concept (e.g., a Midas Muffler outlet or Mailboxes Etc. store). • Significant upfront financial investment is typically required. • Working environment tends to be highly structured (you must adhere to company policies and pay fees on a regular basis for marketing and administration).
Running a Small Business	• You invest in an ongoing enterprise or start your own business. • The business may require financing and backers (e.g., partners). • There is often a substantial start-up period with low (or no) revenues. • The degree of structure varies according to your level of ownership. Full owners have lots of latitude (and risk). Partners may have less of each.
Acting as an Agent or Representative	• You sell the products or services of an established organization on its behalf. • You get many of the benefits of a franchise without the upfront financial investment. • Your efforts are primarily focused on selling established products or services into new markets. • There is often a full marketing, sales, servicing and administration support system.

The Categories of Self-Employment

Kevin Hood, consultant and "Canada's self-employment guru" (according to the TV show *W5*), explains that there are four basic ways to embark on self-employment. They vary in terms of risk, capital required to get started and degree of structure. These formats are outlined in Table 11.1.

What Are Some of the Pros and Cons of Self-Employment?

A Few Positives to Consider

- The potential for success is limited only by your energy, ability and number of hours in a day.
- You can (hopefully) use your true skills and talents to do work that you genuinely enjoy.
- Corporate politics are less likely to affect your life on a daily basis.
- The tax benefits can be significant.
- Your personality can be expressed in the way you do business.

A Number of Negatives to Contemplate

- The world of self-employment can be harsh. There may be no benefits plans, paid holidays or time off for sick leave. Employment insurance and subsidized pension plans are pretty well out of the question.
- You survive on the business that you bring in. Much of your time must therefore be devoted to marketing, in order to always have enough clients to pay your bills.
- Start-up periods can involve long, hard work with little or no income.
- The customer rules. If you want clients to pay you, you'll need to develop a service attitude. (You see, there's always a boss somewhere!)
- Just like traditional jobs these days—there are no guarantees!

How Can I Evaluate My Self-Employment Potential?

- How Entrepreneurial Are You? The Toronto-Dominion Bank's Small Business Resources (**www.tdbank.ca/tdbank/succeed/quiz.html**). Twenty-five questions, automatically scored. To see just how equipped for self-employment you are.
- Are You a Virtual Entrepreneur? Online Career and Management Consulting (**www.dnai.com/~career/ccbus.htm**). If you think starting an Internet-based business is easy, think again. This site provides an enlightening test to see if you have what it takes.

REAL LIFE Of course, you shouldn't rely on a single test (or even a series of tests) to tell you how to run your life. It's important to talk to career advisors as well as small-business experts. Fortunately, much of this can be done online as well. For information on getting career advice, refer back to Chapter 3. To find online advice about starting and managing a small business, read on.

Where Can I Find Information on Starting a Business?

- The On-Line Small Business Workshop (**www.sb.gov.bc.ca/smallbus/workshop/workshop.html**). A comprehensive resource for those just beginning. It is essentially a business start-up manual, brought to you by the Canada/British Columbia Business Service Centre, "designed to provide you with techniques for developing your idea, starting a new venture and improving your existing small business promotion."
- Canada Business Service Centres (CBSCs) (**www.cbsc.org**). Intended to "improve business access to a wide range of information on government services, programs and regulations." Do not miss this excellent resource.
- Self-Employment Development Initiatives (SEDI) (**www.sedi.org**). A non-profit Ontario-based organization founded in 1986 to promote small business and self-employment.

- Entrepreneur, New Brunswick Assistance Program (**www.gov.nb.ca/ael/empprog/english/entrepre.htm**). Help getting started or maintaining your business. Find out if you qualify for provincial government programs and services.

Can I Actually Find Business Opportunities on the Net?

- The Monster Board's "Be the Boss" (**www.betheboss.com**). Focus on franchising. Mostly U.S.-based.
- Independent Business Canada, from The Business Press Group Inc. (**www.rbo.com**). One of the new breed of searchable databases, which charges a modest fee, designed to highlight regional business opportunities throughout the country. Includes businesses for sale and businesses wanted, franchise opportunities, agencies and dealerships available and wanted, investments available and wanted, start-up and home business opportunities, and technology and new product opportunities.
- Canadian Business Networks Coalition (**strategis.ic.gc.ca/SSG/mi00855e.html**). A "state of the art model for encouraging business collaboration among Canada's small and medium-sized enterprises." Great for hooking up with other business to create alliances.

What Tools Can I Use to Prepare a Business Plan?

- The Entrepreneurship Centre in Ottawa (**www.entrepreneurship.com/busplan_eng.htm**). Information on what you need to prepare a solid business plan, from Industry Canada.
- British Columbia Business Service Centre (**www.sb.gov.bc.ca/smallbus/workshop/market/sample/sample.html**). A sample business plan.

CYBER TIP For a general guide to setting up a home office, go to **www.hometime.com/ps/95/ps2offce.htm** or pick up a copy of *The Idiot's Guide to Running a Successful Home Business for Canadians,* from Prentice Hall Canada.

What Kinds of Tips Are There on Running My Business?

- Inc. Magazine (**www.inc.com**). The aficionado's source for information on minding your small business. Here you'll find topics such as Resources for Growing Your Small Business, among other useful features.
- Canadian Home Business Online Resource Centre (**www.discribe.ca/yourhbiz/howto/helphint.htm**). Hosted by DISCribe Ltd., in Fredericton, New Brunswick. The part called Helpful Hints for Home Business is especially informative.
- Canadian Home Business Guide (**www.home-bus.com**). Services such as the Home-Based Business Directory, designed to increase awareness and promote this industry. There is also a mini-magazine containing articles of benefit to both potential "home-preneurs" and those already established. Articles are mainly written by Canadians working in this industry every day.
- Strategis Contact! The Canadian Management Network (**strategis.ic.gc.ca**, then click on "Contact"). An unbelievable place for "Canadian small businesses and their support organizations to meet, learn from each other, develop business opportunities, and connect with people who are otherwise outside of their network."
- Yahoo (**www.yahoo.ca**). For a general search of small-business resources on the Internet, look under "Self-employment."

Where Can I Network with Other Small Business Folks on the Net?

- DISCribe Online (**www.discribe.ca/yourhbiz/yourhbiz.htm**). Canadian discussion groups for small businesses.
- Strategis Contact! (**strategis.ic.gc.ca/sc_mangb/contact/engdoc/homepage.html**). More Canadian discussion forums for small businesses.
- Water Cooler (**www.hardatwork.com/Cooler/Cooler.html**). Primarily U.S.-based self-employment forums.

VIII. CAREER COUNSELLORS

More and more tools for Canadian career counsellors are appearing online, almost weekly. It seems like you've just figured out how to use WorkSearch (**www.worksearch.gc.ca**) when you're confronted with the likes of MazeMaster (**www.mazemaster.on.ca**). Throw in a healthy mixture of cyber-counselling and discussion forums with your peers, and the Internet takes on a whole new light for your practice. These are just some of the questions you might ask yourself.

Where Can I Link to Career Associations Online?

- International Association of Career Management Professionals (**www.iacmp.org**)
- Canadian Career Information Association (**novatech.on.ca/ccia**)
- Canadian Vocational Association (**www.cva.ca**)
- Ontario Association of Youth Employment Centres (OAYEC) (**www.interlog.com/~oayec**)
- Counselling Foundation of Canada (**home.iSTAR.ca/~cfcanada**)
- Canadian Association of Career Educators and Employers (CACEE) (**www.cacee.com/workweb**)

Where Can I Network Online with My Peers?

- Contact Point (**www.contactpoint.ca/html/Discuss1.html**)
- The Catapult on JobWeb (**www.jobweb.org/CATAPULT/catapult.HTM**)
- The Canadian Vocational Association, Discussion Groups (**www.cva.ca/cva/en/disc.html**)

What Other Useful Resources Are Out There for Career Counsellors?

- Counsellor's News: Contact Point (quarterly) (**http://www.contactpoint.ca/html/Counnews.html**)

- CCDF List of Career Conferences (**infoweb.magi.com/~ccdffcac/cgcf/conference.html**)
- Doug's Internet Resources for Counsellors (**bobcat.oursc.k12.ar.us/~counsel**)
- Career Development Practitioner Certificate, Conestoga College (**www.conestogac.on.ca/calendar/career.html**)
- Canadian Council of Human Resources Associations (**www.chrpcanada.com**)
- Upcoming Human Resources Training and Conferences (courtesy of *The Globe and Mail*'s CareerConnect) (**careers.theglobeandmail.com/careerconnect/docs/site/ mgr_conferences.asp**)

IX. WIRED WRAP-UP

What you've just read is the tip of an ever-growing iceberg. In the time since I wrote the first edition of this book, the Internet has expanded exponentially. It has reached a point where it now offers something for just about anyone. Resources for particular groups are a great case in point. There are association Web sites, discussion forums, articles and all sorts of other information available.

Once again, though, the trick is to find what you need, then use it to help you in your career transition. Canada WorkInfoNet (**www.workinfonet.ca**) is a terrific starting point, because it has lots of useful Canadian career links, all organized into categories and sub-categories, and even has mini-descriptions to save you time. Another good starting point is your professional association's Web site. There are a few other of these "master link" sites that I'd like to point out to you:

- HRDC's The Work Place (**www.ns.hrdc-drhc.gc.ca/english/cbreton/workp/index.htm**)
- St. Charles Adult Education Centre (**www.worldchat.com/public/stcharle**)
- Maple Square Search Engine, Employment (**maplesquare.com/bus_subcat.asp?subcat=Employment**)
- Canadian Jobs Catalogue (Keneva Corp.) (**www.kenevacorp.mb.ca**). Charges $10 per year.
- Job Search Canada via The Mining Company (**jobsearchcanada.tqn.com**)

Points to Remember

- No matter what your situation is, you are not alone. The Internet has resources for you based on your economic situation, your age, ethnicity, gender, profession, etc.
- Finding resources for particular groups can be best accomplished by visiting an appropriate association's Web site first. These often have links to related sites. From there, it's a matter of surfing until you find what you need.
- Visiting a "master link" site, like those listed above, will also help you to locate what you're looking for.
- Remember not to restrict your search to the electronic realm. By attending association meetings or by networking individually with other members of your group, you may be able to learn a great deal.

PART 4 STAY WIRED

CHAPTER 12 Hone Your Other Work-Search Skills

I. FIVE CRITICAL COMPETENCIES

Did I just use the word *competencies?* Please...smack me (hard). It's such a business-speak term that I'm shocked to see it in my book. On the other hand, it does describe the fact that there are specific skills you'll need to enhance your search for work. Whaddaya say we let it go this one time, OK?

And let's be honest here: looking for work can be an absolute grind. You should be preparing a plan, doing research, making calls, scheduling and attending meetings, writing letters, preparing for (and sweating through) interviews, sending thank-you notes, coping with emotional upheaval—and that's just for starters. Then, when you finally get an offer, you still have to negotiate the best deal.

Sound tough? It can be. That's why I suggest that you review five specific areas *before* you launch fully into your personal marketing campaign. You want to go into the stage where you actively sell yourself with as many tools as possible to make the process less difficult, faster and more efficient. I'm happy to say there are several things you can do to maximize your chances for success. This chapter looks at those five specific areas and the ways that you can use technology in each:

1. *Planning:* Think ahead about what your work search will look like and how much time you'll spend on each component.
2. *Staying Organized:* Increase your efficiency through time management and record keeping.

3. *Interviewing:* Polish your techniques for formal interviews and networking meetings and prepare for electronic interviewing (e.g., automated voice response and video-conferencing).
4. *Using the Phone Professionally:* Make the phone and voice mail your allies to maximize your chances of reaching the right person at the right time.
5. *Negotiating:* Arrange an offer of employment to your advantage.

II. PLANNING YOUR WORK SEARCH

No marketing campaign is complete without a detailed plan of attack. This really hits home when you start viewing your work search as a personal marketing campaign. In essence, you're trying to promote

Table 12.1 Steps Involved in Planning Your Work Search

KEY STEP	HOW THIS CAN HELP YOU
Make sure that you fully understand what's involved in a targeted work search.	• Improves the odds of covering all your bases • Lays the groundwork for your overall approach
Prepare strategies for each stage of your campaign —in advance.	• Gives you a chance to get orga-nized properly • Forces you to think of contingencies and barriers
Estimate the amount of time you'll spend on each component of your search.	• Allows you to focus your energies • Makes your search more efficient
Anticipate the needs of specific employers.	• Lets you put yourself in their shoes • Helps you position yourself during interviews
Target your messages to match the employer's requirements and style.	• Shows employer you've done your homework • Increases your chances of getting hired

yourself (as a product) to potential employers (your customers). As such, you need to deal with the items in Table 12.1 to increase your odds of succeeding.

Beginning with the Big Picture

Perhaps the best way to approach planning is to start with an overall picture of what's involved. Some questions to ask yourself include:

- How prepared am I to look for work?
- Do I know all the stages involved?
- Am I clear on what I can offer an employer?
- Have I adequately prepared my marketing material (e.g., résumé, cover letter, business cards)?
- Do I have a good idea of what specific employers are looking for?

To help you along your path, I've provided some relevant Internet resources. Here are a couple of informal tests you can take to see where you stand:

- How Prepared Are You? (**www.ventura.com/jsearch/unique/29063/jshome2d.html**). A 24-question quiz that gives you an idea of how ready you are to launch into your search.
- Employment Search Readiness Inventory, CareerWeb (**www.cweb.com/inventory/welcome.html**). This is your opportunity to "discover if you are doing all that you can to find a good job or earn a promotion in your current position." "Employment search readiness" refers to what we should be doing to improve our chances of getting ahead and taking advantage of new opportunities.

Now comes the hard part—putting together a comprehensive marketing plan:

- "Conducting a Successful Job Search," by Taunee Besson (**www.cweb.com/dimensions/Career_Dimensions3.html#Search**). Read about how to prepare your own personal strategy in this article, first published in the *Wall Street Journal: National Business Employment Weekly.*
- Mounting an Effective Job Search (**www.charityvillage.com/charityvillage/job.html**). Great information provided by the Canadian philanthropic association called Charity Village.

- Know Where to Find a Job and How to Get It, Job Coach (**vvv.com/ai/counsel/jc/search.html**). Before you rush out, be prepared. Know everything about the job you're after, tailor your résumé so you make it through the screening process, and get ready for an interview.
- How Do You Rate? CareerOnline (in Australia) (**www.careersonline.com.au/easyway/int/how.html**). Here are some general things an employer might look for in job applicants. Can you match the word with its correct definition?
- You and the Job Market (**www.edu.gov.on.ca/eng/document/brochure/youjob/youjob.html**). Ontario-based quick reference to the job market, with information about the ways that people find work, job market projections and more.

III. STAYING ORGANIZED

It's one thing to make a plan. It's another thing to launch it. And it's something else altogether to keep everything straight. Scheduling meetings, maintaining a record of who said what and following up properly—all this takes time. One of the more useful abilities that you'll need in searching for work is organizing your efforts. (Alright, it also helps if you're good at networking, can write a decent résumé and shower frequently.)

CYBER TIP You can take "proactive steps to your goals and objectives rather than being drawn to different work and learning experiences." Check out Setting Up Your Action Plan from the University of Waterloo's Career Development Manual at **www.adm.uwaterloo.ca/infocecs/CRC/manual/actionplan.html**. Print out the page and write down your *own* action plan!

The Computerized Solution

Organizing means keeping track of everything you do. How many phone calls did you make this week to set up networking meetings? Who did you meet with, and what was said? And where's that darned phone number of the human resources manager who interviewed you last week? Your efforts here produce faster results with less energy squandered.

One way to speed things up is to use your computer and Personal Information Management Software (PIMs). There are all sorts of software programs designed specifically to help you manage your time, schedule your activities and be more productive. They enable you to keep tabs on all your contacts and, in many cases, produce and file professional correspondence.

If you choose to use a PIM, you'll want to decide early on how you intend to use the program. Remember that the two main features of a PIM are *time management* and *record keeping.* If the product you're thinking of buying is weak in either of these, I suggest you shop around.

Hints on Managing Your Time

Time management is all about making the most of whatever time you have. It generally involves some upfront planning, followed by detailed scheduling. This is where the electronic scheduler becomes valuable. You can take your strategy and break it down into an achievable daily routine. For some excellent articles on time management, try:

- "Fifteen Ways to Save Time," by Lucy H. Hedrick. From the Day-Timer® Resource Centre Library (**www.daytimer.com/resource/library/index.html**). Here are just two of the tips that Lucy gives:
  - Do you keep "to do" lists that run on for pages? If you often feel discouraged by what's not crossed off your lists, shorten them. The most effective time managers identify only three top priorities each day. And their sense of achievement is stroked repeatedly when they cross off all three tasks, day after day.
  - There are two reasons why you should group tasks by category (calls, errands, things to do). First, it allows you to focus your efforts and get momentum going. Second, looking at a grouped list of tasks makes it easier to prioritize the important ones first.
- Time Management Skills Quiz (**www.daytimer.com/cgi-bin/quiz.cgi?src=tmq**). Test yourself in terms of the way you control time (or the way it controls you). Again from Day-Timer.
- *Maximizer Internet Newsletter* (**www.maximizer.com**, then click on "Newsletters"). From Maximizer, monthly tips to help you stay on top of your tasks.

- *ActNews Online Newsletter* (**www.actnews.com**). From Symantec Act!, a monthly e-letter on managing time (free trial subscription offered).

Tips on Keeping in Contact

If one side of staying organized is managing your time, the other side is contact management. As you meet more and more people in your hunt for work, you need to remember who's who. That way you can refer to these people later when you absolutely need to. Contact management breaks down into two essential tasks: list creation and record keeping.

List creation is somewhat self-explanatory. It means that every time you plan to meet someone or are referred to someone in your networking, you add that name to your list. With a PIM, it's easy to keep track of hundreds of people. The beauty is that you can also cross-reference people using various criteria and keywords. This can include who referred you to that person, what clubs or organizations they belong to, their title or industry affiliation—you name it.

On the record-keeping side, you'll be most effective if you note the highlights of the transactions you have with each person you meet. This

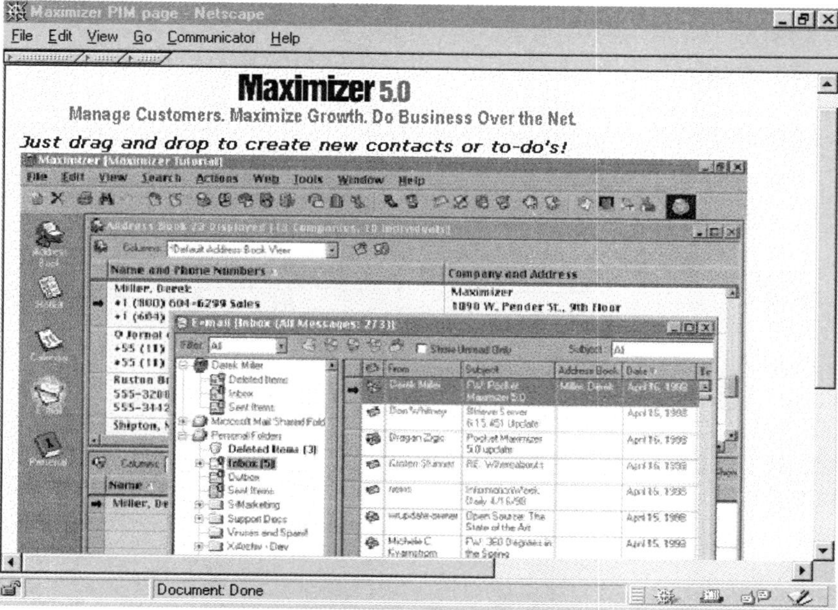

includes when you saw them, what was said, your impressions and thoughts, how you followed up and what's next (e.g., who needs to do what by when). This enables you to keep your marketing campaign going strong. Keep in mind that you'll want to refine your tactics as you go along. You can only keep effective records if you know what's working and what isn't. This will help you make any necessary changes. Of course, you can then record these changes on your electronic calendar!

Some PIM Software to Consider

Personal information managers come in a variety of formats and price ranges. Some can also be obtained online as shareware or freeware. I obviously can't cover every single software package available, but I offer a representative sampling from the more popular programs in Table 12.2. You can learn more about the product and its features at the Web sites I've listed, and even download some free trial versions.

REAL LIFE Don't get sucked into buying bloatware. The PIM you choose should have a good electronic scheduling system and a customizable database. Some PIMs also come with complete word processing and other programs as part of the package—thus, they're bloated. You're better off keeping it simple. Use your existing software (e.g., word processor); otherwise you may spend more than you need to, and the program may take up valuable space on your hard drive.

Table 12.2 Examples of Personal Information Manager Software (and Free Trials)

MANUFACTURER NAME	PRODUCT	WEB SITE
Day-Timers, Inc.	Day-Timer	**www.daytimer.com**
Janna	Contact	**www.janna.com**
MultiActive Software Group	Maximizer Lite	**www.maximizer.com**
Symantec	Act!	**www.symantec.ca**

CYBER TIP You don't have to rush out to your local computer store to get a hold of a decent PIM. If you want some shareware, try **www.shareware.com**. Choose "Selections," then "Business." A list of available PIMs will appear (you can choose IBM compatible or Mac). For those of you who subscribe to a commercial online provider (such as AOL or Prodigy), type in the word "shareware" under keyword, and then navigate to the business software section of your provider and make your selection.

Electronic Organizers

You could always consider a portable database and time manager in the form of an electronic organizer. These calculator-sized wonders are also known as personal digital assistants (PDAs) or digital diaries. They have searchable telephone directories, calendars, schedulers and expense forms. Prices range from $20 all the way up to $500 or more, depending on features and memory capacity.

REAL LIFE To be honest, not everyone is comfortable working with a computer-based PIM or hand-held electronic organizer. These tools can be limiting: if all you need is a person's phone number, you have to pull out your machine, turn it on, go to the address section and look up the name. Plus you always have to update your information to stay current.

With electronic organizers, you definitely get what you pay for. My advice is to try for one with at least half a megabyte of storage (1 meg is even better). I suggest that you spend at least $50 to $100 in order to get the minimum features you require. If you want your organizer to link up with your computer to exchange data (a real time-saver), you may have to spend a little more. See what some of the manufacturers are offering these days, at the following sites:

- Sharp Electronics (**www.sharp-usa.com/main.asp?sect=1&pageid=AE**, or go to **www.sharp-usa.com**, click on "Products," then "Hand Held Devices," then choose from "Wizard Electronic Organizers" or "Mobile Organizer").

- Casio Electronics (**www.casio.com**). Or go directly to the personal digital assistants at **www.casio.com/html/products/digitaldiary.html** and search by product feature.
- 3Com Inc. (**palmpilot.3com.com/home.html**, for information on the Palm Pilot hand-held devices). Or go to the 3Com homepage at **www.3com.com**.
- Franklin Electronic Publishers (**www.franklin.com**). Information on Rolodex products. For a shortcut, try **www.franklin.com/organizers**

CYBER TIP For the ultimate in portability, try the Rolodex "Rex" electronic organizer along with a hand-held computer. Rex actually stores your data and can be used on its own. It can be plugged directly into your laptop, desktop or hand-held computer. For more information, head over to **www.franklin.com/rex.** To see how this can work with a hand-held computer, try the Hewlett Packard site at **www.hp.com/handheld/palmtops.** Note that this option is not advisable for those with pocket-book pains.

IV. THE ART OF INTERVIEWING FOR A JOB

Keeping track of your interviews is all very well and fine, but what about the interview itself? Are there ways to prepare and increase your effectiveness electronically? There certainly are. Quickly think back to your last job interview. (I've blocked most of mine out to protect myself from the emotional trauma.) How'd it go for you? Were you able to answer the interviewer's questions quickly and naturally, or did you sound artificial and over-rehearsed? And what about your level of nervousness—a bit hard to take, *n'est-ce pas?*

Confronting the Dread

Personally, I hate interviews. In fact, I don't know a single (well-adjusted) person who likes them. That excludes, of course, certain interviewers. You know the people I mean. I'm talking here about the type who live to extract pain from their interview subjects. The ones who ask you intrusive, embarrassing—and sometimes illegal—questions. Like the one who asked one of my clients what type of birth control she uses. Or the human resource trainee who made another of my clients wait for two hours in a waiting room, then cancelled and re-scheduled the meeting for later that week, then pulled exactly the same stunt again.

I know, I know...horror stories abound when it comes to hiring time. Is it any wonder then that most people get completely wound up about this process? I had one client who would stay up the entire night before every job interview. Afterward he'd head back home and sleep for 12 hours straight. Another one couldn't walk into an employer's office without being physically ill. Fortunately, he had the good graces to ask for directions to the washroom before doing anything else.

Admit it. Going for a formal job interview is one of the scariest, most nerve-wracking things that you can do. Unfortunately, for most of us it's still a necessary part of obtaining work. Here's something that I know will be of great consolation to you: most of the time, the person who interviews you also tends to experience some discomfort. The big difference between you and those people? If the interviewers blow it, *they* don't go away without a job. You do.

REAL LIFE Remember that there are two essential types of interviewing. The first kind is the *networking* interview (see Chapter 9). The goal here is to build contacts and meet informally with potential hiring managers. The second—and more feared kind—is the formal job interview. It's typically a face-to-face meeting with key people from the organization you're hoping to work for. Keep this in mind: while the main goal of your résumé was to obtain the interview, the primary purpose of the formal interview is to secure an offer of employment.

Beating the Odds

You can greatly improve your odds for success in an interview, be it informal or formal, by preparing thoroughly. The key is to practice the four R's: 1) Reviewing your personal attributes, 2) Researching the employer, 3) Rehearsing your answers, and 4) Realizing that things have changed.

1. *Reviewing.* You can start by reviewing the material you compiled earlier in Chapters 3 through 5. Go over your strengths and accomplishments. Make sure that you can answer typical questions such as "What are your greatest assets?" and "What achievements are you most proud of?" Know your strengths, weaknesses and accomplishments down pat. You're bound to be asked about them during the interview.
2. *Researching.* Then picture your next interview. What will happen when the interviewer says to you, "Tell me what you know about our company." Will you smile weakly and reply, "Gee, I was hoping you could tell me that." Or will you reel off an impressive response, citing the company's products and services, market niche and most recent quarterly results. Research provides you with the power to do this. Go back and review the techniques shown in Chapter 8.
3. *Rehearsing the wired way.* With regard to the actual interview itself, there is a ton of advice available online. So much so, in fact, that it can be overwhelming. Thankfully a fellow Canadian has taken the time to catalogue this information for us. Gary Will, author of *How to Prepare for an Employment Interview,* created the Archeus Web site at **www.golden.net~archeus/intres.htm**. Once there, you can choose from over 50 articles on interviewing, as well as sample chapters from Gary's book. Here is some of what you'll find at the Archeus Web site:
   - If you'd like to know about the latest twists in behavioural interviewing, surf on over to **careers.theglobeandmail.com**, then "Articles of Interest," then "Interview Assistant," then "Alternative Interview Methods."
   - How about answers to the toughest questions you may get asked? They're at **www.adm.uwaterloo.ca/infocecs/CRC/manual/jobwork**.
   - What questions should you ask of the interviewer? At **www.golden.net/~archeus/int-ch14.htm**, Gary recommends that you prepare a list of relevant questions for the employer. If you *don't* have any questions, the interviewer will likely be left with one or more of these impressions of you:
     – You're not really all that interested in this position or this organization.
     – You're so lazy that you couldn't be bothered to put any thought into preparing.

– You're so desperate that you'll go anywhere and talk to anyone to get any kind of job.

REAL LIFE Did you know that a job interview is a two-way street? It may not always seem that way, but it is a chance for you and the employer to get to know each other and to assess if this position and firm are a good fit. Don't be afraid to ask questions about the company's future plans, its corporate culture and what kind of person it's looking for.

Other rehearsing sites to visit as you prepare for your interview include:

- The Hot Seat (**www.kaplan.com:8000/miniapps/hotseat/index.html**). Can you survive the mock interview and land the job? Brave the interviewers' questions and choose the responses!
- Interview Preparation Advice, Hyatt Career Centre at Brandeis University (**www.brandeis.edu/hiatt/web_data/hiatt_interviewing.html**). Your preparation is vital in conveying a positive and polished image and having a productive and successful interview.
- Top 50 Questions and More (**www.student-services.ubc.ca/careers/info/inview1.htm**). The Career Centre at the University of British Columbia brings you this excellent pre-interview advice.

4. *Realizing that things have changed.* Quick, can you name the two newest electronic recruitment techniques? If you answered "cyber-brutality" or "sensory deprivation," you'd be close. I'm thinking more along the lines of *automated voice response* and *video-conferencing.* Never heard of them? Don't fret. You'll likely hear more about them faster than you can say, "What the heck happened to a simple face-to-face interview?" Read on.

Automated Voice Response (AVR) You think that interviews are already dehumanizing? Wait until you remove the human at the other end. That's what AVR (also known as interactive voice response, or IVR), is all about. Basically you have your screening interview with an answering machine. Oh sure, it's a sophisticated answering machine.

Loaded to the gills with PBX, LAN connections and other such techno-junk. The bottom line is still the same: you are being reduced to sound bytes on a recorded message.

If it's so de-personalized, why are more and more Canadian companies experimenting with it? According to Periphonics (**www.peri.com**), a manufacturer of such systems, there are many benefits for the employer. These include reduced costs, fewer errors in data capture and greater efficiency.

One Canadian supplier of AVR is Compu-Skren (**www.compuskren.com**). It calls its system ASIST (Automated Screening Interview Selection Technique) and describes it as "a leading edge employment screening process which uses a 1-800/888 custom designed automated interview that an applicant can easily access from their home telephone." In case you hadn't already noticed, I find this stuff kind of scary. It doesn't make me any more comfortable to read that "the strategy is to use trained interviewers who compile and assess applicant data to determine suitability using custom designed automated telephone screening interviews, follow-up telephone behavioural interviews, work history confirmations and thorough background and reference checks"—all in less than 30 minutes!

You can find out more about AVR by going to:

- **www.compuskren.com/pinnacle.html**. A newsletter from Compu-Skren describing how their customers (such as Home Hardware and Sobeys) are using the system.
- **www.nortak.com**, then "Index," "Client Projects," and "Integrated Voice Response" to see what Nortak is doing with Air Canada, the TD Bank and others.
- **www.peri.com/demo/demo.html**. Online demonstrations of how the system works. Call their toll-free numbers to try them for yourself.

Video-Conferenced Interviews Just to show you how radically things are changing, let me tell you a little story about a recent client in his early 50s (we'll call him Jim). I was at my office one morning in Toronto when Jim called me up excitedly. He'd sent his résumé and cover letter via e-mail to a job posting he'd seen on his professional association's Web site. Boy was Jim pumped, because the firm got back to him the very next day (via e-mail, of course), with a positive response. The reply asked him to e-mail back some additional credentials and information so that they could proceed to the next step.

Sure enough, he did so and the company replied—by phone this time—the next day. "We'd like you to meet with our six board members out here in Calgary," the caller said. "Could we schedule something for later this week?" Jim was especially thrilled about this because he had family in Calgary, and he agreed to meet with them at end of the week (this being a Wednesday). Then off he zoomed back home to start packing for this exciting and important trip.

That evening, he received another dispatch from the Alberta firm. It read something like this: "We're delighted that you've agreed to meet with us on Friday in Calgary. Could you please arrive 15 minutes early at the video-conference studio in Toronto to give the technicians time to prepare for our meeting?"

The next morning Jim—in a somewhat frantic state—gave me a call. "They want me to do a video interview," he blurted out. "What the hell is that? And why won't they let me fly out and visit my parents in Calgary and collect my bonus miles?"

CYBER TIP Make sure that you're dealing with the right kind of video interview here. In some cases, it simply means that an employer wants you to make a videotape of yourself and send it in for assessment. A great example of this is at SuperCamps recruiting site (**www.supercamp.com/staffing/videointerview.htm**). *Video-conferencing*, however, is interactive, real-time visual communication, much like being on a two-way TV.

This Ain't Your Dad's Oldsmobile Welcome to the future of interviewing. The company in Alberta decided that it would save the costs of Jim's transportation and accommodation by not flying him out west. Instead, it hooked him up with a private video-conference facility in an office building not far from his home. This is a growing practice, especially with large Canadian and multinational firms.

So how do you prepare for a video-conferenced interview, especially if you're not sure what it is (and believe me, you're not alone here). You could start by learning more about the process itself. Here are some sites to visit:

- The Video-Conference Service at University of Western Ontario's Student Services Centre (**cafe.sdc.uwo.ca/low/video.html**). These folks are Canadian pioneers in the field of interviewing online. They even have "virtual career days."

- Glossary of Video-Conferencing Terms (**www.camosun.bc.ca/~avserv/technote/glossary.htm**). Developed by the folks at Camosun College in B.C.
- Practicing Your Video-Conference Techniques, Metamorphcomm (**www.metamorphcomm.com**). This is a media training company out of New York that helps you develop your video presence. Go to **www.metamorphcomm.com/videop.htm** for the types of things you need to practice; **www.metamorphcomm.com/qa.htm** is where you can ask questions; and **www.metamorphcomm.com/ppasssv.htm** is the Presenter's Personal Assessment and Survey, which you can do yourself.
- International Teleconferencing Association (**www.itca.org**). Everything you wanted to know about teleconferencing but were afraid to ask.

CYBER TIP A simple way to practice your video interview skills is to get hold of any old video camera and tape yourself in a mock interview. Granted, it works best if you have someone to read out questions and respond to your answers. If you have to do it solo, pretend that you are talking to a real person. You can then review the tape and critique your performance. Watch for your posture, eye contact, facial expressions, seating position, where your hands are and professionalism of dress. Also, check to see that you smile occasionally. If video is a problem, try at least for some audio feedback. Even an old tape recorder can be of assistance in catching your "ums" and "ehs."

Following Up After the Interview

Your quest for work doesn't end after the interview. Immediately after your meeting, it's time to update your records. Go back to your PIM and enter the details. What were the important points? Does it look like a good prospect? Make sure that you schedule in any follow-up activities. These include things such as sending a thank-you note to the people who interviewed you and providing any other material or information that you were asked for.

Always try to send that thank-you note within two business days of the interview. Mention how delighted you were to meet the interviewer. Try to get a word in about how your particular skills fit the requirements of the job. If you're rushed, try faxing or e-mailing the note. You can even send an electronic greeting card, such as the ones at **www.ivillage.com/postcards/cat_busi.html**. But try to send a hard copy—it may have more impact.

V. USING THE PHONE AND VOICE MAIL PROFESSIONALLY

Let's move on to two things that are so basic they are often overlooked as powerful work-search tools: the telephone and the answering service. We all have a phone, and is there anyone left who hasn't had the pleasure of communicating with an automated answering service? The question is whether you have ever been trained to use them as part of your work search.

If You Think You're Already a Pro, Take This Little Quiz

I realize that basic telephones and answering services are not exactly leading-edge technology anymore. If you assume that you're an expert, though, you could be in for some nasty surprises. Here are a few deceptively simple questions to see what you know:

1. When are the two best times during the day to make direct contact with a potential employer?
2. What are three ways to reduce your fear of cold-calling?
3. How many calls does it take, on average, to contact the person you've targeted?
4. What is the best method of minimizing that ever-so-annoying telephone tag?

Phone Tips for the Well Prepared

As you read on, you'll find the answers to these questions. Let's begin, though, by tackling some of the common perils of using the phone as part of your work search.

How about using the phone to ask complete strangers for a job? If you actually enjoy this sort of thing, you're in the minority. Most people hate phone prospecting as much as they do the interview itself. Gary Ames recognizes this fact. He is a licensed psychologist and director of consulting with the R.L. Stevens Career Development firm in the U.S. Gary wrote a useful article called Overcoming Phone-A-Phobia and posted it on the Web (**crm21.com/ames2.html**). Here's how it starts:

"Your heart is pounding, the phone seems to weigh 200 pounds, your palms are sweaty as you grip the phone, your mind is reeling with vague catastrophic expectations as you ask to speak with an executive about a job prospect. These are but some of the symptoms of phone-a-phobia."

Gary explains that many people are terrified by the idea of calling strangers to sell themselves and that most everyone has some phone-a-phobia. As a result, "they procrastinate and decide to do other things, even when they know that a phone call would aid their job campaign."

Two sound pieces of advice from the article are 1) work with a career counsellor to overcome this aversion, and 2) try some "desensitization exercises" by making some safe calls first to people who know you and understand your situation.

REAL LIFE "The following is a pre-recorded message. Phone techniques and voice mail can make or break your campaign. The way we speak and the messages we leave count for a great deal when employers form their impressions of you. Please press the star key to exit and return to the book. Have a pleasant day." Click.

Preparing Professionally Why stumble through another conversation with someone who can hire you when there are simple steps that you can take to prepare yourself? It's not like you get a whole lot of opportunities to make a solid first impression. Plus it doesn't take an extensive amount of time to get ready.

One article that's out there on the Web delves into the ways that you can sound your best each time you pick up the phone. Entitled "Telephone Tips," it's offered by the All Business Network at **www.all-biz.com/26.html**. These are some of the things that these folks suggest you do before making an important call:

- Plan what you are going to say.
- Set clear objectives of what you want to accomplish.
- Write out an actual script, including the points you want to make and potential responses from the person you're contacting.
- Rehearse until you feel comfortable.

Voice Mail and Answering Services

I can barely remember the last time I called someone for business purposes and actually connected to a live person. I'm so used to speaking to some sort of answering service that I actually get flustered when a human being picks up the line.

Today the majority of businesses and organizations use automated answering systems. These range from machines to voice mail to live answering services. Sooner or later, you're going to encounter one when trying to get hold of a potential employer or networking contact. It can either further your cause or frustrate you immeasurably.

Your objective, as always, is to be professional yet natural. That way you convey to potential employers the image that they're looking for, while still being yourself. That article on telephone tips I mentioned recommends that whenever you leave a message, you should remember to cover the four Ws: Who is calling, Why you called, What you'd like the receiver to do and When you're available to receive a return call. A specific request with detailed information increases your chances of a reply.

Another good piece of advice comes from the folks at Mind Tools (**www.mindtools.com/phoneskl.html**). They suggest that if you dial an answering service and you're not prepared for it, hang up and call back. "When you get taken by surprise, you can sound stilted and off-balance. It is much better to hang up, prepare a message, and then deliver it smoothly."

Answering the Call *You* need an answering service, too. Wouldn't you kick yourself if you were out at a networking session and the big call came but no one was home to pick it up? Or what if your seven-year-old answered and forgot to take a message? Why take that risk? (And while you're out at those networking sessions, don't forget to check frequently for messages!)

To avoid telephone tag—that ridiculous game of never calling at the right time—the Telephone Tips article suggests that the outgoing message on your answering machine asks callers to leave you answers to those four Ws, too. So your message should ask callers to leave a brief message stating who they are, why they're calling, what they want you to do, and when you can reach them.

Fortunately, there's no need to plunk a lot of money on an answering machine with all the bells and whistles. You can call your local phone company to see if it offers an automated answering service. It doesn't cost a lot (between $5 and $10 a month, depending on where you live and the features you order). As a bonus, it takes messages while you're talking on the same line, so the caller never gets a busy signal. Plus the caller can leave a reasonably long message without getting cut off.

If you want to take this one step further, ask your phone company for the "distinctive ring" service, too. This provides you with a second phone number for use on your home line. Why bother? Let's say that you use this unique phone number on your résumé and business card. Now when your phone rings with the distinctive ring, you know it's related to your work search. You can answer in a professional manner or instruct others in your home to let it ring and bounce over to your answering service, if so desired.

REAL LIFE When you're looking for work, everything counts. With that in mind, make sure that you return all calls promptly. When an employer is ready to hire, that's when it wants to hear from you. Not two days later.

Now that I've reminded you of how important the telephone and answering systems are to your work search, here are the answers to those "simple" phone questions I asked you at the beginning of this section:

1. Try calling your targeted employers before 8:30 a.m. and after 5:15 p.m. when calls may not be screened by assistants and managers tend to be more reachable. This doesn't mean that you shouldn't call during working hours. It just increases your chances of reaching your target directly.

2. To reduce your nervousness, practice on friends and family first. Rehearse until you're comfortable and set clear objectives before you dial that phone.
3. On average it takes three calls to make contact, so be persistent.
4. Reduce telephone tag by leaving a simple, coherent message, indicating the best times you can be contacted.

VI. NEGOTIATING AN OFFER

The other big skill that you'll use toward the end of your search is negotiating. Once you're presented with an offer of employment, you're expected to respond to the employer in one of three ways:

- An unconditional, absolute acceptance of the offer as it stands.
- A counter-offer, when you add or change things and re-present it to the employer.
- A flat-out "Thanks, but no thanks."

Why Negotiating Is Important

Many people are reluctant to ask for anything more than what is in the original offer. Given the uncertainties of our economic climate, this is understandable. One thing to be aware of is that employers (or companies who hire employees and consultants on contract) often use negotiating as a final test of your self-marketing abilities. They figure that if you can't stand up for yourself at this stage, maybe you'll be prone to backing down on the job.

Try not to misconstrue my message here. I'm not recommending that you storm in and make unreasonable demands. Instead, think of it as a give-and-take process. You're looking for certain concrete elements and the employer has its own position to maintain. Striking a happy balance is usually considered to be the right approach.

Tips on Negotiating

To negotiate from a position of power, it's important that you know exactly what you're willing to settle for *before* the offer comes in, and what perks or benefits you may substitute for a lower salary. Keep in mind that it's crucial to be flexible. Some useful articles on negotiating can be found online, including:

- Mutual Gains Negotiating (**www2.the-wire.com/dweiss/negotiat.html**)
- Basic Negotiating (**www.escape.ca/~rbacal/neg.htm**)
- Negotiating in a Nutshell (**strategis.ic.gc.ca/ssg/mi04745e.html**)
- Evaluating an Offer (**www.adm.uwaterloo.ca/infocecs/crc/manual/workoffers.html**).

It's Not Just about Salary Some people get completely stuck on the issue of salary, as if it were the only component of the job offer. Be careful of this trap. There are all sorts of other ingredients to consider when haggling over an employment offer, such as:

- benefits, sick leave and vacation allowances;
- training and education expenses;
- travel (frequency and duration, plus expense coverage);
- performance evaluation (how often, on what basis will you be measured, minimum and maximum pay increases);
- other perks that may be appropriate for someone at your level; and
- compensation package (base salary, bonus or incentive plans, flat salary versus commission on sales, stock purchase plan, etc.).

Check Your Assumptions Here is some additional advice for when the offer actually comes in. It suggests that you ask yourself several key questions before deciding whether to accept a job.

- Is the offer solid? Sometimes it's easy to look at any phone call as a positive sign. Be sure the offer you're getting is real and that the person is not just saying, "You're still in the running." If possible, get the offer in writing.
- Does the job fit into your long-term career plans? You may not want to accept something completely unrelated to the field that interests you most. On the other hand, any work can be good work if it enables you to move gradually toward your real goals.

Tips for Students and Recent Graduates When I speak to students, I find a significant polarization in their attitudes to negotiating. At one extreme, there are people who believe you might as well ask for the world. Sometimes they go in and make preposterous requests that end up blowing them out of the running. At the other end of the

REAL LIFE The best time to negotiate is shortly after a formal offer has been presented to you, but *before* you accept the position. Once the employer gives you an offer, its interest in you is confirmed. If you start negotiating too early, you might scare off the employer. After accepting the offer, you're no longer negotiating—you're asking for a raise.

spectrum are those who take whatever is handed to them. No matter how frugal or basic the offer is, they say, "Yes, thanks. When do I start?"

I propose an approach somewhere between the two extremes. This is illustrated well in the words of author Stephen Kaplan, past president of the Canadian Association of Career Educators and Employers. He states that "While it is true that they have less negotiating power in today's market, students, while basking in the ecstasy of getting a job, should not forget that one of the most crucial components of launching a successful career is the art of negotiation."

Kaplan goes on to say that students often believe that "negotiating the terms of an employment contract are the sole domain of the agents' high draft picks of professional sports teams—nothing could be further from reality. It is the responsibility of every employee and employer to ensure that every aspect of the job and the expectations of both parties are clearly understood."

Make It a Win-Win Situation

Whether you're a student or the president of a billion dollar company, the art of negotiating is all about leaving both sides relatively content. I use the word *relatively* because neither side gets exactly what it wants. Note that the word *content* also snuck its way in, indicating that there is some degree of satisfaction on both sides.

Do not be afraid to leave something on the table. This means that you may have to give up something you want a little bit to get something you really want a lot. On the other hand, both you and the employer lose if you accept a lowball offer. You will not be a happy employee and odds

CYBER TIP Be as informed as possible before you start your negotiations. On the salary side, you can get some rudimentary information by typing in the words "salary survey" (quotes included) in the AltaVista Canada search engine (**www.altavistacanada.com**). Look for something in your industry or profession. To refine your search, add a key word such as "marketing," and see what comes up. Best of all, meet with people in the field to find out about compensation standards.

are that you will be constantly looking for something better. This could easily affect your performance.

Remember that after all the bargaining is over, you have to work together with your new boss. So while you may not get the new Porsche and the condo in Spain you'd asked for as part of the package, take comfort in knowing that your new employer had to pay you more than the $1.70 an hour that it had hoped to get away with.

VII. WIRED WRAP-UP

Baseball coach Casey Stengel is famous for his quote, "It ain't over 'til it's over." Searching for work is a lot like that. There are so many tasks involved that it can become a full-time job in itself. Each requires planning, execution and follow-up. And until you've negotiated and accepted a firm offer of employment, it ain't over!

We've now looked at the key steps you have to go through to get to that final stage. If you've been through a search before, you know how exhausting all of this can be. The process is wide-ranging. From self-assessment to writing your résumé to interviewing and negotiating an offer—a full-out job search takes an incredible amount of energy and a great deal of your time.

On a positive note, you can use a variety of electronic tools to help you get ready and stay on top of things. Web sites with advice, discussion forums, PIM software, electronic diaries and video cameras can all give you an edge. And in today's employment market, you want every advantage you can get!

Points to Remember

- Assess yourself honestly when it comes to those five critical competencies involved in honing your work-search skills. That way you can fill any gaps by upgrading your skills.
- Planning is the basis of success for your marketing campaign. A solid plan covers the who's, where's, how's and when's of your approach.
- Staying organized undoubtedly increases the effectiveness of your marketing campaign. It allows you to keep on target and track your success.
- Interviewing well can make the difference between securing an offer and going home empty-handed. Remember to practice the four R's: Review, Research, Rehearse and Realize that things have changed.
- Using the phone and voice mail professionally increases your chances of connecting with decision makers and making a positive impression.
- Negotiating is a powerful skill that can help you get what you want, while keeping the employer happy.

CHAPTER 13 Get Wired, Not Mired

I've certainly thrown a lot of stuff at you, haven't I? From self-exploration to negotiating your employment contract, we've covered a lot of wired ground. For those of you who are just becoming cyber-literate, it's easy to feel overwhelmed by all this technology. Even veteran technocrats can get mired in all the new resources—and the many choices they bring.

In this final chapter, I hope to encourage you to use technology in ways that are meaningful for you. Such as keeping up to date on changes to our economy and the nature of work. Or understanding the latest recruiting techniques and Internet tools. I never claimed it would be easy. I did state up front, however, that by sticking to it, you can create a competitive advantage for yourself. After all, that's the bottom line when it comes to finding and keeping the work and lifestyle that you really want.

I figure that the best way to bring this home is to finish off with some tips on covering your bases. That's why the first part of this chapter is devoted to anticipating the future. Looking at the changing world of work, spotting recruiting trends and staying on top of technology, for example. Then it's back to the present, and how best to succeed in the employment you've secured for yourself. Finally, I'll mention some ways to stay connected and exchange your ideas online.

I. EMPLOYMENT TRENDS

Even as I write this edition of *Get Wired, You're Hired,* the world of work continues to change. The Canadian economy is in flux, prodded by such things as the "Asian Flu," the "Russian Bear"and the resurgent issue of separation. New jobs are being created and old ones are being re-engineered. Still, it is not at all easy to secure "good" employment, particularly in traditional or shrinking industries. And through it all, contingency hiring has proliferated. Outsourcing and contract hiring are becoming more and more the norm, particularly in the high tech sectors.

Outsourcing and Self-Employment Are on the Rise

We can expect this trend to continue. Many companies are expanding and re-hiring. However, they are reluctant to over-staff and get caught in the cycle of recession and lay-offs that ran rampant in the early 1990s. Hence the shift to outsourcing—but not in all cases, by any means. A growing number of firms are relying on a core group of "permanent" employees to provide continuity and expertise as the economy dances its unpredictable rhythms.

Self-employment, meanwhile, is steadily creeping ahead. By the year 2000, it is predicted that close to 20 percent of the Canadian workforce will be working for themselves. Witness the phenomenal rise in home-based businesses and consultants registered as sole proprietors.

Staying Ahead of the Trends Who benefits from reading what the experts say about employment trends? Only those who are trying to match their skills and experience with the changing needs of employers (in other words, everyone!). So where can you go for predictions on the changing nature of work? Online, of course.

- Canadian Workplace Research Network (**www.cwrn-rcrmt.org/eng/cwrnet_e.html**). This site is dedicated to fostering "research on workplace change and innovation" and promoting links among researchers, practitioners and policy makers in industry, labour and government. High-level stuff, but there are some good discussion papers here.
- Workplace Innovations (**labour.hrdc-drhc.gc.ca/wip**). Your source for "information on innovative workplace practices produced by the Canadian Workplace Information Directorate." Users can share and exchange work-related information, practices and interests.

- The Information Highway Workplace Issues: Challenges and Opportunities (**www.reflection.gc.ca/doc/e/foreward.html**). The final report of the Collective Reflection on the Changing Workplace offers "an opportunity to initiate broad dialogue on the nature of changes in the workplace, and what kind of workplace we want in the future."
- Brave New Work World (**www.newwork.com**). A terrific source for U.S. and worldwide updates on how the nature of work is shifting. As the author says, "the historic link between academic credentials and economic security has been broken...Conventional educational institutions have lost their monopoly. We're watching the revolution, and we report on it here."

II. RECRUITING IN THE FUTURE

Several times in this book I've used the terms *scanning*, *tracking* and *keyword résumés*. These are the watchwords for the next few years, as more and more companies turn to electronic recruiting. No, this doesn't mean the end of face-to-face encounters with human resource folks. But it does mean a rise in the use of automated voice response for screening, and video sessions for interviews (as discussed in Chapter 12).

The Further Electronification of Recruiting If you think we've seen the peak, guess again. Look out for the following advancements in online recruiting:

- *More job postings on company Web sites.* There is a phenomenon on the Net known as "disintermediation." Simply stated, this means that companies are going straight to consumers (or potential employees), rather than using intermediaries. The same thing is happening with job postings. The idea is that companies can save money by listing available positions without having to pay for as many advertisements in newspapers or job banks. I predict that this practice will grow, but don't expect a quick demise for other forms of classified advertising.
- *Consolidation of Job and Résumé Banks.* As I stated back in Chapter 10, there are hundreds of Canadian job and résumé banks, with thousands more in the U.S. How on earth can all these separate sites survive? The answer, of course, is that they can't. History shows that new industries and services (such as job banks, for instance), start out with many different competitors. Ultimately, there will be

mergers and the strongest shall survive. That's good news for job seekers, as the victorious sites will be better organized and flush with posted vacancies. Of course, you may be paying higher fees...

- *Intelligent search agents.* Touted as the next generation in technology, intelligent agents are coming close to reality. Picture this. An employer is looking for a new hire with the following qualifications:
  - at least five years experience in management,
  - minimum of seven years as a non-manager,
  - a three-year degree or diploma in a specific field,
  - computer and Internet literacy,
  - the ability to make group presentations and write formal reports.

Now picture the employer inputting these qualifications into a piece of software called a search agent. The search agent surfs the Internet for résumés that match these criteria and delivers them right to the employer's desktop. Sound farfetched? I'd review Chapters 6 and 7 if I were you, to be on the safe side.

Other sites to visit if you want to keep track of recruiting methods:

- Electronic Recruiting News (**www.interbiznet.com/hrstart.html**)
- ResTrac Systems (**www.restrac.com**)

III. THE NET GROWS UP

The pace of transformation on the Internet is expected to accelerate, not slow down. What are some of the implications for work seekers? First, employers are demanding greater levels of computer and Net literacy from their employees when it comes to hiring time. Second, even established jobs and so-called "manual labour" are being integrated with computers. For example, a forklift driver may now have to use—or at least be comfortable with—scheduling and space management software for maximum efficiency. Third, the Internet plays a growing part in keeping us informed and connected.

Faster Connections

One of the major complaints of Netizens is that the Internet has always been, and still is too slow. With increased traffic, plus extended use of graphics, streaming video and sound bytes, bandwidth and speed have become major issues. You might want to go back to Chapter 2 and review some of the ways of connecting to the Internet—there are some sophisticated alternatives already on the market.

- *Speedier modems.* At the time of writing, almost every computer comes with a 56.6 kbps modem. Keep an eye out for some radical changes in this area as manufacturers vie for your dollars.
- *Integrated Services Digital Network (ISDN).* Those transmission speeds of 64 to 128 kbps are estimated to increase as time goes on, while prices begin to decline.
- *Asymmetric Digital Subscriber Line (ADSL).* Transmits data 50 times faster than a standard 28.8 kbps modem. Needs a special modem, which will probably be supplied free in the future.
- *Satellite.* The high price of this way of transferring data from satellite transmission to a modem might come down some time soon.
- *Cable.* The dedicated connection offered by cable companies is likely to increase from the current maximum speed of 500 kbps, while access to this service spreads across Canada and prices come down to compete directly against phone-line ISP's.
- *Your wall socket, and other strange ideas.* It seems like everyone has a concept for speedier Net access. One version will come through your standard electrical outlet. Another will use existing phone lines, but will blow the socks off whatever you're using today (and still allow you to receive calls or send faxes while surfing).

Lower Rates, More Fees for Service

Another thing we're seeing is a levelling-off of Internet access rates. That's because the larger companies such as Bell Canada's Sympatico, Sprint, AT&T, PSINet and Netcom have helped turn the service into a commodity, while many of the "mom and pop" service providers have merged or folded up. Sure, there will always be room for local ISPs, but the consolidation trend will probably continue. Other things to watch for include:

- *Cheaper flat-rate plans.* More Internet providers (both ISPs and commercial online providers) are lowering their monthly fees and providing unlimited use of the Net for a flat monthly fee ranging from $20 to $25.
- *More choice of plans.* The ISPs recognize that not everyone needs unlimited access to the Net. More are offering tiered service, at 5

hours a month, 20 hours, 40 hours, etc. This means you pay less and use only what you need.

- *More fee-based services.* Until recently, most of the stuff out there in cyberland has been free. Now banks, credit card companies and others are providing relatively secure financial transactions online (can you say "secure socket layer protection"? I knew you could!). You can expect to start paying for everything from information downloads to résumé critiques. The positive side is that the quality and usefulness of information could increase, as should the ease of retrieving what you really need. Will that be cash, or digi-charge?

Increasing Sophistication, But More User-Friendly Services

Back when I started writing the first edition of this book, all you needed to surf the Net was Netscape version 2.0 and a 14.4 kbps modem. Admittedly, it was slower than molasses in July. But at least you could turn off the graphics and scoot along merrily. Now many sites won't even load up for you unless your browser can handle frames, Java, HTML 3 or 4 and inline pictures. Look what's going on.

- *Frames.* Web sites are often subdivided into separate areas (frames) on the same page. Each frame has its own URL. Your browser must support frames, although some sites still provide a version for browsers that can't (for now).
- *Java.* The hot new programming language that just may revolutionize computing. Right now you can use it to put animated graphics on your Web site. Someday it just may become the biggest competitor to Microsoft's operating system. Personally, I find it brings my old laptop to a near standstill, and I could do without the shimmering images and fancy features.
- *Virtual Reality Modelling Language (VRML).* The ticket to 3-D Web sites. Watch for increased interactivity, such as realistic job-interview practice sessions, for example.
- *Net Telephony.* How about free phone calls to virtually anywhere in the world? That's the promise of Net telephony. It enables you to hold real-time voice conversations with people all around the globe—without incurring long-distance charges. Both you and the person (or people) you are talking to must have compatible telephony software

and an Internet connection. (Try **www.cadvision.com**, then "Help," then "Internet Phone" for more details.)

- *Text-to-Speech.* Tired of having to boot up your computer and log into your ISP just to get your e-mail? It will soon be common to pick up your e-mail messages by phone. Thanks to text-conversion software, words and phrases can be converted into more "natural" conversation.

Other Stuff to Watch For

There are a few more interesting developments that you should know about, if you want to consider yourself truly Net literate. Of course, you can still get by with the basics, but remember—there are varying degrees of cyber-experience, and you'll need to use the following if you want to be more advanced.

Push Versus Pull Most surfing is done these days by digging into the Web and "pulling out" the information you need. That's changing rapidly with the advent of "push" technology. A good case in point is the Canadian version of PointCast (**www.pointcast.com/download/canada.html**). It's a free software program that you can personalize in terms of your information preferences. For instance, you can select business news, information on specific industries and companies, plus late-breaking news. The program hooks up through your Internet service for periodic updates. All you have to do is check your screen from time to time to read the latest headlines in your area(s) of interest. A neat service, although it kind of gets in your face if you're expecting a nice, calm little screensaver.

Personalization It used to be that the search engines were impersonal, despite their funky names like Yahoo! and DejaNews. Now you can look forward to more sites like "My Yahoo!" (**my.yahoo.com**) and "My DejaNews" (**www.dejanews.com/rg_reg.xp**). Site designers are taking interactivity a step further. They're allowing you to personalize their Web site to suit your tastes. Much like we saw with PointCast above, the information is then "pushed" out to you on an ongoing basis.

Intranets and Extranets Many companies are installing private Net-like systems that allow employees to share information online. These so-called Intranets are the newest wave in data exchange. They work much like the Internet; however, people outside the company cannot access the information. Be prepared to use an Intranet for internal e-mail, company announcements, group scheduling and project management at your new job.

The flipside of this particular coin is the Extranet. Here you have companies sharing critical data with key suppliers. It's like an Intranet except that it's only accessible to a company's major clients. Usually Intranets and Extranets are protected by things called firewalls and passwords. Want some good news? *If you can surf the Internet, you can pretty well surf the Intra and Extra versions too.* It's easy to transfer those skills. In fact, I advise my clients to brag about it on their résumé. It's a skill many employers are looking for.

There are many sites that provide you with regular updates on where the Internet is headed, and the new components that are constantly being churned out. Here are but a few:

- The Financial Post Technology section (**www.canoe.ca/fptechnology/home.html**) for the Canadian viewpoint.
- The Convergence Magazine, from Toronto Star (**www.theconvergence.com**).
- ZDNet Internet User (**www.zdnet.com/products/internetuser.html**) for a U.S. perspective.
- The Berst Alert at Anchor Desk (**www.zdnet.com/anchordesk**, then subscribe for free at the "E-mail Alert" icon) from a guy who shoots from the hip.

IV. HERE'S TO A NEW BEGINNING

And so we draw to a close. I thought long and hard about how to conclude this guide. After all, how can I reach an end-point when everything I'm writing about is in the midst of rapid change?

So I looked at the notes I prepared when I was putting my first draft together. I was searching for key ideas or some overriding theme. My goals were simple enough: to leave you with a sense that you've taken the first steps in a very exciting journey, and also to remind you that this journey has, in some ways, only just begun.

Avoiding Obsolescence Then it hit me. This book is all about helping you move from the past into the present—and on to the future.

It focuses on some of the cutting-edge Internet applications with regard to career-management and the work search. The irony of it all is this: now that you have the book in your hand, some of the material is already outdated.

Talk about revolutionary change. As you read these words, there are new Web sites being added, while some old ones are gone or have moved to a new location. Maybe "the next big thing" is already lurking on the horizon. That's how quickly things are moving. It would be a shame for me to leave you hanging without a bridge to the future.

That's when it all came together. I thought to myself, "What better way to keep you apprised of online happenings than by doing it online?" Seems like a logical conclusion. That's why I'm inviting you to visit the new *Get Wired, Your Hired* Web site at **www.wiredhired.com**. Here are some of the things that you'll find there:

- *Updated Internet resources.* This covers changes to the Web sites and Usenet newsgroups that you've found throughout this book.
- *Discussion groups.* A place where you can exchange your ideas and experiences online with other Canadian work searchers.
- *Answers.* You'll find the answers to your most Frequently Asked Questions.
- *Resource guides.* You can link to the best resources for job hunting, self-employment, career search and self-exploration and more.

Visit **www.wiredhired.com** regularly to take full advantage of this book!

V. WIRED WRAP-UP AND CONCLUSION

As we approach the year 2000, change is still the one thing that we can count on. In fact, the pace is speeding up, and competition is intensifying at every turn. Not a very comforting thought, if you were hoping for security and predictability. But if you can accept this as the premise for planning your career from now on, you may have already won the toughest battle of all—adapting your way of thinking to the new realities.

Every week I work with people who have just been thrust out into the new world of work. Many of these were loyal, hard-working team players in jobs where they were competent, established and comfortable. Suddenly they've been tossed into the maelstrom.

Grasping the New Rules

On the whole, the folks who end up succeeding are those who try to understand the rules of the new game. They ask questions like, "I'm more comfortable being part of a larger organization, but I've heard consulting can be a good route. Is this true?" or "I realize now that my skills are not very current. Are there any retraining programs and grants so I can polish up my abilities?"

As a two-time recipient of the "Layoff of the Day" award (that is, having been fired twice), I know that change is neither a quick nor painless process, regardless of whether the change is voluntary or involuntary. The most common initial reaction of my clients is: "I want to replace what I had with exactly the same thing, only better." Unfortunately, that "same thing" often no longer exists. To make matters worse, the work-search methods that these people learned two, five or ten years ago may no longer give them the advantage they now require.

When my clients, men and women ranging in age from mid-20s to their early 60s, start investigating the new world of work and begin using the Net as one of their work-search tools, I know they are poised on the brink of success. Their potential has far less to do with my magical abilities to conjure up jobs than it does with their attitude. They recognize that things just ain't what they used to be, and that it's time to move on.

Go at Your Own Pace, and Follow Your Own Path

There is one piece of advice I give people when they reach this critical stage: Treat your career and life as an ongoing journey: enjoy it and learn at every stage.

The suggestion that life is a journey is what I'd like to leave you with. Difficult as it may be, you've got to hold on to who you are—and what you're truly striving for—even while you're looking for employment. Here's an excellent quote I use to remind myself and my clients:

"As a general rule, you have to accept that no matter where you work, you are not an employee; you are in a business with one employee—yourself." (Intel's CEO, Andrew Grove, on "Managing Your Own Career" in *Fortune Magazine*.)

Make Your Own Choices

The crux of this quote is that today you work only for "Me Inc." You alone are responsible for ensuring that the type of employment you choose, go after and secure is meaningful to you. Your friends, family, colleagues and career consultants can be a great source of feedback and comfort during this process. But they can't make decisions for you. Recognize, too, that you don't just go through this process once. It continues throughout each cycle of your career—and your life.

If this book has enabled you to move even a little bit closer to this realization, then I've achieved my main purpose. Remember what I told you at the outset. It was not my intention to turn you into some sort of high-tech, lean, mean, job-finding machine. Instead, I've provided you with choices that can help you to open new doors. Now it's up to you to use the appropriate tools and techniques in ways that will suit you.

I hope you use technology, along with the tips I have given you and advice from people you trust, to assist you in reaching your genuine career and life goals. If you do, you'll be more than just *wired and hired,* you will also be truly *inspired!*

CYBER TIP Remember to visit **www.wiredhired.com** for regular updates to the Internet addresses found in this book.

INDEX